HARD LINES

HARD LINES

ROUGH SOUTH POETRY

EDITED BY

Daniel Cross Turner
and William Wright

The University of South Carolina Press

Published by the University of South Carolina Press
Columbia, South Carolina 29208

www.sc.edu/uscpress

Manufactured in the United States of America

25 24 23 22 21 20 19 18 17 16
10 9 8 7 6 5 4 3 2 1

Library of Congress Cataloging-in-Publication Data
can be found at http://catalog.loc.gov/.

ISBN 978-1-61117-635-3 (cloth)
ISBN 978-1-61117-636-0 (paperback)
ISBN 978-1-61117-637-7 (ebook)

This book was printed on recycled paper with
30 percent postconsumer waste content.

CONTENTS

Preface xi
William Wright

Acknowledgments xiii

Introduction 1
Daniel Cross Turner

BETTY ADCOCK 11
Burnt Offerings
Rising Star, 1985
If Their Voices Were Visible Entities

DAN ALBERGOTTI 15
Notes for a Poem in Which God Does Not Appear
Lesson of the Elements: Fire
Lesson of the Elements: Earth

PAUL ALLEN 19
Altar Call
After an All-Nighter Camping with a Young Friend at Cape Romain Wildlife Refuge, South Carolina

BRIAN BARKER 23
In the City of Fallen Rebels
The Trees of the South
Dog Gospel

COLEMAN BARKS 27
Lard Gourd
Grace
Luke and the Duct Tape

JACK B. BEDELL 32
Travail
Saturday Night Crab Boils
Loup Garou

DESTINY O. BIRDSONG 35
Sugar

DAVID BOTTOMS 37
Shooting Rats at the Bibb County Dump
Under the Vulture-Tree
Under the Boathouse
In a U-Haul North of Damascus

BESMILR BRIGHAM 42
The Hurricane
Winston Weathers

KATHRYN STRIPLING BYER 44
Dagger
Bait
Delivery

FRED CHAPPELL 48
The Artful Dodger Out of the Bag

KELLY CHERRY 51
Wild Dogwood
The Heat Down South (Richmond, 1955)
Gulfport

MICHAEL CHITWOOD 54
A Childhood
The One Day
Skinning

JIM CLARK 57
Black Dog Shadrick Mayhew
Waking Up Drunk
Once More, the Night

ALLISON ADELLE HEDGE COKE 61
Off-Season
Packin' Four Corner Nabs

DANIEL CORRIE 67
Sleeping and Waking

KATE DANIELS 68
Autobiography of a White Girl Raised in the South
Louisiana, Late Summer
The Figure Eight

KWAME DAWES 71
Thief
Reburial

JAMES DICKEY 74
Cherrylog Road
The Sheep Child
Canebrake

R. H. W. DILLARD 80
A Friday Night Kind of Sonnet
Event; A Gathering; Vastation

CLAUDIA EMERSON 82
Ephemeris
Practice Blood
Third

TARFIA FAIZULLAH 85
Nocturne in Need of a Bitch
The Streetlamp above Me Darkens:

FORREST GANDER 88
From Life of Johnson Upside Your Head
Lovegreen

GEORGE GARRETT 90
Whistling in the Dark
Buzzard
Luck's Shining Child

JESSE GRAVES 93
River Gods
Firing Order
Elegy for a Hay Rake

JEFF HARDIN 96
On the Eve of a New Millennium

ASHLEY MACE HAVIRD 97
At Stonewall
Lunar Eclipse

DAVID HAVIRD 99
In Seventh Grade
Downriver with Uncle Paul

TERRANCE HAYES 103
Ode to Big Trend
Palmetto State

HASTINGS HENSEL 105
Jump-Start
The Rope in the Motor
Filet

RON HOUCHIN 108
Meanwhile
Outhouse
The Broken Eye

REBECCA GAYLE HOWELL 110
No One Was Born Here
We're on a Need to Know Basis
The Quick and the Dead

DAVID HUDDLE 112
Even Then I Knew
Evidence Contributing to a Late Illumination
Trotlines

ANDREW HUDGINS 116
The Names of the Lost
My Daughter
In
Out

T. R. HUMMER 119
Slow Train through Georgia
The Antichrist in Arkansas
Greek

TJ JARRETT 123
Of Late, I Have Been Thinking about Despair
Late That Summer
Meridian, MS, 1978: Miss Polly Attends the Altar at Mt. Zion

RODNEY JONES 126
The Power of the Quote

JUDY JORDAN 130
From Pete's Lake

TERRY L. KENNEDY 134
Concerning the Hunt
Concerning the Puppies

YUSEF KOMUNYAKAA 136
From Requiem
The White Handkerchief
Augury at Sunset

JOHN LANE 141
The Day Andy Griffith Died
Tony Dorsett and His Band
Wreckage

NATON LESLIE 148
Completion
Country

ED MADDEN 150
Inferno

AL MAGINNES 152
Pornography
Firefly Gospel
Music from Small Towns

JEFF MANN 156
A Brief Christian Visit; or, The Butch Bottom Sends Old Ladies Packing
The Shepherdstown Sweetshop

JEFF DANIEL MARION 158
Hand-Me-Down Days
Orpha
Winter Watch

LINDA PARSONS MARION 161
Chicken Pickin'
My Stepmother Takes Me to the Fair
Repossessed

CHRISTOPHER MARTIN 164
Parable of the Carolina Chickadee
Visiting Wildman's Civil War Surplus and Herb Shop

CHRIS MATTINGLY 167
No 'Count
Summertime

MICHAEL MCFEE 171
Yaller
Breaks
Cottonmouth

RAY MCMANUS 174
Dog Box
Disturbing Remains
Staying in the Truck

THORPE MOECKEL 178
Spittoono Lily
Cold Range, Hot Range
Living by Water

ROBERT MORGAN 182
Manure Pile
The Gift of Tongues
Man and Machine

RICARDO NAZARIO Y COLÓN 185
Mi Nuevo Hogar: Kentucky

TARA POWELL 187
Watching Deliverance *with My Students*

RON RASH 189
The Skeleton in the Dogwood
Winter Lightning
Animal Hides

JANISSE RAY 191
Land of Milk and Honey

PAUL RUFFIN 193
Frozen Over
Circling
Gigging Frogs
Sawdust Pile

STEVE SCAFIDI 197
To Whoever Set My Truck on Fire
The West Virginia Copper-Wing
The Hillbilly Break-Dance and the Talking Crow

JAMES SEAY 201
It All Comes Together Outside the Restroom in Hogansville
Kelly Dug a Hole

DAVE SMITH 204
How to Get to Green Springs
In the Yard, Late Summer
The Tire Hangs in the Yard

R. T. SMITH 209
A Local Doc, over Rocky Lunchtime Bourbon, Speaks of Barter and Hopeful Home Remedies
Horton's Store
Dar He

SHERYL ST. GERMAIN 215
Addiction
Always Wear Clean Underwear, You Never Know When You Might Get in a Car Accident
Wild Ones

LEON STOKESBURY 219
To Laura Phelan: 1886–1906
Midway

RICHARD TILLINGHAST 222
Lost Cove & the Rose of San Antone
Allen's Station: They

DENO TRAKAS 226
End of August, 2005
Walking to Work on a Snowy Morning

NATASHA TRETHEWEY 228
Disclosure
From "Native Guard"
Dr. Samuel Adolphus Cartwright on Dissecting the White Negro, 1851
Onlookers Gathered at the Traveling Chair's Arrival

ADAM VINES 231
Prologue and Return
Mine Rats
The Old Salt's Brag

ELLEN BRYANT VOIGT 234
Bright Leaf
The Trust
Cow
Owl

G. C. WALDREP 238
Elberta
Vertigo
Sustainable Agriculture

FRANK X WALKER 241
Spell to Give the Woman a Head
How to Swallow an Elephant
Cure to Eliminate the N-Word

ROBERT WEST 244
Mountaintop Removal
Cornfield

JAMES WHITEHEAD 245
A Local Man Remembers Betty Fuller
The Alabama Man Remembers All He Can about the Battered Children and the Woman with Almost Perfect Skin in Mobile Seven Years Ago

AMY WRIGHT 247
In That Place

CHARLES WRIGHT 249
Driving through Tennessee
Lost Bodies

WILLIAM WRIGHT 253
Trumpet Creeper
Rabid Cat
Triptych for the Days before Her Passage

JAKE ADAM YORK 259
Collect
Self-Portrait in a Plate-Glass Window
Letter Written on a Hundred Dollar Bill
Inscription for Air

The Contributors 265

Suggestions for Further Reading 283

Index of Authors and Titles 291

PREFACE

Brutal Grace

William Wright

Hard Lines: Rough South Poetry was born from two conversations. The first comes in book form and keeps talking: *Grit Lit: A Rough South Reader,* published by the University of South Carolina Press in 2012. Eight years in the making, *Grit Lit* is raucous and visceral and captures the dark and gritty South so well that it's best read slowly, as the textures are heavy, harrowing. I thank Tom Franklin and Brian Carpenter for their dedication to *Grit Lit,* a wonderful book and the central catalyst of our inspiration to compile this collection of poems.

The second conversation consisted of a discourse between the poet and editor G. C. Waldrep and the environmentalist, poet, editor, and essayist John Lane, both of whom yearned for a book of poems that featured "rough" South poetry. Fortunately they suggested that Daniel Cross Turner and I create this volume, a collection of work that, more than any other edition in which I've taken part, has helped elucidate not only "Rough South literature" but also southern poetry in general.

Editing helps clarify a book's purpose, of course, and the purpose of *Hard Lines* is twofold, appropriate to the two conversations that brought it into being. As well as its centering on the darker side of southern experience, Dan and I want with this volume to revivify literature-loving audiences with an exposure to poets who have for some decades formed the heart of southern poetry; second we wish to introduce readers to poets perhaps unfamiliar but who we think will become significant facets in southern literature. Indeed our hope is that this text serves as one of the best anthologies of southern poetry for contemporary readers for some time to come.

To define the term "hard lines" is impossible, other than to say that each of these poems, often in extremely distinct ways, reflects some aspect of the South and the burdens with which it freights anyone who was born here or has lived here long enough. Some of the poems, for example the opening piece, Betty Adcock's "Burnt Offerings," are dulcet and quiet but harbor a tension, an internal roughness, that amplifies with each reading. Other poems, such as Brian Barker's "In the

City of Fallen Rebels," prove violent, gothic, charged. We have the quintessential poets herein, the writers who helped establish southern poetry during the last several generations: in addition to Adcock, one will find almost all of the greats—including David Bottoms, Rodney Jones, Natasha Trethewey, Charles Wright, Kathryn Stripling Byer, Yusef Komunyakaa, and James Dickey. Just as necessary are poets of a younger generation, including the late Jake Adam York, whose poetry will forever thrive for many readers, sensitive as he was to identity, the importance of memory, and the roughness, the grittiness, woven permanently into the South's history. Present too are poets whose work exists on the fringes, including the under-known Besmilr Brigham, whose entire life was steeped in a nomadic spontaneity, an adventurous and gritty existence. Readers will encounter the dreamlike cadences of Forrest Gander, the ecopoetry of Janisse Ray, and the image-rich meditations of Jeff Daniel Marion. There are the dramatic monologues and heartbreaking narratives of R. T. Smith, the Saxonic lucidities of Ron Rash and Robert Morgan, the lush and tactile lines of Ellen Bryant Voigt, Dave Smith, and Kwame Dawes. And there is more, a lot more.

Though we are proud of this bounty, we of course were limited by the natural obstacles of a literary anthology: in many cases we could not include as many of a poet's poems as we wished to. Most poets have two to three poems in the book, but some have one, others four. These slight vacillations from the average have to do less with our selection process or the poets' literary reputations and more with the complex world of permissions. Too, we could not include everyone whom we know belongs here—Robert Penn Warren, A. R. Ammons, Cathy Smith Bowers, Jim Wayne Miller, and Gerald Barrax, to name just a few. For the conspicuously absent, we feel obliged to acknowledge that we *did* try to gather them to the table. That's OK! While we would have liked more folks to join in this grand cacophony, the book we've made is one we truly love.

If anything we hope this book illustrates plainly that rough southern poetry is myriad and ultimately uncontainable and that grittiness need not be only blood, ash, violence, hate, and history, even as the poems in this book explore these motifs thoroughly. Whatever their styles and thematic centers, these works are true; they do not suffer false nostalgia, looking back to a nonexistent southern history with melodramatic lugubriousness. These poems do not stew in the sweet-rotten effluvium of magnolia in the moonlight. What they share is a harsh, sometimes brutal grace, tragic hints and downright screams, the strange, conflicted, essential beauty that blooms from the South's potent ground.

ACKNOWLEDGMENTS

Daniel Cross Turner

Many thanks to John Lane for getting me involved in *Hard Lines: Rough South Poetry* in the first place after a dynamic *Grit Lit* reading by Ron Rash and George Singleton at Hub City Bookshop in my native town of Spartanburg, South Carolina. And many thanks to Jonathan Haupt at the University of South Carolina Press for his new vision for the Press and for his unwavering encouragement of Will and myself to edit and compile this volume.

A huge thank you to all the contributing poets for allowing us the opportunity to feature their excellent work in *Hard Lines,* verifying the continuing vitality and diversity of poetry written in and about the South in poems that speak to the region's pasts and its futures in crucial ways.

I am grateful, as always, to the patience of my wife, Keaghan, a writer herself, who willingly, generously yielded the floor to *Hard Lines,* ceding time away from her own projects so that Will and I could produce this collection in good order. She's wonderful, as are our two sons, both marvelous works-in-progress who fill our lives with life.

Last, but absolutely *not* least, an especial thank you to my coeditor, William Wright, who quite brilliantly shouldered so much of the responsibility for this collection's coming into being, from deciding on the scope and sweep of *Hard Lines* and judiciously determining which poems were essential to include to his expert managing of the devilish details of correspondences and formatting issues. Will has proven an ideal collaborator.

William Wright

I would like to thank John Lane and G. C. Waldrep, whose dialogues about southern poetry were catalytic to this volume. Without their encouragement, enthusiasm, good humor, and acumen, this book would not exist. I'd also like to thank Jonathan Haupt for his enthusiastic support.

Many thanks to the poets in this edition, all of whom were gracious and giving. Thanks to David Bottoms, especially, for his encouragement and guidance.

Thanks to Michelle, my wife, and to my mother, father, and sister for their patience and love.

And thanks to Daniel Cross Turner, who joined me in the editorship of this book with much enthusiasm and a luminous perspicacity. Without his unique knowledge of southern poetry and his love for literature in general, *Hard Lines* would not be the collection it has become.

✦

We both would like to thank Louisiana State University Press's Erica Bossier for her generosity and patience, as well as its permissions department. Too, we thank the University of Arkansas Press and Mike Bieker for their generosity. Generally we appreciate the publishers of the fine poets herein for believing in this project and entrusting us with their work.

Introduction

Rough Rhythms

Daniel Cross Turner

Tom Franklin and Brian Carpenter's excellent prose anthology, *Grit Lit: A Rough South Reader* (University of South Carolina Press, 2012), presents one hell of a rough-and-tumble collection of fiction and essays from some of the contemporary South's finest—and gutsiest—writers. As editors of this collection devoted to rough South poetry, William Wright and I believe firmly that the poets contained herein rival the wild-blooded crew of *Grit Lit* writers in hostile spit, grit, grime, and gristle. In *Hard Lines: Rough South Poetry,* we've selected southern poets who are not only awfully good but also good at offering awe-filled spectacles and scenes born of the American South. Their poems, you'll find, administer full doses of tour-de-force, hardcore backwoods noir.

To some rough South poetry might sound oxymoronic. Poetry and toughness, it seems, seldom align in the popular imagination. Poetry is a literary genre known for formal restraint and fastidiousness and is often viewed as genteel, replete with ornate diction and fancy rules of versification, from sonnets to sestinas. Most general readers couldn't tell a ghazal from a villanelle and couldn't care less, either. Poetry is too often seen as a particularly and peculiarly stylized genre, an erstwhile bastion of romanticism and false nostalgia, a luxury set clear apart from the everyday. "Visions of dancing daffodils wandering lonely as a cloud in the mind's eye" sort of thing. This anthology, we aver, overturns such flowery notions. Here we get the dirt beneath the flowers, the churned-up earth, thick and clotted in our hands, that teems with life, also death. *Hard Lines* gives us the things themselves, not just feelings about the things. We get a poetry that's tactile and turbulent, that eschews the highfalutin to get down to the nitty-gritty. A poetry that *matters*—in all senses. A poetry that summons up all the messy *materia,* the sheer physical fact of the multifaceted world we inhabit and that inhabits us. A poetry that keeps things real. A poetry that evokes a full-bodied drive of ineffable, unstoppable rhythmic sensory overload. Wan lyrical cooings and waxing philosophic are a no-go for our poets. The poems assembled here care little for nightingales tender as the night, and anyhow birds don't last long in these Southscapes pulsing with peril, peeling right through to the red, living heart of things. Serpents, cockfighting, rabid cats—all sundry dark creatures of the night burn bright on the pages of this anthology. Herein we have a number of poets and poems that take as gospel truth the piercing reverb, the stunning backfire and wheelrip that roars out of the famed final line from "Cherrylog Road" by one of the most original and visible rough South poets, Georgia-born James Dickey: "Wild to be wreckage forever."

What can you say to that? You tell me, and we'll both know, as my father used to say, who grew up "rough as a cob" and fatherless in Depression-era Louisville, Georgia, he who could cuss like a sailor and soldier both, having been both—with tours in the U.S. Navy (1946–48) and the U.S. Army (1952–53), the latter as commander of a tank platoon who saw active combat in many battles of the Korean War, including the bloody Christmas Hill and Punchbowl encounters.

Maybe, according to "Lost Bodies," set in Tennessee, a poem by Charles Wright included in the very book you have in hand, you could say this:

> What can you say to that?
>   everything Jesus promised
>
> (My five senses waiting apart in their grey hoods,
> Touching their beads,
>   licking the ashes that stained their lips)
>
> And someone to tell it to.

Those lines might appear neither rough nor southern. But then you take a look at what comes just before, the bare, shattering image that has fired such ethereal rumination:

> The cross was opposite Fleenor's Cabins below the hill
> On U.S. 11W.
> Harold Shipley told me, when I was twelve,
>   he'd seen a woman undressed
>
> In the back seat of a Buick, between two men,
>   her cunt shaven clean,
> In front of the motel office.
> They gave him a dollar, he said, to stick his finger up there.

Therein lies a peculiar commingling of a visceral, gut-level realism on the one side and a lofty, ascetic high-mindedness on the other. A backcountry prostitute, rough life, shitty work, her legs splayed and displayed for male consumption off a backcountry road in nowhere Tennessee, back of beyond. Not a pretty picture; not a pretty poem. Any promise of redemption won't radiate pristinely from that cross opposite the rundown tourist cabins on a now-bypassed roadway but has got to be dragged through the smut and the mud first. Nothing's sole or whole that's not been rent, to echo W. B. Yeats, though in Wright's telling, it's not love but money (a dollar) that pitches its tent in the place of excrement. These excerpts from Wright show a poet not afraid to let language get fouled, to dirty things up so as to sting our senses into awareness of a rough world down South, where a woman is hard-pressed into wretched service, treated like trash, disposable. Like Wright the other poets we've included in *Hard Lines* don't mince words. As you'll see—and *hear* (for poetry is aural-bound, meant to ring in the ears) and *feel* (for poetry is a full-bodied experience, meant to beat in the blood)—the poems included here can earn their keep, their lines taking a hard line on southern hard times. Weighing the cost of living with the price of dying, atrocities committed on all sides in such a place as this, our poets put the *versus* back in *verse*. Such collisions between body and soul as we see—*hear, feel*—in Wright's unflinching words, such clashes of the abstract and the abject, are at the center of what we conceive of as rough South poetry. These poets are as tough-minded as they are high-minded. However, rough South poetry, in our eyes, doesn't merely include molten-muscle-kickass poetry, but also offers poems in an elegiac mode, such as Jesse Graves's "Elegy for a Hay Rake" or Kathryn Stripling Byer's "Dagger." There is plenty of raucousness to be found in this anthology, and yet the cultural conflicts that ignite southern wildness are often lyrical without becoming lugubrious, mournful but not maudlin. Some of these southern poets are coming to terms with a visibly transforming culture—a "roughness" in and of itself—and indeed many of these poets are part of what's changing the definition of the South.

So what's so different, then, about poetry that requires a separate gritty-lit anthology, beyond prose, all to its own? Well, here's the thing: to *hear's* the thing. The true pleasure of this and all poetry lies not in properly splitting hairs between terza rima and pantoum but in its sound patterns—what Robert Frost called "the gold in the ore" (439), the dynamic interplay of sound and sense brought on by poetic rhythm. Poetry should contain some feeling of words breaking across a (relatively) repeatable rhythm. That is not to suggest that only works that follow traditional meters should be considered poems or even good poems. Rather it is to emphasize how poems engage in playing sound with and against sense, even those written in free verse. In fact free verse poems are never entirely "free" of the influence of rhythm; instead, to work as poetry, they invoke what T. S. Eliot called "the ghost of some simple metre" (85) in "Reflections on Vers Libre" (1917), which haunts their more open-ended structures. From this vantage poetic rhythm is not unlike the music that reinforces or contrasts the meaning of lyrics in songs. This argument for the centrality of poetic rhythm has a long history—comparable, for instance, to Edgar Allan Poe's assertion in "The Poetic Principle" (1850) that poetry is "the rhythmical creation of beauty" (175)—and has enjoyed a critical renaissance in the past decade. Poetry's attention to form is most evident in its redoubled focus on rhythm, for the rhythmic structure of poems underscores the materiality of words in themselves. The acoustic impulse of rhythm creates a compelling experience of language as pure physical sensation momentarily separated from the conditions of meaning. Since sound/rhythm is meaningless in and of itself, we must draw on the images and ideas of a poem in order to "translate" this physical experience into meaningful terms. According to Amittai F. Aviram, "the sublime power of rhythm in connection with the body" (7) approximates theories set forth by a continuum of major modern philosophers, mirroring Friedrich Nietzsche's Dionysian reality, Sigmund Freud's drive, Jacques Lacan's order of the real, and Julia Kristeva's *sujet en procès.* Charles Bernstein argues similarly that "it is precisely because sound is an arational or nonlogical feature of language that it is so significant for poetry—for sound registers the sheer physicality of language, a physicality that must be the grounding of reason exactly insofar as it eludes rationality" (21). Poetic rhythm stresses sound divided off from sense; the driving, unconscious flow of rhythm allows primal sensation to counterbalance abstract sense. Poetic rhythm thus offers the participant a feeling of liberation from strictures of social codes of value. Reveling in the driving momentum of language as meaningless sensation, we experience a momentary stay against confusion: we avoid confusion not by *outthinking* it (a matter of a poem's content, its sense), but by *unthinking* it (the sublimely negating effect of a poem's form, its sound). Poetry's insistent aural repetitions speak directly to our physical being-in-the-world, and this is something that our poets seize upon in their verse. In our selections for this anthology, Will and I made sure that the rough South poems we chose are founded on the same bedrock deep-seated at the heart of form. That something you'll see, *hear, feel* is rhythm. Poetic rhythm awakens a kind of muscle memory, and the poems herein use that somatic power to make memorable people and places down South rough-cut by hard labor, whose futures are damaged goods, whose pasts reckon heavy losses.

If you don't believe me, or Frost, or Eliot, or Nietzsche or Freud, or Lacan or Kristeva, for that matter, then perhaps you'll put some faith in a legendary badass, the ultra-haggard, rugged, ragged, gun-toting, knife-wielding, bourbon-swigging, jaded, faded junkie guitarist—Keith Richards of the Rolling Stones. The former choirboy who sang soprano for the Queen has patched together a fifty-year career riffing off the rhythms of southern blues-based rock and roll. He knows a thing or two about the power of rhythm. And about the rough South to boot. Whereas Mick Jagger has been knighted, his ever-benighted ragtag counterpart can be canonized a surrogate southerner. Sir Mick and Saint Keith, we'll say. Of the bodily effects of rhythmic sound, Richards proclaims that "what matters is what hits the ear" (236), for "what you're looking for is power and force, without volume—an inner power" (237):

> There's something primordial in the way we react to pulses without even knowing it. We exist on a rhythm of seventy-two beats a minute. The train, apart from getting from the Delta to Detroit, became very important to blues players because of the rhythm of the machine, the rhythm of the tracks, and then when you cross onto another track, the beat moves. It echoes something in the human body. So then when you have machinery involved, like trains, and drones, all of that is still built in as music inside us. The human body will feel rhythms even when there's not one. Listen to "Mystery Train" by Elvis Presley. One of the great rock-and-roll tracks of all time, not a drum on it. It's just a suggestion, because the body will provide the rhythm. Rhythm really only has to be suggested. Doesn't have to be pronounced. This is where they got it wrong with "this rock" and "that rock." It's got nothing to do with rock. It's to do with roll. (244)

And so too with poetry—it thrives on rhythmic Zen: "Hypnotic. Trance. Relentless beat" (343).

As you'll see—*hear, feel*—from poring over this anthology, poetry can more than hold its own with regard to illustrating vividly the roughness of the American South. The numbers are in our favor. More than 150 poems by more than seventy poets impart an immense range of perspectives on the pressing realities of the region, reflecting the sheer multitudinousness of the rough South. In terms of the myriad ways in which these poets create the sublime force of lineated rhythm, our writers work in a remarkable spectrum of forms, making exemplary and exceptional use of traditional meters and structures as well as more open verse formations. Relative to other U.S. regions, the poetry of the South is typically known for its attention to traditional forms, an association that is often perceived—or *mis*perceived—as an affiliation with the influences of cultural, if not political, conservatism. This idea that southern poetry reflects a more conservative mind-set is set in opposition to the more experimental or avant-garde movements linked to other areas, such as New York- and California-based aesthetics of Language and concrete poetries. However, one could—probably *should*—take issue with the notion that experimentation with conventional poetic forms is any less radical than other versions of poetic experimentation. Indeed one could argue that this play within and against forms is every bit as experimental as other modes, while at the same time maintaining a thriving connection with the grounding force of rhythm, hypnotic, trancelike, relentless. Formalist poems sing in their chains like the sea, and the singing may be all the more beautiful for the very strictures of its insistent repetitions, a given form's compulsion to repeat. That many southern poets keep close to formal constructions tends to heighten the metrical power of their verse, a fact duly noted in a perusal of the lions of post–World War II southern verse, from Warren's expert manipulations of iambic baselines to Dickey's resonant rising trimeter, his "primal" anapests, to Ammons's heavily enjambed *terza libre* (series of unrhymed tercets), to that fine set of poets who carried the lights onward from the 1970s, including Dave Smith, David Bottoms, Kathryn Stripling Byer, Fred Chappell, Betty Adcock, Rodney Jones, Kelly Cherry, and Robert Morgan.

And yet many of the selections in *Hard Lines* show southern poets shifting away from strict formalism, such as poems by Besmilr Brigham, Judy Jordan, and Brian Barker. The poems collected here show an admirable mix of form and free verse. And even when the verse is more free, the ghost of meter usually looms beneath, beyond the lines, passing through the hollows of the unaccented syllables, materializing at the appointed stressed sound; after all rhythm, per Saint Keef, "really only has to be suggested." Though writing in open form, Charles Wright, for instance, attends to the rhythmic power source that fuels his staggered lines jutting and jagging across the page: he counts each and every syllable of each and every line of each and every poem. One would be hard-pressed not to *hear, feel* the aural call to the body electric firing through Yusef Komunyakaa's brilliantly compressed, muscular free verse, when it seems at times as if the words have veritably been nailed to the page. And even when the poems return to form overtly, we often find our chosen poets regrooving received measures, forging hybridizations of past practices, new variants of old forms, like the tense and tender strains of Natasha Trethewey's unrhyming sonnets; Andrew Hudgins's conversational pentameter, freed from the lilt of iambs to record realistic talk; or Jake Adam York's austere couplets, each pair hard-edged, daring the next line to complete its rhythmic run, or Dan Albergotti's fused variations that make us appreciate both the artistry of the half-sculpted figure and the brute beauty of the stone from which it is in process of emerging. All the poems gathered here share the common denominator of rhythmic drive, even as the astonishing multiplicity of poetic forms carries over its long division across the dozens of included poems.

Likewise southern poetry is traditionally marked by a strong narrative impetus—the compulsion to tell, tell about the South. This penchant for storytelling is evident in such rough South founding fathers as Warren, whose volume-length narrative poems *Brother to Dragons* and *Audubon: A Vision* brim with gore, like poetic slasher movies. Dickey, too, filled his verse with hard-edged storylines animated with his concept of "country surrealism" (*Sorties* 107–8). One need look no further than "The Sheep Child," which tells the tale of farm boys who are a little *too* wild, taking the idea of "being one with nature" to its illogical extreme as they couple with anything, making every living thing out in the country nervous, especially, as the title suggests, sheep. And many of Warren's and Dickey's poetic heirs, such as Dave Smith, Bottoms, Rash, and John Lane, are no strangers to narrative verse: storylines fill their lines. But among our constellation of selected poems there are also a number of nonnarrative poets—those who prefer to let their images do the work. Ammons might perhaps be the figurehead of this lineage of contemporary southern poetry, and imagistic and impressionistic verse has its say down South too, in the work of luminaries such as Charles Wright and Komunyakaa. Ammons's span of imagery is immense, amalgamating snippets of gritty southern dialect (drawn from his youth spent on a North Carolina tobacco farm) with the opaque Latinate discourse of theoretical science. Immense, too, is his formal experimentation, from quick-hitting, epigrammatic poems to beautifully sprawling, rolling book-length poems, as is his tonal range, commingling the comic and the plaintive. Ammons's career-long engagement with the landscape relumes in the work of many of our included writers. Narrative or not, what seems to really matter in making poetry matter is that all good poetry takes the familiar and makes it strange in some way. This strangeness is there lurking between the narrative talking points and in the flashpoints of imagery too, as we see, hear, and feel in the poems of T. R. Hummer and Forrest Gander.

The astonishing amorphousness of the poetry of the contemporary rough South, its amazing multiplicity of poetic forms (from lyric to narrative and from received structures to free verse), is reflected in another level of diversity at work in the poems included in this anthology. The poems in *Hard Lines* expand out from the traditional equation of "southern writer" with whiteness and maleness. Rough South poetry certainly records, at times critiques, southern whiteness as a distinct ethnic category, but it also reveals the many ways southern poetry moves us beyond the stereotypical frame of whiteness and marks the current South as a nexus of diverse ethnic strands. The poems collected here help us to explore as multifariously as possible how rough South poetry speaks to (or against) racial, ethnic, sexual, gendered, social, and other forms of power. When I asked her during our interview if she considered herself a southern writer, U.S.—and Mississippi—poet laureate Trethewey provided a compelling affirmation of her experiences as a mixed-race person growing up in the Deep South:

> Geography is fate. Of all the kinds of fate swirling around my very being, this place in which I was born and this particular historical moment matter deeply. The story of America has always been a story of miscegenation, of border crossings, of integration of cultures, and again, I embody this in my person. To me, I fit in as the quintessential Southerner. Perhaps even now my role is to establish what has always been Southern, though at other points in history it has been excluded from "Southernness." We just hadn't found the right metaphor yet. (Turner, "Southern Crossings")

This anthology also fleshes out what has been excluded from that narrow understanding of southernness. Our poems respond to a region always in process of changing, a place of transregional, even global connectivity. That stark female body we find astonishingly in Wright's "Lost Bodies" yields to the many bodies rendered, reflected, and refracted by other poets of the rough South within these pages, like the wiry strength of the part-Native, female field- and factory-worker who must fend for herself in Huron-Cherokee-Creek writer Allison Adelle Hedge Coke's poems. Or the dead bodies that loom large throughout Trethewey's verse: from the corpse of her murdered mother, victim of domestic violence; to the amalgamated blood, bone, and tissue of the black soldiers who served as the Louisiana Native Guard, treated as cannon fodder by their white Union military leaders; to the corpses of electrocuted criminals executed in the electric chair that traveled around Mississippi county seats in the 1940s. Or the dead bodies unburied by monsoons in the war-torn junglescapes of Vietnam that rhyme eerily with the corpses of blacks lynched and lost to Louisiana swamps in Komunyakaa's work. And there's more to see here, from the likes of Kwame Dawes and Frank X Walker as well as magnificent up-and-comers such as Tarfia Faizullah, TJ Jarrett, and Ricardo Nazario y Colón. Rather than insist on a common, consensual definition of the South and southernness, our collection enlarges the traditional definition of a southern poet to account more fully for the remarkable range of contemporary poets writing verse not merely in but all about the region and its multiethnic, transregional histories. Indeed several of our poets hail from elsewhere, born and/or raised in regions beyond the cartographic gridlines of the South, including Ohio-bred blue-collar poet Naton Leslie, a self-described "tough old hillbilly" with unshakable Appalachian roots. The gritty South is variegated, multiethnic, female as much as male, working-class as much as middle-, and bursting at the seams with mixed, often vexed ecologies, both humanly and naturally formed.

In *Hard Lines,* then, we encounter poetry as an enworlded force, fraught with the agreements, entanglements, and antagonisms of heavily striated *southernnesses*—multiple, even contradictory. And we are called, time and again, by these poems to take stock of the transforming landscape of the South, the often dark and bloody proving ground of its human and nonhuman animals that mark, even mar, the land that they labor upon. All told, this is pretty rough stuff. Rough in its demeanor, its steel-eyed gaze at the blunt facts of fate in these grim Southern scapes. Yet pretty too, as the lines herein add some stark beauty, if not grace, to the region's histories, dark and deep, otherwise unredeemed.

Works Cited

Aviram, Amittai F. *Telling Rhythm: Body and Meaning in Poetry.* Ann Arbor: University of Michigan Press, 1994.

Bernstein, Charles, ed. *Close Listening: Poetry and the Performed Word.* New York: Oxford University Press, 1998.

Carpenter, Brian, and Tom Franklin, eds. *Grit Lit: A Rough South Reader.* Columbia: University of South Carolina Press, 2012.

Dickey, James. *Sorties.* Baton Rouge: Louisiana State University Press, 1984.

Eliot, T. S. "Reflections on Vers Libre." In *Selected Prose of T. S. Eliot,* 31–36, edited by Frant Kermode. New York: Harvest Books, 1975.

Finch, Annie. *The Ghost of Meter: Culture and Prosody in American Free Verse.* Ann Arbor: University of Michigan Press, 2000.

Frost, Robert. "The Figure a Poem Makes." In *The Robert Frost Reader: Poetry and Prose,* 439–42, edited by Edward Connery Lathem and Lawrance Thompson. New York: Holt, 1972.

Poe, Edgar Allan. "The Poetic Principle." In *The Collected Works of Edgar Allan Poe,* vol. 1, 164–97. Cambridge, Mass.: Belknap, 1969.

Turner, Daniel Cross. "Southern Crossings: An Interview with Natasha Trethewey." *Waccamaw: A Journal of Contemporary Literature* 6 (2010). Accessed May 20, 2015. http://archived.waccamawjournal.com/pages.php?x=324.

BETTY ADCOCK

Burnt Offerings

The sun's flare on my father's folly: an ornamental
pool whose fish moved like fugitive lantern-light,
long tails trailing as in a water-wind—

                                        green flame of a live-oak
spreading sunset's arson, my swing hanging by two
rough ropes in a glittering stillness—

                                                compacted coals
of a fallen pomegranate broken open on the ground,
and smoldering with birds—

                                        dark red silk
fires of the rooster's back, slick as oil and wet
with a morning rain—

                                even the chill white
blaze of a March dogwood trapped into early radiance,
the scorched lips of those petals—

                                    always
the medium of memory is glass, fire's child,
molten, cooled into forms that can fix a sun's
brilliance, inexplicable and *inknown,*
on gone flesh or leaf, on lost house or touch,
anywhere   any life   out of time   fierce
reigniting of the past to its old dazzle
shattering and ash.

Rising Star, 1985

—For B. H. Fairchild

We'd passed the town a dozen times, traveling that stretch
of highway across Texas west to east by way of Dallas
and other diversions, mostly

by way of tough small towns.
Potosi Clyde Rowden Pioneer—
then, incongruous as song erupting from the prickly pear
that collaborates with mesquite to kill the grass,
a sign said *Rising Star.*

We'd left Abilene in the dark, early to make time
past dreaming ranches. Only windmills were awake,
creaking their water-anthem among cattle still as fenceposts
just paling into view
November sky
turned gray with a trademark chill west Texas
dawn, and a numb horizon opened almost
abruptly beyond the pocked town sign and lit
the single street, its stoplight dancing in a little wind.
Oil wells whined along the railroad tracks, black pump-jacks
lifting and falling, huge up close, like grotesque versions
of the toy drinking birds I'd bought as souvenirs
on this ride with my father when I was ten years old.

Breakfast in Rising Star, you said, *what better place.*
What I remember now is the peculiar light that spilled
out of plate glass windows of the one café.
With ashen daybreak all around, the street held pooled
yellow light that was somehow old, a slow color
like 1950's lakeside summers; or the deeply sudden drench
of Saturday afternoon when the double feature ended,
the color of Sunday night streetlights blooming
onto asphalt beside an empty church.
Warmer
than sepia, but like that could turn
any view it touched into another time—
it was as if some magic bulb in that café
could cast the past onto the sidewalk at my feet.

The wide plate glass was crudely painted over
with that thin, almost transparent stuff
that washes off, so the glow from the interior
outlined an outsized quarterback, pale gold,
with a brown ball, a tepid flag, a girl with pom-poms
like red explosions. *Go Wildcats!*
lettered in black.

Inside, we sat on hard chairs listening to the talk
of ranch-hands, roughnecks, the guy from car repair.

Their voices washing over us illuminated local
weather, stock prices, carburetors, and what to expect
at Friday night's championship game when Tank
Johnson's boy would surely bring it home.
We ate something, and then we walked
into bright day and the chance of making
Dallas long before noon.
                                        We didn't talk.

Where now is Rising Star? Half sunk—
or utterly—beneath bluebonnet-colored skies?
Vanished maybe, with the read wildcats, their yellow shining,
and with my remembered light that had even then
been gone so long it might as well have come
from any distant star.

If Their Voices Were Visible Entities

Sacred Harp Singers, Georgia, 1930s

If their voices were visible entities
flying from the deep South's fading
churches, startled from the throat
of an earlier century by hope revived,
they would be birds.
                              Ordinary
                                             starlings. Or swifts perhaps,
a flock of embers
                              cohering, dispersing, action-
painting against cloud or blue, form into dissolving
form. Turn on turn ascending,
they clot and flow, shift like wind-
tossed silk against the sky, their lift and dive
from pumping hearts that hold
the wingbeats' bellows to the burn
of being.

They make and remake,
undoing and reweaving the garment of light
to puzzle all earthly suitors. They work
the air to patterns of return. And colorless
with height, they show only light
underwings or their black backs,
a moving kaleidoscope of contradiction.
Watch this story whose form is motion.
Listen. It is neither language nor music but flesh
become no thing, word become space
where the missing third wrings open
this harmony, and the design folds
and folds in rough fugue all the way to *gone*
to God, the mystery that unfurls the sky.

DAN ALBERGOTTI

Notes for a Poem in Which God Does Not Appear

Assemble materials on a white table.

Images or fragments that form nothing
on Taw Caw Creek, summer 1976.
Drought has hardened the earth enough
to break a shovel. The air is dry, the sky
cloudless. *Do not make the bright sun irony.*
Only let it burn, apart from everything.

Metaphor is the indifferent drone
of the motorboats on the lake, the music
of this world. *Yes.* Metaphor could be
the thin tentacles of memory that entwine
certain hours in certain light. Nothing
on Taw Caw Creek, summer 1976,
but a small, weak boy. *Yes, make him weak.*

But do not try to make his little fists
an emblem of weakness.

Only make them fall on the Collie
to no effect. The indifferent Collie is beauty
clenching its strong, dirty jaws around
the Chihuahua's torso. *What does the Collie feel?*
It does not feel the blows or hear the screams.

And the parents inside do not hear the screams
for a long time. *Make them hear something.*

They hear something. They think it comes
from the television they have left on.
Make them talk on with their guests,
the guests who have brought the Collie.
They hear something or nothing while they talk.
The boy and the dogs. The great sky.

When the parents know what they hear
and rush outside, when the Collie releases
his jaws, the mother falls on the boy
like a blanket on a burning man.

The sky is opened
and opened again.
God should not appear.
He does not.
But if he must,
He does not.
But if he must,
He does not.
But if he must, make him
the Great Father.

The Great Father with his pistol, disappearing
round the corner of the house, following the bright,
torn flesh dragging the ground behind the small dog
that flees, that will hide behind the azaleas
and tremble, licking at its opened side.

And make his majestic voice

His majestic voice is the report that echoes
over the cove's surface and through the pines,
that finally settles in the distant land of small skulls,
dry earth, and trash. In the land of every measured word.

Lesson of the Elements: Fire

When he was a young boy, the man
            would light the heads of his plastic army men
                        and then become the flame that ate downward,

melting helmet, rifle, canteen, and boots,
            until he was the perfect disc of swirled green
                        and black on the driveway pavement.

But tonight he cannot become the flame
            that he starts on the burn ward of the hospital.
                        Tonight he can only hear its god-like words.

You could burn it all clean, you know.
You could make something new out of fresh ash.
You could be the end and the beginning.

They sound to the man like the voice of God,
but those words are ours. We say *Ilium* and *auto-da-fé,*
napalm and *Nagasaki.* Our words are like tongues

of flame atop toy soldiers, consuming us as soon
as we utter them. We speak swirls of fiery stars
back at the cosmos. Our words make flames rise

like the screams of victims or like the body
of a god ascending into heaven. We say
Alpha and *Omega,* one and another word of the fire.

Lesson of the Elements: Earth

And when the rains came, the people there
could not tell dust from ash from clay. They could not
distinguish what was of the earth or of the ocean.
Nor of the air or of the flame. We could tell them
that we are all of the flame, composed of the stuff
of ever-burning stars. That we are of the water,
more than two-thirds water. That we are of the air,
respiring spirits. That we are of the earth, from dust
to dust. But none of that would give them comfort.
Our answers are no better than Horatio's
to Hamlet in the graveyard. *E'en so, my lord.*
We stand on the rock that is only the rock
and the dirt and the flesh. We stand on an old world
that is handful after handful of dust. In fear,
the woman taken in the act of adultery—*the very act,*
O lord—stood on this earth before her accusers.
Christ wrote in the sand and she lived.
But the day before or after, was there not
another woman in that same circle of men?
Think of her—younger, prettier, a girl, really—
with only smiles for her judges. Think of the first stone
catching her square in the eye. That one puts her down
and makes it easier for the rest of the men to pour

their heavy pieces of earth onto her prostrate form.
Think of the stone in each man's hand with the heft of sin.
Think of the young woman's last vision of this world,
its dusty floor growing darker, each stone pressing her
harder against it, the friction of her face on the grainy sand
making the whispered word of the earth.

PAUL ALLEN

Altar Call

Montgomery, AL, 1964

One goes to the whore as one comes to God,
goodness not a factor, but release,
relief from innocence, finally feel—
after all the life and thought and thought and life—
pure feeling in the death of everything else.
There's usually a guide. For me there was,
my first time boldly naked, fully abed,
not making do in a car with hand or head.
My guide, a senior teaching me the bones
in the lab on the third floor of Bellingrath.
The skeleton we used (campus legend?)
was that of a slave girl, a century removed,
now wired together. We had a name for her
but for the life of me, I can't recall it.
We went over it and over it,
naming, memorizing, stumbling the rich
words' consonants and rhythms: ilium,
pubic, sacrum, patella, fibula, ulna—
o, we tracked her hour after hour,
naming all the antique frames of her spaces.
Some nights we lost all track of time in her.
Other nights it was the opposite,
losing track of her in the grinding time.

I'm not sure where we were when he brought her up,
the whore he knew in town whose liquor he drank
maybe once a week. I do know though
where we were just before we stood
at the side door of the Graystone Hotel.
I could show you exactly, except, I hear the streets
were changed, revitalization of Old Town,
and changed again in the slow, sad failure of that.

We entered the exit. He tipped the porter and called
him by name. The porter went through his door
and I could see the marble and crystal lobby
for a second. *Go up,* my tutor said, *go up.*
You first, I said, worried it might be a trick.
We climbed the service stairs between the walls.
He taught me protocol, a last cramming—
how to knock on her door, how not to hand
her the money but lay it on the dresser
fanned out so she could see the numbers, 20,
10—without grossly looking.
Taught in whispers, turned at every landing
to make sure I was following, and punctuate
some detail I might need to know so
as not to give offense, a last unlearning
of things my past had taught me about love.
Or maybe to see my face where eyes and mouth
might show reluctance, some losing of resolve.
I remember thinking on a couple of landings
he wanted this for me, like this might render
me new, make future conquests easy.
I knew he wanted it deeply, for both of us.
It was something more urgent than free sex and Scotch
she'd give him another night because of this night.

He graduated. I named all the bones.
At our 40th, someone near spoke
his name. With *dead.* The word and name, coupled,
called him from the tomb my years had purchased
for him. His name had never surfaced before.
His career, his after-college life:
He'd been a preacher, Methodist, they thought,
his church somewhere down on the coast, and big.
I thought of the girl's wired bones, the woman's flesh
and saw in my wine, him, in the raised pulpit,
him climbing down the spiral steps,
holding his vestments so he wouldn't stumble
and stepping to the center of the chancel
at the final hymn, glad, stopping the song
at each verse, saying *come down, come, come down.*

After an All-Nighter Camping with a Young Friend at Cape Romain Wildlife Refuge, South Carolina

You're surprised that we believed you last night?
How could we not believe your vision of a ghost dog?

When we were an "I," the astrologer said I was Gemini,
twins, two. The shrink said bi-polar. Two more.
That made four of me in the cramped camper of my skull.
We didn't always get along.
Cowboy kept his cards close to the vest.
All hours were high noon, all meetings, a showdown.
He liked women who liked horses.
Poet liked women who were going through something,
said they were always going through something,
so he didn't have to use poem-thought to think up new responses.
Priest was downright eremite, avoided religion.
He said their god's too small, a voodoo Ken-doll
which people dress in "sundry best" as occasion or whim demand.
He liked women who'd given up on God.
And one of us was just plain queer. We didn't care.
For a long time we bumped and shoved each other
in the line that led to the gate. Historically,
it was our Thirty Years War, a period
of numerous skirmishes and battles, hand to hand,
for tribal chieftain, clan leader, alpha male—
Pyrrhic victories all. What did we ever know of "me"?

With the new millennium, our skin began
to crack, then fissures opened, festered, our body
began horribly dividing. We tried to stitch our
selves together, drank any potion,
but nothing would stop it; the sutures ripped,
our voices became howls, our disagreements
with each other more violent.
The ex couldn't stand to watch,
couldn't stand the sound of splitting flesh,

the thump of joints disjointing,
the tick of snapped ligaments, our screams.
We hid in the seven swamps,
in eight dark forests we slept.

When it was over,
our four bodies, four heads, eight legs, eight arms
moved in sync and we stayed close, so close
that from a distance, you might have thought us still
one creature. No one is first anymore, none last.

So after you and we watched from the canoe
the alligator the size of our canoe
emerge from the marsh grass and sink beneath us,
then darkness come on, paddled against the tidal creek
and, where we four saw only an abandoned pier,
you saw the slobbering ghost-dog,
spirit-dog forming itself out of the blacker black of land,
as though the world we'd known
had unleashed it, ravening, coming for us across the water,
and you were afraid. You thought we'd tell you
it wasn't there, make a joke about what you smoked?
We couldn't do that.

How could we not have believed?
Look at who we are (are now!),
the selves we've shown to you—
four old beings, one beast:
Cowboy, Poet, Queer, Priest.
Manticore, Griffin, Minotaur, Unicorn.
Matthew, Mark, Luke, John.
Conquest, War, Famine, Death.

Of course we believed.

BRIAN BARKER

In the City of Fallen Rebels

—After Jaime Sabines

Here comes the boy again, dragging his death
by a string. Here comes the gun he waves above his head.
Here comes the light raked loose
like salted slugs, how it fizzes over liquor bottles
and magazine racks, and he must feel it, yes,
like ulcers puckering his skin, for he hugs himself
with his other arm, high-stepping in place, trying to hold in
the filthy, burst mattress of the soul.
But here it comes nonetheless! Christ, look at it!
It won't stop jumping out
to bang on the scuffed Plexiglass window
of heaven. Here come the angels,
they hear him, those starved revenants
trampling the riverbank of his mind. But the gods,
they refuse to blink, *he's nothing more*
than a speck of shit on the eyelash of infinity, they say,
spitting sideways into the dust,
though they come anyway, like Confederate marauders
spurring their wormy, wide-eyed horses
up from the shallow graves.
They're peat burnt and staunch, they're flashing their bleary sabers.
One has a face that keeps fuzzing out,
and one has biceps like a pit bull's flanks splattered with blood,
and when he shoots at them, wailing, bottles explode,
rum tumbles down shelves, trickles
toward the feet of Mrs. Wen.
Here she comes too, fumbling the keys,
trying to coax the register open.
Here come the five English words she knows,
flitting about her like flying mice.
Here come the gods again (they never give up),
and the boiling sargassum of blood she can't hold inside her chest,
as some fusty, ferruginous fog blows in

from the backside of the ghetto.
Here come the dead, they smell it, waking in vacant lots,
shoeless and soft in the weeds. Here come
the screwworms and roaches, the black ocean seething in its bowl
and a whole century like a ship on fire.
In the park, where the boy buys his tinfoil surprise,
the severed heads of history nod all night on their rotten branches.
He blows the gates. He sleeps
his dreamless sleep, curled fetal beneath a bench,
his eyelids blue and blotched with bruises.
Here comes the poet. (What does *he* want?)
He's scared of the dark; he'd like to turn into a sparrow,
fly into a steeple, hide beneath a broken bell.
But a desiccated bat hangs at the back of his mind.
He keeps poking it with his pen until the godawful
gods come again. (They never quit!)
Here they come, galloping across the river
of a dead king rising, surpliced, bearded in flames,
blowing their battered bugles.
They want a word with the boy, they say. They take him
into the trees. And there he goes, still half-asleep,
dragging his death by a string.

The Trees of the South

Deadfall and new growth, trees of the past
sunk in red clay—
the Japanese cherry that flared
like an Easter boutonniere, and the scraggly
mimosa where a crow perched once,
flashing a quarter in its beak.
Or that stand of pines you raced through,
where her dress snagged on bramble
and buck brush, where soft needles spread
a gentler earth above the earth.
Magnolias, their coppery bangle,
their waxy blossoms drinking up the light
like delicate teacups,
the finest in a cemetery in Richmond
where all summer scholars drowsed

with musty books tenting their chests,
thirteen thousand crosses
fluttering behind their eyelids.
The gnarled roots of the live oak
that churned the courthouse steps back to dust
as the old laws vanished into the night's vault,
turning backwards on wind and rain
to leaf, to pulp. And the sweet gum in Selma
battered by shotgun blasts,
the cottonwood somewhere outside Charleston
with a foot of rotted rope still dangling
from a branch. There, where the cicadas
climb their wire ladders of song,
and the frantic shadows scissor in the wind
like the arms of a man
flagging down help roadside;
there, where the forest runs out of breath
and the light breaks so suddenly
you have to shut your eyes.

Dog Gospel

When I dare at last to imagine hunger,
I see a farmer wandering his parched fields
knowing nothing to do, finally, but sleep
the day out in the barn's long shadow,
dreaming of the family dog he drove
deep into a neighboring county
and abandoned by the side of the road.
Weeks later a boy finds it in a ditch—
timid and gimp, a halo of gnats
festering between its swollen testicles
and wormy flanks—and he coaxes it
into some pines, tethers it with a tentstake
and a chain as the late summer light
spirals and drapes over the branches,
a mirage the dog slavers and snaps at.
Consider the boy's amusement
as he imagines the animal jerking the light
down and the ruckus of bells that clang

and catapult from the treetop belfries,
the canopy rent like a piñata, spilling licorice
and circus peanuts, coins and fluttering dollar bills.
The real possibilities are beyond him.
The dog as a parable of pain or loss.
Hunger as some small iridescent thing at work
inside the animal, hovering around its heart
the way a lone dragonfly skirts the dry pond crater,
dismantling the day—light unstitched
from dust, dust unbuckled from air.
By now, the dog's given up, and the boy
watches its tongue loll in the pine needles,
the heave and fall of its stomach, its eyes
following birdflight in and out of the shade.
Restless for something he cannot name,
he imagines the music he might make
if he thumped the dog's belly like a drum.
Imagines its eyes are the color of iron.
Imagines the unimaginable and does it,
the tire tool and the belly unwilling instruments,
and the dog's caterwaul is not like music
at all and when night comes the cricketsong
dulcifies nothing, the dog's body
is just a body, is not paltry, is not glorified.
What hunger is this that haunts the boy,
that haunts the man sleeping in the shade?
Watch as the dragonfly dips into his open mouth
and keeps going, a blur between bone and sinew,
a wet thread collapsing soft caverns of flesh,
gone to where his body is a field
honed by sleeves of sunlight,
to where the boy ceases to be and the man wakes.
He knows what flits through him now
keeps the time with its thrumming,
carrying him away from himself
into himself, to where the dog roves in the shadows—
ravenous, luminous—its tail bobbing
in the heat, a winnowing sliver of light.

COLEMAN BARKS

Lard Gourd

In the 19th century in Georgia
there was a clever dog who found he could
secretly dig his way under the foundations
into the back of a meathouse.

The meat was hung to smoke too high
for his leap, but there were gourds
loaded with lard nearer his level.

The night he made his entry
was early in the century. The new residents
of the land were intruders themselves,
scared and cruel, so when they heard
the banging about, they did not investigate
until morning. The dog had gotten his head stuck
in a lard gourd. He could not see,
and he almost smothered out there
in the helpless percussion of his night.

This ancient color
allegorizes three of my troubling conditions:
blind desire, panic, and blackout drinking.

I have felt at times that I might be carrying
the living thread that connects
the sufi and zen currents,
also the vedantic and high mountain shaman.

Then I get drunk, talk trash to a sweet saint
woman, fall out of my top bunk, scare the children,
pee indoors, and I know the golden thread
I hold is puissant bad behavior
and not being present for the events of my life
I am a bad dog with sex and alcohol.
I do not lead a pure life.

Then I remember the dog inside his lard
inside his gourd inside himself,

the dog that grows still and quiet.
I have somehow achieved these breathing holes.
I cannot see where I am going,
but I can breathe. Others have died
on nights like this. Maybe some human type
will find me and ungourd my head
and scrape this shit off
and groom my face with turpentine.

I fall on my knees to beg forgiveness
for meathouse-rude intoxication
and give all praise to the being
that lives and watches out, dog or not,
from the gummed-together eyes
of the lard gourd dog.

For those not of a monkish cast,
I'll explicate. The lard is the mind.
The gourd the container of that.
The meathouse, this temptatious world.
The dog is me. What gets quiet
behind the dog's eyes, survives and looks out,
has no name, except maybe *you*.

Grace

There's an eruptive quality on mother's side,
    One Thanksgiving my
        cousin Tom Lamar was asked to say grace,

which was a joke since Tom was way too religious for
    church and so began,
        "May the big pumpkin eat the little pumpkin and

all the buzzards left of the river descend to the leafball
    nest in the willow tree
        where the sparrow lice are waiting for the squirrel

to return, praise be." Aunt Edith adds quietly, "Thankyee
    Jesus," and everyone sits
        down deadpan till Sally's small one, Mary,

says, "Can I open my eyes now?"

Luke and the Duct Tape

Nothing can save us. All this sweetness dies and rots.
Luke was a thirty-year-old pharmacy graduate
student who worked at Horton-Add Drugs,
at the post office in the back
that stays open until seven p.m., my post office.

It also has a lunch counter.
He sometimes did things behind there,
like make a tuna fish sandwich
and fill a glass with ice and diet coke.

He mopped the place and swept up,
as quick and accurate with the broom-jabs
as he was at calculating my strange Tasmanian mail.
Hey, Finland! Once, I sent out seventy-four books
priority mail. He said, It looked like Christmas
back there. In the storeroom where
the mailman picks up.

He laughed so easily with his quiet industry,
something out of Norman Rockwell.
He's maybe the most promising thing we are,
Luke, young American man just before
he meets a woman and raises a family
and does church group and Little League,
and every good thing stored in his strong hands
comes building out into the air.
Luke, master of small fixing.

Now on the glass double door, this handwritten
posterboard for his memorial service.
11 a.m. today. I missed it.
Would I have gone? *Luke Poucher.*
I never knew a last name.

One day we had some talk about how he knew
my name from all the mail, but I didn't know
his. Luke. That's a great name.

He was killed instantly last Thursday
in an automobile accident down the street
on Lumpkin at Old Princeton Road,
where he lived, not half a mile from me,
not a week ago I had not heard
and don't now ask the Horton family for details.

Car wreck. Luke's dead. Luke 17:21.
The kingdom of God is within you.
He was so lightheartedly that,
it took your breath.

It is with his death I fear my own
before the loving here gets as open
as it might could get in such as me?

It may be Luke is off somewhere profound
and myriad, though I feel him close
and still-mortal as I write this, waiting
for the fooling satisfaction
of my own phrasing.

What is the sudden subtraction of a young man,
who might just as well be my son,
a filament of ocean beauty
I do and don't see today, do.

I grieve the death of Luke Poucher
for the place he swept and tended so well,
this fivepointed threshing floor
of stores and walkers and apartments,
mailmen, depositors, lunching retiree,
chemo-waver, body-worker, skateboarder,
UPS, any bunch that knows each other's
half-grin in hurried irritation
out doing errands.

Let this be Luke, this end of the parking lot
around the mailbox, Luke Poucher Place.
The air, the few flowers,
and the people as they meet going in
to buy lunch or stamps or shampoo,
their small nods of helplessness.

I asked for duct tape once.
You know, we ought to carry that,
but we don't. It's about all I know
how to do to fix anything.

I've got some broken ducks.
I need to get them in a row.

Let this low-talking, the love and the joking
we do fumbling for courtesy
here at the door to be Luke, Luke
looking up from the stroke
of his all-hallowing broom, *Beautiful*
out there, idn't it?

JACK B. BEDELL

Travail

Handling serpents doesn't impress me.
I've done it too often to feel any real breath
on my neck from the act. I've come home
too many spring mornings from the marsh
at the back of my neighborhood with a pillow case
full of snakes snatched from the water's edge,
thrown them on the cool concrete under the carport
to set while I ate lunch, then spilled
the slow curves out between my feet
to see what I'd caught. Snakes
of all colors and moods—copperheads, moccasins,
pygmy rattlers, angry hognoses,
I've held them all, fangs or not, and lived fine.
No, there's no real trial to serpents.
They're too easy to stun with cold
or the throb of a three-piece band
pulsing in the boards of some old church.

That row of Mason jars full of strychnine, though,
all crystal clear and lined up on the altar,
that there is a different kind of test altogether.
No matter how cold or loud the church is,
it sits there still, willing to wait for you
to work up the nerve to snatch a jar off the wood
and hoist it over the dancing crowd,
unscrew its lid and tilt it toward your lips,
knowing your muscles are going to cramp
so tight they'll lock down your lungs,
the trismus spreading with every stomp.
And when that liquid slithers down your throat
into the cul-de-sac of your stomach,
there's not but a couple of ways to pass
through that kind of test to the other side.
Both of them involve pain and grace,
only one offers a tomorrow.

Saturday Night Crab Boils

By the time the kids came in from playing chase or four square or horseshoes, the tables were already piled high with blue crab, potatoes, and corn. All of it steaming hot and full of pepper and lemon, right off the butane and out of the pots. The eating was straight noise, everybody cracking shells with the handles of butter knives, picking out meat, and telling stories over somebody else's beat. The women drank highballs in gold-rimmed glasses. The men pulled beers from salted ice in every kind of can you could imagine—Pabst Blue Ribbon, Schlitz, Pearl, Falstaff, Jax. Then in no time flat, the shells were rolled up in old newspaper and thrown into garbage cans outside, the tables were folded up, and somebody cranked up the music for the fais do-do. As soon as the eight-track came on, our folks danced like the garage was a V.F.W. hall. They turned up the Frankie Laine and spun each other out into the oyster-shelled driveway, right into the street sometimes, spinning and juking to "Where the Wild Goose Goes" and not caring who heard or saw or wasn't invited to the party. They made joy, and we watched. Our folks moved and laughed and sang like nothing had to be cleaned or put away, like Monday wasn't going to be hard for any one of them.

Loup Garou

Some nights a shadow bends the sugar cane
towards the back porch, and what wind there is
carries a scent that starts the dog to grumbling.

It doesn't matter that all the locks are latched
and all the knives are put away. The moon
has risen over the fields, and coons and treefrogs

press their bellies against cypress and keep quiet.
These are nights mothers warn their children
to keep hands and feet over the mattress;

the Loup Garou is coming for their fingers and toes.
It doesn't have to come as the wolf, or fog.
It could easily be the blue heron creeping

just behind the children's cane, or the nighthawk
razing each row for field mice. Any light-footed shape
can bring it close enough to make frissons.

And nothing, not even an infant's calm breath,
can keep it back, until the sun climbs
over the cane and burns its eyes away.

DESTINY O. BIRDSONG

Sugar

I

Late harvest frenzy could fell a full-grown man:
Fighting for space with the sun, the snakes, the heat.
The tug-o-war with stray dogs. River rats.
Shit, a half-wit and a machete could split your guts
Open before either of you knew.
So men like my father learned to work quickly
And move on. To leave some things undone, without amends.

II

Every so often my friend Christina's father,
Drunk as a drain with rum on Saturday nights,
Would slice stalks into slippery little slits
Just big enough for me and her. We'd sit
In our thin nightgowns, savoring the juice.
The real thing, he would say. *The first real thing*
Anything expensive ever tastes like,
And it's growing right under
[he'd kiss my lips] *your nose.*

Drink cost money. Women did. Men too.
But cane and little girls were always free;
They grew on every side of the road we knew.

III

A Zulu man once strangled nineteen women
And threw their bodies in fields just north of Durban.
When workers burned cane at the end of the season,
Swollen black bodies burst into syrupy flame.
He lived in a nearby shanty township
So dangerous the white policemen wouldn't enter.
They knew his name by the seventh victim, but waited, afraid.
Patrolling for bones scattered by wild boar.

IV

My grandmother died in January, the coldest month
All year. But even so, great gusts of sleet
Couldn't blow the bittersweet smell of gangrene away.
Doctors had already cut off what they could:
Her buttocks. A leg. Two pounds of flesh from one thigh.
Pieces of her piled in the basement at Waste Management.
Her daughter was twenty-two. I was unborn.

Well, that all happened a long, long time ago,
My mother said. *You should forget about those things.*
She slipped a pecan pie into the oven and looked away.

DAVID BOTTOMS

Shooting Rats at the Bibb County Dump

Loaded on beer and whiskey we ride
in the dump in carloads
to turn our headlights across the wasted field,
freeze the startled eyes of rats against mounds of rubbish.
Shot in the head, they jump only once, lie still
like dead beer cans.
Shot in the gut or rump, they writhe and try to burrow
into garbage, hide in old truck tires,
rusty oil drums, cardboard boxes scattered across the mounds,
or else drag themselves on forelegs across our beams of light
toward the darkness at the edge of the dump.
It's the light they believe kills.
We drink and load again, let them crawl
for all they're worth into the darkness we're headed for.

Under the Vulture-Tree

We have all seen them circling pastures,
have looked up from the mouth of a barn, a pine clearing,
the fences of our own backyards, and have stood
amazed by the one slow wing beat, the endless dihedral drift.
But I had never seen so many so close, hundreds,
every limb of the dead oak feathered black,

and I cut the engine, let the river grab the jon boat
and pull it toward the tree.
The black leaves shined, the pink fruit blossomed
red, ugly as a human heart.
Then, as I passed under their dream, I saw for the first time
its soft countenance, the raw fleshy jowls
wrinkled and generous, like the faces of the very old
who have grown to empathize with everything.

And I drifted away from them, slow, on the pull of the river,
reluctant, looking back at their roost,
calling them what I'd never called them, what they are,
those dwarfed transfiguring angels,
who flock to the side of the poisoned fox, the mud turtle
crushed on the shoulder of the road,
who pray over the leaf-graves of the anonymous lost,
with mercy enough to consume us all and give us wings.

Under the Boathouse

Out of my clothes, I ran past the boathouse
to the edge of the dock
and stood before the naked silence of the lake,
on the drive behind me, my wife
rattling keys, calling for help with the grill,
the groceries wedged into the trunk.
Near the tail end of her voice, I sprang
from the homemade board, bent body
like a hinge, and speared the surface,
cut through water I would not open my eyes in,
to hear the junked depth pop in both ears
as my right hand dug into the silt and mud,
my left clawed around a pain.
In a fog of rust I opened my eyes to see
what had me, and couldn't but knew
the fire in my hand and the weight of the thing
holding me under, knew the shock of all
things caught by the unknown
as I kicked off the bottom like a frog,
my limbs doing fearfully strange strokes,
lungs collapsed in a confusion of bubbles,
all air rising back to its element.
I flailed after it, rose toward the bubbles
breaking on light, them felt down my arm
a tug running from a taut line.
Halfway between the bottom of the lake
and the bottom of the sky, I hung like a buoy
on a short rope, an effigy
flown in an underwater parade,

and imagined myself hanging there forever,
a curiosity among fishes, a bait hanging up
instead of down. In the lung-ache,
in the loud pulsing of temples, what gave first
was something in my head, a burst
of colors like the blind see, and I saw
against the surface a shadow like an angel
quivering in a dead-man's float,
then a shower of plastic knives and forks
spilling past me in the lightened water, a can
of barbequed beans, a bottle of A.1., napkins
drifting down like white leaves,
heavenly litter from the world I struggled toward.
What gave then was something on the other end,
and my hand rose on its own and touched my face.
Into the splintered light under the boathouse,
the loved, suffocating air hovering over the lake,
the cry of my wife leaning dangerously
over the dock, empty grocery bags at her feet,
I bobbed with a hook through the palm of my hand.

In a U-Haul North of Damascus

1

Lord, what are the sins
I have tried to leave behind me? The bad checks,
the workless days, the Scotch bottles thrown across the fence
and into the woods, the cruelty of silence,
the cruelty of lies, the jealousy,
the indifference?

What are these on the scale of sin
or failure
that they should follow me through the streets of Columbus
the moon-streaked fields between Benevolence
and Cuthbert where dwarfed cotton sparkles like pearls
on the shoulders of the road? What are these
that they should find me half-lost,
sick and sleepless
behind the wheel of this U-Haul truck parked in a field on Georgia 45

a few miles north of Damascus,
some makeshift rest stop for eighteen wheelers
where the long white arms of oaks slap across trailers
and headlights glare all night through a wall of pines?

2

What was I thinking, Lord?
That for once I'd be in the driver's seat, a firm grip
on direction?

So the jon boat muscled up the ramp,
the Johnson outboard, the bent frame of the wrecked Harley
chained for so long to the back fence,
the scarred desk, the bookcases and books,
the mattress and box springs,
a broken turntable, a Pioneer amp, a pair
of three-way speakers, everything mine
I intended to keep. Everything else abandon.

But on the road from one state
to another, what is left behind nags back through the distance,
a last word rising to a scream, a salad bowl
shattering against a kitchen cabinet, china barbs
spiking my heel, blood trailed across the cream linoleum
like the bedsheet that morning long ago
just before I watched the future miscarried.
Jesus, could the irony be
that suffering forms a stronger bond than love?

3

Now the sun
streaks the windshield with yellow and orange, heavy beads
of light drawing highways in the dew-cover.
I roll down the window and breathe the pine-air,
the after-scent of rain, and the far-off smell
of asphalt and diesel fumes.

But mostly pine and rain
as though the world really could be clean again.

Somewhere behind me,
miles behind me on a two-lane that streaks across
west Georgia, light is falling
through the windows of my half-empty house.

Lord, why am I thinking about this? And why should I care
so long after everything has fallen
to pain that the woman sleeping there should be sleeping alone?
Could I be just another sinner who needs to be blinded
before we can see? Lord, is it possible to fall
toward grace? Could I be moved
to believe in new beginnings? Could I be moved?

BESMILR BRIGHAM

The Hurricane

raging tonight off Brownsville

waves raising lions of the sea
flat sands boca del toro

beat over the tall-palm ways
dip mesquite earth in wet
                                                        lay down the still
will in the heart /still whirling back

                                                                and I:
sit in a house in Arkansas. to take a train
                                                                       a bus
drive down into that earth the blood races
                                                    people rushing out filling
cars with last electric gas. they will board their
windows
huddle my mother with her sons my father
walking the drip-deep floor. The storm is

not outside us.
What do we fear?
losing the things a man loves
                                                        shelter
(if the roof falls babies crying

once in a rare time the rage the blood-rage /there
is something to meet it: we are not alone—the storm

comes in to meet the spirit of a body
and the body to let it wash clean-over

I will sit in the house of my heart and receive him

Winston Weathers

animals along the highway in arkansas & louisiana

After fog
burns from the valleys
in Southern

mountains/highways
emerge like naked
veins, petrified

veins in
the Southern body/
& small

animals—sleep
with broken

ribs & frozen
jaws on the dark
shoulders

of these state
& national monuments/
they dream

of blind
mechanical blood/they
stiffen into

highway
signs/directions/brief
warnings

/& we are
reflected (light & motion
through the Southern

night) in
the mirror of their
dead eyes.

KATHRYN STRIPLING BYER

Dagger

Don't sing love songs
lest you waken the blade

that seeks marrow, my heart's
muscle, bone-chain

that carries me deep
into shady groves where

I hear naught but my own
blood dissembling.

No dulcimer stringing
its lies, no more wandering

into the dark where I lay
beneath silver leaves dangling

their keys to a door
I saw closing, its light fading

surely as maidenhair weaving
its warnings in vain.

Oh my bridal shroud
now laid aside in the rosewood!

His brazen ring knotted
from wild vine! Don't ever

again sing me love songs
or I'll snatch the strings from the neck

of your mandolin, I'll slash
the warp of my mother's web

winding me fast to her ribside.
Her whet stone. I'll sharpen

my sorrow till nothing's left,
nary a spindle of seed sprouting,

mayapple ripening, false
stab of Solomon's seal rising

out of the leafmold where
never again will I suffer

the pulse in my throat
to be reft of its last loving cries.

Bait

Her lips dribbled what looked like bug juice
when she called me over. *You there.*

Never the name of her first grandchild
for whom I knew I'd been christened,

nor even my everyday name,
nicked because I was so small at birth

they thought I'd never grow into who I am now,
still inhaling the air of her sitting room,

hearing her yellow piano keys clacking
through afternoons holding me hostage

to self-pity whining like flies in her cuspidor.
Too long have I cast my lineage as hook

line and sinker, swallowing cornpone
she handed out Sundays to each of us children.

Now I sniff her slop jar and jiggle
the grin of her teeth in their water glass,

tiptoe on gritty soles
over her kitchen linoleum,

knowing the darkness in which she lay
down never lasts. Must I stare again

into her open mouth waiting for chocolate
dipped cherries we brought every birthday

and Christmas Eve, hungry to suck to the quick
every sweet nothing I never offered,

its syrup escaping her lips
like a pleasure too guilty to speak of?

I dare not. I do what
I can for her. I wipe her chin.

Delivery

1

Pulleys and hooks
or his own hands
my father would use
to pull out the calf,
else it would die
inside its mother.

2

The doctor said *don't worry,*
you could be tied to a tree
and your baby would fall out
neat as a melon.

I should have let her swim out
like the Pisces she is
and not let him maul her with forceps.

I know he was weary. Past midnight,
he wanted to leave. Like my father
who'd waited for hours alone in a field.

3

Last week a friend showed
me photos—her daughter
in bath water nursing
her newborn. I emailed
my daughter the images,
to which she messaged
No way would I sit
in a bathtub if you'd
given birth to me there!

4

Wheeled to Delivery,
cervix forced wide
by the doctor who told me
to stop yelling,

I felt like one of those heifers
my father had tried
to save, both bloody hands
grabbing hoof,

tail, or head,
anything he could pull
out onto grass and declare
it delivered.

FRED CHAPPELL

The Artful Dodger Out of the Bag

Interviewer. *So many have heard of your Great Escape,*
The way you survived to lend us hope,
They clamor to hear your true Life Story.
Were you always destined for Glory?

Glory, you say? We didn't know any.
We lived in shameful poverty.
Old Man decided that we were too many
And desired us chained to the bottom of the sea.

"Old Woman," he said, "bag up them cats.
Snivel and bawl, I don't give a durn.
It's all we can do to feed our own brats.
They're headed for the River of No Return."

"But William," said she, "don't be unkind.
They're oh so funny and oh so cute.
I'll share with them, I really won't mind."
The Old Man said, "I don't give a hoot."

She pleaded, she wailed, she begged and she cried,
But Old Man's heart was hard as a rock.
When she petitioned his lenient side
He drew back his fist and gave her a knock.

So we knew what was up and we scattered away,
Three under the bed and two in a shelf.
She couldn't catch any, try as she may.
"You're useless," says he, "I'll do it myself."

He came at us now with his big clumsy hands.
We made ourselves small and cowered away.
He overturned tables and candlestands,
He busted to flinders her mama's tea tray.

I laughed so hard I was helpless as soup
To watch the Old Man fumble and blunder;

The cabinet fell, it knocked him for a loop;
He dropped to the floor with a thump like thunder.

The Old Woman ran to help him arise,
And I went to sniff him took down a peg,
But when I got there he opened his eyes,
And reached out and grabbed my right hind leg.

Into the burlap, spitting and yowling;
Out of the house and into the lane.
I decided right then to give up my howling
And try if I could employ my brain.

I unsheathed a claw, one single claw,
And severed the sack-threads one by one,
Think to free my right front paw
By the time we reached the deep mill-run.

We got to the water just before dark.
The Old Man stood on the bank of grass
And said to the world, "This is Wholesome Work,"
When I extended around and tattered his ass.

He let go the totesack and grabbed at his butt,
He yelled Blue Murder, a hair-raising screech.
When the sack touched the ground I squirmed right out,
Aiming to keep just past his reach.

He leapt at me twice and then once again;
I was dodging along the edge of the mill-race;
When he lunged the last time he went over and in,
Receiving his baptism with surly ill grace.

He splashed and he thrashed and he kept going down;
It looked like he'd met a well-deserved doom;
But then with a shout that alarmed the whole town,
He managed to grapple the lip of the flume.

When he pulled himself out I made tracks for home
To warn my sisters the Old Man was coming;
Drenched from his bootsoles plumb to his dome,
Wild as a cockfight, he'd be cussing and fuming.

He banged through the door and stood in a daze.
From his clothes there arose an Almighty Stink.

She took him all over and Old Woman says,
"Will, you was always a one for the drink."

Int. *Your heroic exploits inspire one and all.*
Is there anything further that you'd wish to say?

"That's all of the story that I'm willing to tell.
So I wish you Good Health and I bid you Good Day."

KELLY CHERRY

Wild Dogwood

1

Her betrothed had brought her
a bloom. The mountain was mad with it,
the froth and foam of it. He tucked
the bloom behind her ear and smoothed
her hair over the stem.
Sometimes,
when he's not there,
when he takes his rig to
Atlanta or Birmingham,
she pushes aside the book
she has been reading and walks
on the mountain in moonlight,
stopping under the poplars and the pines to watch
the wind pulling at white petals
like a girl asking a daisy
if he loves her or loves her not.

2

The wild dogwoods are dying.
The bright, tumbling clouds of them are disappearing.

A breath blown into history.

The Heat Down South (Richmond, 1955)

The heat does something wonderful
and difficult for Northerners to grasp.
It says a silent benediction,
it houses us in torpor.
A halo of humidity

surrounds the porch, the people
are robed in sweat and none contrive
to do much more than read a magazine.
To turn the fan to "on" is strenuous
and so is reaching for a beer. Night
may bring relief or trouble but
tonight's forever from now.
A six-foot floor-fan shuffles the air,
which doesn't cool the room,
and no one stirs, and nothing else
is moving. Telephones won't ring:
Forget the will to power,
we haven't the will to say hello.
No one knocks. You are secured
from all assaults upon your consciousness
and there is nothing to keep you from
imagining a wiser nation might
arise among the fields and woods,
the birds at liberty,
the lions lying down with lambs.

Gulfport

Grandma insisted we learn the catechism
while we were there—my sister and I—and so
we did.
The mom-and-pop grocery store,
where, with pennies, we bought bubblegum
and jawbreakers, had a simple wood floor
so cool to our feet when we came in barefoot
that we thought ourselves in heaven, and the sweets
confirmed us in our heathen theology.
A single door chimed to announce our presence,
as if we were the owners' salvation. "Back
for more," we said as one, as if mom-and-
pop might misunderstand why we were there,
ragamuffins with Tootsie Rolls on their minds.
The momentary respite from heat and light,

the (to us) seemingly oceanic Gulf,
convinced us we were blessed, or if we weren't
the devil had a better time in hell
than hosts of angels in the blistered sky.

MICHAEL CHITWOOD

A Childhood

A boy is given the gift of a hatchet
and goes out to cut something up.

It doesn't really matter what.
Behind the garage are some sumac.

They'll do to start. Their center is soft like putty
he discovers when he's hacked one down.

Wonder what the blunt side of the head
would do to the concrete floor of the garage?

It makes a pleasant *thock*. The handle is smooth
as skin. He would like to try it on something else.

He finds an old baseball and lets the hatchet
hit it. The ball turns and the blade strikes dirt,

nicks a spark from a rock. There's a smell
like a struck match. Behind the garage again,

an old tire propped with black water in the bottom.
The hatchet jumps off the tire's top, leaves a scuff.

In the boy's hand the hatchet considers its next strike:
what would it like to come down on?

It would like to go off somewhere, to a new place.
It would like to be with the boy when he says goddamn,

when he looks around and says I will chop
any goddamn thing I please. Any goddamn thing.

The One Day

We were behind on the job
so waited out the rain in the pickup.
Because the backhoe would mire

he shouldered the four-foot pipe joints
and brought them to us in the ditch.
The red mud clutched and tugged at his boots
and Bill laughed at his "Swan Lake"
as he fought through, lurching and staggering
when the mud would suddenly let go.
But he kept them coming, lugging the red joints
to us and then slogging back for another
while we slid on the gasket and fit the pipes together.
You can see how, pushing like that, he wound up,
two years later, with the tiny plastic piping of IVs
feeding into both arms and the three drainage tubes
snaking from under the patch on his chest.
His skin was a shade away from being same as the sheet
when I saw him in the ICU,
and he couldn't have lifted the drinking straw
on the bedside tray.
But that one day he brought two hundred yards of pipe
and even the red earth couldn't stop him.

Skinning

How many times did I hold them up for him
and watch how easily something that had lived
comes apart? In each hand I clutched
an unlucky foot and splayed them, belly-side
to him, and he'd pinch the fur at the crotch
and with the knifepoint separate the fur
from the muscle and fat underneath. He'd cut
all the way around until it seemed the rabbit's
long shirt had ridden up and then with one tug
he'd pull the fur down the body and over the head
the same way you'd tug the pajamas off a child.
From being plush, they suddenly looked frail, naked,
even old though most had known only two autumns.
Then with three or four quick flicks of the knife
he took the head and always the little headless nude
swung back and struck me in the chest.
Carefully, so as not to nick a gut, he slid the knife
under the belly skin and opened the little body.

Intestines, bladder and lungs spilled out but he would
have to pull them free, the glob in pink folds
like a sopping handkerchief dangling from his fingers.
He'd toss it over into the weeds and say a meal
for something passing in the night. In the night
when I startled out of sleep in the chair beside his bed
his bare, shrunken chest seemed so suddenly old
that again it knocked terribly against me, the dead weight.
Hold it up, he would say, higher. And I did.

JIM CLARK

Black Dog Shadrick Mayhew

I'm the one they won't tell about,
barn burner, horse thief, cheat.
In the hills of Corbin County, near
the Kentucky line, in the curve
of Horseshoe Bend, I carried
fifty-pound bags of sugar and corn
to my daddy's still when I was ten.
I stirred the mash and kept cold
the water that cooled the worm,
and clapped my hands at the first
clear drop that clung from copper,
then fell into the waiting jug.
Underneath the chestnut tree
my daddy snored, drunk on profit.

When I was seventeen I asked
Abigail Simpson to be my wife.
Yes, she said, but hadn't reckoned
on her Pa's tight-lipped No, sudden
and final as a shotgun blast. That night
I sloshed kerosene on stable floor hay
of his new barn, struck the match
and held it, eye level, till the flame
licked my fingers, then dropped it.

I lit out for Tompkinsville, and there
lived for five loose and lawless years,
vowing never to ask another man
permission of what I wanted.
And what I wanted I took and people
all along those Cumberland ridges
gave me wide berth, and a name—
Black Dog Shadrick Mayhew.

Then war came, and fire and death
and thievery marched the valleys,
a smoky cloak of pestilence hugging

the ridges I rode. Under cover
of a uniform, gray, with a little box
of a hat, I robbed and killed and burned
my way back to Corbin County.

When they slapped the horse's rump,
and I felt the stiff hemp bite
into my neck, I danced above the earth
and watched the smoke plait and curl.

Waking Up Drunk

1

In North Carolina, in mid-afternoon,
a man rises
through levels of alien sleep
like a stuttering moon
hoisted on rusted pulleys.

He thinks, or dreams, of hammers
tearing at the scaffolding of his sleep.
The room where he drifts
beats like a giant heart
as though the sluggish atoms
of desk, dresser, and bed
might suddenly wake
from their dense sleep
and flare, divergent,
wholly out of their jigsaw prison.

Sinking again,
he dreams of sleeping in the woods,
and in that sleep dreams
of waking and finding his ankle
gnawed half through by a rabid 'coon—
his faithless dogs
running far out under the frosted moon.

Slowly, slowly,
he rises, like a bubble in oil,
feeling his way up the rough sides
of sleep's dark well,

and cracks slightly
his matted eyelids.

2

On his feet now,
his body an old drafty house
whose windows shatter as he walks,
he makes for the bathroom
and cringes
before the awful grin of porcelain and steel.
He splashes up cold water
and his face washes down the drain.
This won't do, he mutters,
caught in the towel's strangling folds.

He stumbles to the front door
and throws it open.
Rivers of sunlight and wind
course through the cells
of his body's frayed network,
and whatever is in him that remains intact
lights up like a grid of stars
and he is awake.

Once More, the Night

Black rock under no moon,
stars, Jupiter cradled
in the dip of the southern ridge
where the power lines scissor up
toward the horizon's faint borealis.

Below, on the black mirror of the lake,
a small fishing boat purrs
into Bonner's Cove. Ripples shatter
the starlit water. A single match
flares, goes out, the orange coal
of a cigarette brightening.

"I'm getting married," you say,
cracking another beer.

I shift my weight against a rock
and smile. I know her, the quiet
dark-skinned woman with strong hands.
I look down at the boat, drifting
in the cove. Years from now,
it will be you down there,
and your wife and children, baiting
the hooks by a hissing yellow lantern,
setting the jugs afloat, the children
shrieking with delight at the huge
channel cat floundering in the boat.

The cooler between us empties.
I don't tell you I've decided
to go west, soon. You get up
to take a piss and startle
an owl in the cedars behind us.
"*Otus asio,*" you say,
"The common screech owl. Bane
of faint-hearted campers everywhere."
Laughing, you walk unsteadily
toward the woods. Your white shirt
ripples in the breeze, outlined
against the dark. From where I lie
you could be a spirit, moving
intently through a familiar wood—
William Bartram come ghostly downriver,
notebook in hand, eyes
full of bluebell and trillium,
a tale of the fierce alligator gar
on your tongue.

When you come back
there's already a glow in the east
and the fishing boat's making for
Redmond's Landing. You hand me a beer
and we finish the last two.

ALLISON ADELLE HEDGE COKE

Off-Season

For Fieldworkers and Framers Like Me

Early, on grayest morning, when we
nettled deep in between rows,
tobacco and sweet potato,
both two seasons away from planting,
you reasoned I belonged there,
flowing like creek water
below our bright leaf fields,
then showing only golden stubble and root.
You said I'd never make it
swinging hammers and teething
saws for Inland Construction.
I raised my back wings, those muscles
wrought from priming rows, muscles
which cradled my ribs and sides. I
chucked tools in the flat bed, headed
north, to the city sprawled out like
scattered masonry and split rails, Raleigh,
smoked factory winds and speakeasy halls.

A white chicken fell off a Tyson rig,
just a bit ahead of me on Saunders Street.
I called her "Hooker"
from walking down the red light street.
The Inland guy hiring was big and red,
sat behind a door laid flat for a desk on cinder block.
He chuckled much like you
at the sight of me but the fields and breaking horses
justified my ninety pounds of lean.
Next day he had me start out on a crew full of men.
Men who'd never seen a woman work
that way in town, first
time I had a chance to operate a backhoe,
first time I got to frame, and when I swung the hammer

full leverage, three pounds drove in sixteenpennys straight.
In six weeks, I made foreman.
Just before I drove back to you.
"Hooker" almost got pecked to death
by our bantams—citified as she was.

I laid out so much money, I beat
what you pulled in for fall. We settled in
for the long freeze. You ate ridicule and haste.
We never were the same,
until spring when the fields reclaimed
us as their own and we returned
to what we both knew and belonged to.
The off-season only an off-shoot
in what we were meant to be.
You never did know this part
of what I am. Fieldworker, or framer,
I only showed you what you said I couldn't be.

Packin' Four Corner Nabs

For All the Cracker Packin' Girls

fourteen, I'm packin'
crates Fairmont Foods—Cary, NC
only mixed-blood "Indian blonde" girl around
only factory workside worker not black
all of us under white Super's thumb

tho when shop stewards hound dues
I don't know what's what
thinkin' this work here
is dues enough
what's a union do for me?

Sadie, she took my arm, said,
"Listen, you stick close to me
when you go out back,
they're gonna get ya.'"
Me, I follow

suit down, shower up
snack bar and closing

fourteen, I'm still wild yet
don't know enough to be scared
so I never am
that's how I got these scars here.
Anyway, I follow Sadie

she's about fifty
and weighs five times that
just before the door she
grabs a hunk o' rebar
and latches my hand

we start out back
light up a Camel straight
look left, *there's about twenty,*
eyes, rebound right, *twenty count more,*
they semicircle in

memory rings—I hear my dad's voice advising me 'bout
        fightin' white girls
"Circle 'em they're easier to pick off"

Sadie swings the rebar
and calls 'em all on down
warning, "Touch one corn-silk
on this girl's head and
I'll kill ya'. I will, too."

Her eyes round and circle wild
her big bosom heaves breath
she swings round and wide
hoping for reason to let out some rising steam

half a century's factory work
crackers, all those crackers
four corner nabs under her belt 500 gallon vats—peanut butter
stink so strong the smell
lasts a lifetime and more
crackers flying by 'bout ninety miles per

pull and pack ten
thirty, if you're a stacker

pull and pack ten filled and
wrapped on belt conveyors
drop in cardboard containers

pull ten more
till ten times ten makes
one hundred count boxes—
Austin Foods—all the scrambled ones
go to feed dog, or hogs

somewhere, they say,
somewhere far, far, away

lookin' at Sadie swing rebar
you know she's packed plenty
I wish I was packin' more 'n fists
studying Sadie I surmise
her punch'd be good as my drop cut

on the so-white preacher's daughter's nose
when she called me a heathen
I was proud of breakin' it in one jab but
my dad said I maybe just
proved her right

Hell, I didn't even know what a heathen was
guess this union thing must
be like a club for preacher's daughters
I decide and slide
shuffle step slide
in to back up Sadie's swings

swing low, swing high, swing 'round and back

never had an older woman
fend for me before
defended plenty though
guess it's fair in all
Union guys they

just pull in and pull back
like a boxer afraid to land
case he might get landed on
Sadie is so big to me
she's the midnight blue of sky

just swings and swings with fear of God
human pendulum momentum
strutting her stuff through the crowd
straightening 'em out like scolding babies
"Didn't your mama hold you?"

"What you big men wanna
beat a tiny girl like this for?"

I look down my upper arms
fully bulged from field work—
furrows and packin' crate and
concrete block—heavy work side I live

they just don't fit my build
so I look like a monkey
when I look in mirrors
big muscular arms and back on
a skinny little frame

kinda wiry, funny, even to me
the biceps aren't tiny, I think
and pull back my jacket
to show 'em off
let 'em ripple with blood pumping

never did know when to be scared
even when I was really shy

Sadie steps through
Austin Food's finest forty
like walkin' water, she steps
I walk right on by behind her
they begin shuffling, shuffling

away at her words and
at the Super's floodlights

now circling us and flashin'
like a prison yard
counter escape
warden super packin' something else
we're past and out

I look at Sadie
she whispers low, only to me,

“Better get them dues paid.
Next check, okeh?”
I nod, duck out the lot

hitch a semi home down
highway 50   smellin’ like crackers
and peanut butter from packin’ four corner nabs
even after the shower down
spot a teamster card on the visor

DANIEL CORRIE

Sleeping and Waking

I am the next layer on those things that have happened already.
Andy Goldsworthy, as quoted in River and Tides

My mother bragged that she would stab my father
some night in his sleep. Who was this Southern girl
who finally drank herself into my mother?

Before he entered guestroom sleep, my father
slid a magazine inside his shirt to shield
his heart from sudden steel and from my mother.

Arms tightening in drowsiness, my father
dodged a kitchen knife his dreams could feel.
His waking arms crisscrossed to block my mother.

To tame his dreaming arms, my father
cut the ends off Quaker oatmeal
cardboard tubes. Fighting off my mother,

he wore those sleeves. That way, my father
rode through the scenes of sleep with elbows held,
locked in the cereal cylinders my mother

emptied making breakfasts for my brother
and me, on mornings when the kitchen smelled
of bacon frying. In the bedroom, my father

buttoned his colonel's jacket, by its lapel
the Silver Star. Some other day, my mother
left. We seldom spoke of her to one and other.

Wrong and right seemed dreams, each like the other.
Time bled my past, reddening like a future.
I would stitch each year, slow suture after suture.

KATE DANIELS

Autobiography of a White Girl Raised in the South

In any self-portrait from the '50s, you'd have to see the me
that was not me: the black girl trudging along the side of the road
while I whizzed past in my daddy's car. Or the not-me
girl in the bushes, peeing, while her mama kept watch
and I relieved myself inside, daintily, in the sparkling facilities
of the Southside Esso, labeled WHITES ONLY. All those
water fountains I drank from unthinkingly, the lunch counters
where I disdained my lunch—she was there on the wooden benches
bleached by sun out back of the store, or squatting on a curb
sipping from a Mason jar of tepid water lugged from home,
or eating her sandwiches of homemade biscuits and a smear of fat.

From the beginning, then, there were always two: me and not-me.
The one I was, white and skinny, straight brown hair. And the one
I wasn't, but could've been—that black or brown girl, hair coarser
than mine, eyes darker, skin gleamier and smooth, free of freckles.
I didn't even know where she lived, only saw her in public
when she stepped up on my granny's back porch with a paper bag
of okra, accompanying her mama, selling turnips and tomatoes,
or her daddy, with his tools, come to sharpen the knives.
Then, we eyed each other, I recall, hands behind our backs,
faces solemn and shy, our hair plaited, mine in one long, compliant
tail—but hers in a dozen marvelous sprouts, each tied off
with colored twine. Now, I think it's odd, cruel even,
I never shook her hand, showed off a toy, or asked her out
to my special place in my grandmother's yard,
the powdery patch of gray dust beneath the cherry tree,
where blossoms plopped down in tiny clouds of air and color.
There, cross-legged, knee to knee, we might've touched
each other and satisfied our terrible curiosity—
whether she, in fact, was just like me, and I, like her.
For a moment, sheltered by the blossoms of a flowering tree,
the universe might have seemed to us like the garden

it once was—various and multitudinous, aswarm
with rich textures, interesting odors, a wide palette of color and hue.

Instead, I kept my head down and watched her toes, bare and curled
in the powdery gray-brown dust, and felt envy for her going free
of shoes, and had no idea of the images that might be passing
through her mind. Then I heard my granny's much-loved voice,
calling from the porch, to come away and go inside. She sent away
the not-me's daddy without a sale, and chastised me throughout our lunch
for what she called "familiarity." And through the back screendoor,
I saw the not-me girl, walking away behind her daddy, not
looking back, and I heard his voice, querulous, too, chastising
her, as well, for something bad, whatever it was we almost did
but didn't, finally, dare to do.

Louisiana, Late Summer

Because our bodies have been claimed
by humidity, we walk around in our heads
in the heat, squatting in the backroom
to paint a baseboard, sweat
pouring down in fragrant runs,
the ghosts of different body parts
asserting themselves with distinctive odors.

Overhead, a fan twirls lackadaisically,
collecting spoors. Far back in the closet,
a light mold, transported here by some
primeval wind, festers on the toe
of a suede shoe. It pours its cheap
mold life into ignominy and plans
the destruction of the entire world.

The Figure Eight

The swan's path is a calm infinity in Boston Common's
public pond. In it, closing back on itself after every turn,
I see the fragile image of my younger brother

in the years before his marriage failed, the rented farmhouse
south of Richmond he shared with friends, laborers
like him at DuPont Chemical. In the evenings,
their gray uniforms dark with sweat, their hair flattened into oily mats,
they squat together on the worn wood steps to smoke
a few joints and guzzle cheap beers, tossing the empties
towards the edge of the wood. They ignore the shattering.
A few minutes of silence before the alcohol kicks in,
its spidery fingers scrambling gratefully in their guts.
And then they're bitching themselves into a state of restlessness—
they've finished with the niggers and the god damned democratic
president, dispensed with the northerners' spiel
on collective bargaining. They're onto women now—
what cunts they are, how all they want is to take you
for a ride. Pissed at the child support somebody's
paying, the abortion another one's wife refused to have.
And without even speaking, they rise and walk down
into the meadow, their cigarettes gleaming weakly in last light,
to the place where the old car rests, a junker someone finagled
for $85 and a lid of hash. An Oldsmobile or something that
glamorous, from the 1950s, once turquoise and sleekly desirable,
Elvis blaring from the perforated speakers in either door,
a shapely car hop leaning down to latch a silver tray of fries
and shakes on the rim of the driver's window . . .
One of them hotwires it alive and my brother slides in, grinning,
lit now, somebody at last, both hands gripping the wheel, and takes off
around the meadow as if—this time—he might really be going somewhere.
His buddies howl when the car stalls out in a deep rut
and then roars to life again, blue smoke breaking
through the back of the engine. The car is whining and popping
with breakage, its back end swinging back and forth, the way
a wounded dog keeps going, homing for its master. The wheels
are straining, like that, trying to moving forward,
but he's just going around and around, around
in the mud stiff ruts, somewhere there in the dark cab,
his head cloudy, his mind set on nothing but the figure eight
he's making in the mud, inscribing it deep in the earth
so when God looks down He'll see the sign for infinity,
the same shape of the neat path the swan swims
in the pond at the public gardens where I sit, years away
several lives distant, a universe removed, my hands
shaking, my mouth dry, writing down the words of this poem.

KWAME DAWES

Thief

after Caesar

A grown man, even a boy, standing on the corner
laughing or looking, his empty hands dangling,
that is a thief. Pick him up, lock him up.

A thief still has shame, doesn't want a soul
to know he is a thief. Can't look you in the eye.
A thief is worse than a murderer, he has shame.

Nobody will thief from you with blood
in his head. No, a thief will walk by you,
smile with you for a whole week, and then strike.

Give a thief money, he won't know what
to do. Put a quarter on the table, walk
away, a thief will know what to do.

You can't fix a thief. It is in the blood.
A thief will look on your body and say
he wants what it can do. He will hire you.

A thief can see a woman's soul, know
her spirit, know how to talk to it. He will
make her cry out, take that sound and run.

When a thief is done with you, he looks
like God the way he comes when you don't
know, the way he makes you pray for peace.

But laugh with an open mouth in front of a thief.
He will steal your breath, leave you with
five years less in your future, leave you bereft.

A thief comes by where there is plenty. He
will stand around and watch your song floating
from your throat. Next thing, he makes a record.

When a man comes to you with a box to
say he wants to take your picture, you got
to know that every time he does, you fade a little.

Only one thing to do with a thief. Hound him,
call the world on him, let everyone get
a piece of him; let the dog lick his blood.

Reburial

Sometimes a man is one same song,
that is all there is to him. Maybe it wasn't
always that way with him, maybe one time
he had a wide open brain, and tomorrow
was like a window to him; a sky
so wide you could tell that all kinds
of songs were living there; and the man
could count laughter as a song, or
the sly calculus of desire, another,
or the slow contemplation of ordinary
happiness, the peace of sinlessness;
and when you saw him coming
you didn't know what song
you would hear because that man
had many songs. But like seasons
come or grey in the beard, a stone
can rise at a man's feet and cause
him to stumble, cause the world
to change, make the window
close; gather the grey and mauve
in the sky and leave him with this
one blanketing song, this shadow
over all he does. And this citizen
let a man die over stolen nails,
or broke his wife's heart with his
infidelity; or made God wink
with a constant weakness; and soon
this is his only song, the shadow
of dusk. A man like that will do
anything to learn a new song, to shake

this one song from his skin. So
he follows the instructions
of the diviner, bathes until his skin
is blistered and waterlogged, and
then he enters the sky that makes
a poet wish he could manage the seeping
of watercolors—he enters naked,
and starts to travel the magic
ship that will take him beyond
water, beyond light, deep into
the City of Bones where we must
leave the unwanted things
and then pray we may return
to the surface of things, filled
with new songs and laughter.

JAMES DICKEY

Cherrylog Road

Off Highway 106
At Cherrylog Road I entered
The '34 Ford without wheels,
Smothered in kudzu,
With a seat pulled out to run
Corn whiskey down from the hills,

And then from the other side
Crept into an Essex
With a rumble seat of red leather
And then out again, aboard
A blue Chevrolet, releasing
The rust from its other color,

Reared up on three building blocks.
None had the same body heat;
I changed with them inward, toward
The weedy heart of the junkyard,
For I knew that Doris Holbrook
Would escape from her father at noon

And would come from the farm
To seek parts owned by the sun
Among the abandoned chassis,
Sitting in each in turn
As I did, leaning forward
As in a wild stock-car race

In the parking lot of the dead.
Time after time, I climbed in
And out the other side, like
An envoy or movie star
Met at the station by crickets.
A radiator cap raised its head,

Become a real toad or a kingsnake
As I neared the hub of the yard,

Passing through many states,
Many lives, to reach
Some grandmother's long Pierce-Arrow
Sending platters of blindness forth

From its nickel hubcaps
And spilling its tender upholstery
On sleepy roaches,
The glass panel in between
Lady and colored driver
Not all the way broken out,

The back-seat phone
Still on its hook.
I got in as though to exclaim,
"Let us go to the orphan asylum,
John; I have some old toys
For children who say their prayers."

I popped with sweat as I thought
I heard Doris Holbrook scrape
Like a mouse in the southern-state sun
That was eating the paint in blisters
From a hundred car tops and hoods.
She was tapping like code,

Loosening the screws,
Carrying off headlights,
Sparkplugs, bumpers,
Cracked mirrors and gear-knobs,
Getting ready, already,
To go back with something to show

Other than her lips' new trembling
I would hold to me soon, soon,
Where I sat in the ripped back seat
Talking over the interphone,
Praying for Doris Holbrook
To come from her father's farm

And to get back there
With no trace of me on her face
To be seen by her red-haired father
Who would change, in the squalling barn,

Her back's pale skin with a strop,
Then lay for me

In a bootlegger's roasting car
With a string-triggered 12-gauge shotgun
To blast the breath from the air.
Not cut by the jagged windshields,
Through the acres of wrecks she came
With a wrench in her hand,

Through dust where the blacksnake dies
Of boredom, and the beetle knows
The compost has no more life.
Someone outside would have seen
The oldest car's door inexplicably
Close from within:

I held her and held her and held her,
Convoyed at terrific speed
By the stalled, dreaming traffic around us,
So the blacksnake, stiff
with inaction, curved back
Into life, and hunted the mouse

With deadly overexcitement,
The beetles reclaimed their field
As we clung, glued together,
With the hooks of the seat springs
Working through to catch us red-handed
Amidst the gray, breathless batting

That burst from the seat at our backs.
We left by separate doors
Into the changed, other bodies
Of cars, she down Cherrylog Road
And I to my motorcycle
Parked like the soul of the junkyard

Restored, a bicycle fleshed
With power, and tore off
Up Highway 106, continually
Drunk on the wind in my mouth,
Wringing the handlebar for speed,
Wild to be wreckage forever.

The Sheep Child

Farm boys wild to couple
With anything with soft-wooded trees
With mounds of earth mounds
Of pinestraw will keep themselves off
Animals by legends of their own:
In the hay-tunnel dark
And dung of barns, they will
Say I have heard tell

That in a museum in Atlanta
Way back in the corner somewhere
There's this thing that's only half
Sheep like a woolly baby
Pickled in alcohol because
Those things can't live his eyes
Are open but you can't stand to look
I heard from somebody who . . .

But this is now almost all
Gone. The boys have taken
Their own true wives in the city,
The sheep are safe, in the west hill
Pasture but we who were born there
Still are not sure. Are we,
Because we remember, remembered
In the terrible dust of museums?

Merely with his eyes, the sheep-child may
Be saying saying

I am here, in my father's house.
I who am half of your world, came deeply
To my mother in the long grass
Of the west pasture, where she stood like moonlight
Listening for foxes. It was something like love
From another world that seized her
From behind, and she gave, not lifting her head
Out of dew, without ever looking, her best
Self to that great need. Turned loose, she dipped her face

Farther into the chill of the earth, and in a sound
Of sobbing of something stumbling
Away, began, as she must do,
To carry me. I woke, dying,

In the summer sun of the hillside, with my eyes
Far more than human. I saw for a blazing moment
The great grassy world from both sides,
Man and beast in the round of their need,
And the hill wind stirred in my wool,
My hoof and my hand clasped each other,
I ate my one meal
Of milk, and died
Staring. From dark grass I came straight

To my father's house, whose dust
Whirls up in the halls for no reason
When no one comes piling deep in a hellish mild corner,
And, through my immortal waters,
I meet the sun's grains eye
To eye, and they fail at my closet of glass.
Dead, I am most surely living
In the minds of farm boys: I am he who drives
Them like wolves from the hound bitch and calf
And from the chaste ewe in the wind.
They go into woods into bean fields they go
Deep into their known right hands. Dreaming of me,
They groan they wait they suffer
Themselves, they marry, they raise their kind.

Canebrake

Morning; it shows
Its suppleness, and the massed green bones of strength.
Beyond, the river rises
Like a serpent touched at the tip of the tail,
And sprung, thereby, in a flurry of feathers to the eyes.

The road is still, and does itself no good,
As you kick its ruts into the little field.
From your feet, far out above

Your head, is a silence made of sounds.
Is it the pencil leaves
Of the stalks, you hear, or the river sprouting, unseen?

Making not the shadow of a thing
Beyond the naked stems, the sun
Casts a game of jackstraws on ground.
It might be better if,
Feeling it hopelessly exposed, you put your hand
On one of the light, slim, jointed tubes.
Thus, in a dream some years from now, you may have entered

The sway of the sprinkled leaves on top,
And seen the serpent lift his blinding head
Out of the side of the river,
The hot green wind come forth,
Come in and thatch a staler roof
To the roof of your drying mouth.
Insect-like, among the grassy posts,
You still may learn which gradual sound

Is the river's, and which the fending of leaves.
Here is another place that moves within
If motionless. Stand, swaying a little, here,

Your hand a support of classic, columned
Yet untameable air, and feel for the needle's
Word to be split, in peace, on the tongue of the serpent
An army of angry children would stomp to death,
Afraid it would speak, as it will.

R. H. W. DILLARD

A Friday Night Kind of Sonnet

Hell, I once hit a man so fucking hard
He's still falling, about two years ago,
So you think I'm scared of you?
You? No fucking way, Joe Zay.

That was right after I had to duck
A fucking cue ball or maybe it was
The eight ball, more fitting if it was,
Damn near busted my head wide open.

I heard about some damn moose tried
To take on a whole fucking freight train
Head on. Talk about dumb. Thought
It was another moose or something.
Bout as dumb as you, I'd fucking say,
You try to get anything on with me.

Event; A Gathering; Vastation

> If the natural world is so double-faced and
> Unhomelike, what world, what thing is real?
>
> *William James,* The Varities of Religious Experience

Rolling in glass, drunk
As cauliflower, knowing
The flaw but not knowing
Its nature, swamped:

Blue as an old orange,
You grip the sash,
Hear the day like a noise
In an empty hall, warped,
Discolored, open, endless.

You have blown out the candle,
Taken the required beating,
Opened the gifts: raw knuckles,
Crisp skin, the bruise.

Old as any hour, eroding,
Caught in a mirror, thrown
Back bent and peeling,
You have celebrated too well,
Too soon, are alone too soon.

The old day mocks you,
Dies with the blind twist
Of a moth, flying by stars,
Downed by electric light.

And the night covers you up,
Small scars, the large deformity,
Leaves you on the rug, pinched
In your own shadow, a day
And years older, on a bed of shards.

CLAUDIA EMERSON

Ephemeris

The household sells in a morning, but when
they cannot let the house itself go for
the near-nothing it brings at auction,
the children, all beyond their middle years,
carry her back to it, the mortgage now
a dead pledge of patience. Almost emptied,
there is little evidence that she ever
lived in it: a rented hospital bed
in the kitchen where the breakfast table
stood, a borrowed coffee pot, chair,
a cot for the daughter she knows, and then does not.
But the world seems almost right, the near-
familiar curtainless windows, the room
neat, shadow-severed, her body's thinness,
like her gown's, a comfort now. Perhaps
she thinks it death and the place a lesser
heaven, the hereafter a bed, the night
to herself, rain percussive in the gutters—
enough. But like hers, the light sleep of spring
has worsened—forsythia blooming
in what should be deep winter outside
the window—until it resembles the shallow
sleep of a house with a newborn in it,
a middle child she never saw, a boy
who lived not one whole day (an afternoon?
an evening?) sixty years ago in late
August. And as though born without a mouth,
like a summer moth, he never suckled
and was buried without a name. She had waked to that—
that cusp of summer, crape myrtles' clotted
blooms languishing, anemic, the cicadas
exuberant as they have always been
in their clumsy dying.
                                        This middle-born
is now the nearer, no, the only child.

The undertaker's wife has not bathed
and dressed him; the first day's night instead
has passed, quickening into another
day, and another, and he is again awake,
his fist gripping a spindle of turned light,
and he is ravenous in his cradle of air.

Practice Blood

From late spring through summer, the county paper
runs grainy photographs of anomalies
from gardens, an entire page—tomatoes big
as melons held up by people who grew them,
conjoined pumpkins, the absurd, misshapen gourd.
But when hunting season opens, a full page
won't hold them: first turkey, first doe, first buck,
killed by boys mostly, though not all, children
as young as six or seven holding gobblers
by the feet, wing spans wider than they are
tall, others posed holding up bucks' heads
by their antlers. The day comes long awaited,
inevitable as the wedding on another page.
They cannot recall when the first of the opened
carcasses appeared suspended from the tree
beside the swing. They were told the joy of it
before being waked up to see the gutting,
dressing, before being brought along to watch,
all part of practicing: *inhale, exhale*
by half, squeeze, don't pull. The captions name
whose child, whose land, what make, caliber—shotgun,
muzzleloader, rifle, sometimes detail
about the kill, the points in the rack's expanse,
a dropped tine.
                    All their eyes are open,
as though in compliance, wet, luminous—the same
whether heart shot and dropped mid-graze or lung shot,
found hours later having tried to outrun the blood-
raveling wound; the lens of the eye still shines
as though from dawn fog, or the field of frost
after the understory died—exhaled by half—

this the look of a mirror in a vacant house
that seems to hold a light no longer there.

Third

He survived the first beach landing and an entire
world war for this: the textile mill, buildings
looming over the river, windows painted
black during the war so they could run the third
shift he came to choose—easier he found
to black out the days, shutter them, so that the hours
that had been for drinking or the dreams
he could better sleep through, to wake evenings
for cigarettes and coffee. The trick—not to wake
too much, avoid the gaze of the face in the mirror
as he shaved it, watch static on the television screen
or the crosshairs of a test pattern. Nights were
easier bright and loud—rooms the size
of airplane hangars, close as circus tents,
dye room, spinning room, his the weave room,
voiceless, lit with sound, rows of looms,
their ceaseless weft and warp, shuttles swift,
percussive—clawhammer-like—air thick
with the smell of cotton, lint in their lungs, their hair,
sheeting like dyed, transfigured fields, or fields
bleached to blinding, a collective shroud.
Graveyard shift
made them all equal, orphaned; those with families
saw them Sundays, afternoon its own ghost.
It was easier to bear what no one else wanted—
a world just lightening when his shift ended, the river
they all crossed running with the night's dye.

TARFIA FAIZULLAH

Nocturne in Need of a Bitch

Forget the sounds of glass shattering,
the alleyways I walk past, hunger
knifing me cleaner. Forget the schizophrenic

I still see, for years now—forget his voice
burning past me. *Bitch, I need you.*
Bitch, I need, I need, he moans,

and it's not me he wants, but
the night is a varnished peeling wall
against which I always want to be

roughly pressed. How many other nights
has he stumbled across this sidewalk,
pleading with someone else

who isn't there—cars blast by:
earthquake of bass, crackle of voices,
thigh, throat, clavicle, crook of elbow,

curve of breast, *bitch, I need, I need—*
and I can't forget those summers
all of us spent sleeping underground

in that old peach-carpeted basement,
can't forget how my sister was still
safe and warm beside me the night

I heard footsteps that weren't hers
or mine—I took her hand,
waited until the footsteps finally

stopped: dream-summoned,
alive or ghostly, I'll never know.

But what does that have to do with lips,
tug of earlobe, palms macerating
palms? *I need, I need,* and the hunger

inside me isn't for food, and I can't forget
we don't belong anywhere: not this city,
not in childhood's bed or the adult one

I slide alone into after praising Your name,
Lord. Tell me why being human is so lonely,
why this man turns now to embrace

no one beside him. Tell me why my sister
is a ghost stepping lightly across the floors
of strangers, their children asleep below.

Tell me why, Lord, you made it so that taking
a kiss full on the mouth feels like weeping:
the helpless swell, its delicious spill. I need,

I need. Take then, as You took her too.
Take the morning's sandpaper sunlight
in which I'll wake again to offer You

another day of hunger. Take from me
this razor humming inside my body
You made for any kind of breaking.

The Streetlamp above Me Darkens:

for this, I am grateful. This elegy
doesn't want a handful of puffed rice

tossed with mustard oil and chopped chilies,
but wants to understand why a firefly

flickers off then on, wants another throatful
or three of whiskey. This elegy is trying

hard to understand how we all become
corpses, but I'm trying to understand

permanence, because this elegy wants
to be a streetlamp dying as sudden as

a child, who, in death, remains a child.
Somewhere, there is a man meant for me,

or maybe he is meant merely to fall
asleep beside me. Across two oceans, there

is a world in which I thought I could live
without grief. There, I watched the hands

of a vendor reach with hands made of lace
towards a woman who leaned into him.

There, I fingered bolts of satin I never
meant to buy. There, no one said her name.

How to look down into the abyss without
leaning forward? How to gather the morning's

flustered shadows into a river? To forget
my sister was ever born? Tonight, I will

watch a man I could have loved walk past,
hefting another woman's child. He won't

look at me. I won't have wanted him to.
This elegy wonders why it's so hard

to say, I always miss you. Wait, she might
have said. But didn't you want your palms

to be coated in mustard oil? Did you really
want to forget the damp scent of my grave?

FORREST GANDER

From *Life of Johnson Upside Your Head*

✦

The Devil hummed around the tonic, the blue third and the fifth
he snatched this out air
to cock it on the wall, controlling timbre
while cotton pickers *prastered off like a load of bokros*

Smashes the sound box with his palm
sheep went astray the moon shot an octave
a cruel glare floods his skull zissified
on stump-likker bit a raw yellow onion

Then screws up slab of face
distorting linear time severing brambles
and readjusts his mouth cavity
takes off his jacket to reveal a downpour

The Devil intimated to make a long piss short
he slides tone around axis dragging limp bags
through cotton fields railing in embers on levee chipped
tooth doing jake leg and yawns tin can over
what young plant awaiting the revenant's
hallelujah immersed in 1932 brief, mosquito-bitten, gone

✦

The voice the dead man's voice is young and tight and high
the naturalness of it as language a man's voice
tuned a little sharp the image of the voice
a pressured high and letting out
the dead man's falsetto counterpointing a drum beat
in lower register his guitar breathing the blinds
of syllables his chair squeaks voice undulating
outside the wire-thin loops of swallows in his voice
the diphtheria epidemic in his voice the barn fires
his father a drunk in the dark
mistaking carbolic acid for cough medicine
bottleneck slide groups of triplets
in the treble strings tuned high-brown thumb

for hard rhythm intensity inside him his mouth
a little slack the concentration inside
the voice an orphan who ate match heads
his wife on the cooling board his baby buried
pain's medium voice contours of landscape eroded
mortal erotic upwelling to warp as the degree
of emotion the power to be funny
jammed through oblivion like crowbar cotton
fields frog gig pissing in wild sweet pea
sweat lubricating the voice sex speeding up the dead
man's voice orphaned from its mouth

Lovegreen

That the trunk, submerged in air,

whirling leaves, thresholds-out. On the bark of

its leader stem, a black-capped

chickadee pins caterpillars and lacewings.

Its water-sprouts and spurs unpruned,

unbraced, the Yellow Transparent tree's

boughs release the girl open-mouthed

pumping her two-wheeler

across a meadow softly-furred

as a bumble bee, her plastic bag

pendant with hard apples

from one handlebar swaying—

Coffee cut with honeysuckle.
The unprimed pump won't give up its water.
Mosquito hawk clings to the barn wall's shadow.

GEORGE GARRETT

Whistling in the Dark

What has happened, my friends, is this:
we are saying the same things over and over again
because we have to, because there is no other choice.

We are singing the old songs, whistling the same tunes,
each like a small boy in the dark, in a graveyard,
maybe, whistling to reassure the rotten dead

that he, of course, is careless, indifferent, fearless.
We are saying the same things in exactly the same tone of voice
because we have to, because there is no other choice,

except, perhaps, that purity of absolute silence
to which our noisy music does aspire,
with which our music will be well rewarded

all in due time. Meanwhile, my friends, we must
say again and over again the same few things
(wise or foolish no matter, beauty of bounden duty)

without which the world goes wild and the silent dead
rise up to rattle us daft with their dancing bones
because they have to, because there is no other choice.

Buzzard

I've heard that holy madness is a state
not to be trifled with, not to be taken
lightly by jest or vow, by lover's token
or any green wreath for a public place. Flash
in the eyes of madmen precious fountains,
whose flesh is wholly thirst, insatiate.

I see this bird with grace begin to wheel,
glide in God's fingerprint, a whorl
of night, in light a thing burnt black,

unhurried. Somewhere something on its back
has caught his eye. Wide-winged he descends,
like angels, to the business of this world.

I've heard that saintly hermits, frail, obscene
in rags, slack-fleshed, with eyes like jewels, kneel
in dry sand, among the tortured mountains, feel
at last the torment of their prayers take shape,
take wings, assume the brutal rush of grace.
This bird comes then and picks those thin bones clean.

Luck's Shining Child

Because I am broke again
I have the soles of my shoes repaired
one at a time.

From now on one will always be
fat and slick with new leather
while his sad twin,

lean and thin as a fallen leaf,
will hug a large hole like a wound.
When it rains

one sock and one foot get wet.
When I cross the gravel parking lot
one foot winces

and I have to hop along on the other.
My students believe I am trying
to prove something.

They think I'm being a symbol of
dichotomy, duality, double-dealing,
yin and yang.

I am hopping because it hurts.
Because there is a hole in my shoe.
Because I feel poor for keeps.

What I am trying not to do
is imagine how it will be in my coffin,
heels down, soles up,

all rouged and grinning above my polished shoes,
one or the other a respectable brother
and one or the other

that wild prodigal whom I love
as much or more than his sleek companion,
luck's shining child.

JESSE GRAVES

River Gods

In the lapse-time of remembering, my life
folds back through the warp of this city
the way the Tennessee River winds through it,

and I live again on the north bank, in Maplehurst,
watching the slow seep of barges downriver,
my blood renewed and coursing old arteries again.

Years break apart, become sediment in the stream
of those distant days, their blue-lobed nights.
Twenty-two and alive only to feel.

Still, I dared it only once, walking the rail trestle
where Cormac McCarthy's hillbilly Ulysses
docked the houseboat and dragged his trawling line.

Since no one wants to cheat a foolish death alone,
I convinced my friend to leave his satchel on the bank
and we stepped out a hundred feet over the night.

We sprang from tie to tie, hoping for solid wood,
for no rumbling train engine beyond the south hill,
our nerve soldered by a half-pint of Maker's Mark.

Lights from downtown Knoxville laced bright letters
across the water, and we stood, staring down
into a floating book, our bodies swaying like kites,

far above the circulations of ancient, whiskered fish,
held aloft by the confluence of blind river gods.
So much of the unknown rushing beneath us.

Firing Order

I

We found no warmth under the open hood,
Stranded mid-field where the truck's engine failed.
This work preceded all other, hay baled,
Stacked high and waiting on the metal bed.
Cows in winter, like broken furniture leaned
Against a wall, braced in zippery wind,
Staring out from their mysterious minds,
Hipbones like arched frames carved from wood.

My job was simple: I held the wrench
While his fingers set to work pulling wires,
Clearing rust and debris from the engine
Block, pocket knife flashing quick and sure.
His hands in the open heart of a machine,
Old plugs scraped clean enough to carry fire.

II

The field reveals no human history,
Logs none of the hours my father spent
Disking its soil, sowing down seeds, back bent
Like a tire iron, his fair neck blistered.
Bitt Rouse's sleeve once caught in the corn thresh
Keeps us careful, mindful of accidents—
Blood spilled here seeps through webs of buried roots.
Subsoil remembers, but topsoil forgets:

Forty summers ago, high heat of June
Salting the air, a young man's good right hand,
The one that bowed his famous fiddle tunes,
Churned to paste well before the pain began,
His feet tearing marks like ancient runes
Etched in the dirt, his signature on that land.

III

Under the pond's frozen face bright florets
Of algae swirl out and spread through the wild
Energy of their iced-over lives,

Deeper cold approaching with sunset.
Late November drawing down, so much less
Than it started with, early cold, crops shriveled,
The leaves tell it all in luminous wreckage.
He remembers, and I do, but the ground forgets.

What work gets done today will come again
Tomorrow, the day after, on and on,
Until he gives out, and the ground reclaims
What my father and I set in motion,
An engine turning, our family name
Stamped on the place that takes us back in.

Elegy for a Hay Rake

To every thing its season, and to every tool
its final turn; to the Farmhand rake my father
bought hard-used in 1976, rust has eaten away
all your labels, all your sheen and simple function;
to what I hope is my last sight of you, unhitched
and standing in the field like a photograph
from the Great Depression;
                                        farewell to the cut hay left
scattered on the ground to rot, nothing ate you
but the soil that birthed you; to the tractor tire
those long grappling points missed by inches
on every sharp turn, you survived without puncture;
to the long afternoon hours spent digging clumps
out of the balers' clenched teeth, good money
cannot buy you back;
                                        so long to the lucky machine,
lucky I won't sell you as an antique, that no one will
paint you red, white, and blue and plant you in a garden,
or hang you on a restaurant wall; goodbye to the five
leaning wheels, their crooked tines turning, reaching up
like broken fingers to wave hello, hello, goodbye.

JEFF HARDIN

On the Eve of a New Millennium

Drunk off his can and pissed at the ruse of another day,
back-ache a bum rap and woodpile shrunk to kindling,
the old man stood at the kitchen sink and stared out
at his neighbor's cow. *What a filthy beast,* he thought.
What a stinking, cud-chewing, gas-spewing waste of a field.
And then, because what else should happen on a day as dull
as this one, what better way to stun the silence out of all
it cannot say, he stumbled through the ashen rooms to find
his gun. The front room table spilled its stack of magazines
and pens. He was not a man who cared one whit for what
you might have thought of him. He spat cruel words and mocked
your God and cheered the buzzards dropped to feed on roadkill.
What was all this talk about a new millennium to him?
Weren't the evening and sun the same as always, and nowhere?
Even drunk, he didn't miss, and the cow tumbled down
dead-weight and draining blood, and the good earth shook
on its foundation, knocked off its axis for a visible second,
the good earth clutched at the blood, drug it down, down,
and the neighbor boys hid in the back of their closets.
Here was a stretch of road a man like him could tuck himself
back down and not have to answer to a soul, least of all
some dimwit codger whose cow would stare him straight in the eye.
And then what happened, you'd like to know, as if stories
have endings that conclude or explain, as if stories heal loss,
stop time, weep light, speak truth, change lives, dream souls.
He tumbled himself into his truck, took off toward town
slinging gravel and missing the ditch, his arm out the window
conducting last light on the maples and shagbark hickories,
damning them all to hell, even the burnt stalks of corn
and the useless rail fence and the pigs caked with mud
lost somewhere he was tired of looking, and those bible verses
learned fifty years ago of the good soil and the bad soil,
and it took just a mile before he saw a car coming, and aimed.

ASHLEY MACE HAVIRD

At Stonewall

I'm wading through a clearing,
knee-deep in khaki weeds and
coreopsis so yellow my eyes burn.

Over the pines a pair of buzzards
sharpen the groove
of their same circle.

Horseflies—a nimbus—
find my sweaty tangles
trickish as a web.

I kick the head off the blister
of a fire ant mound to open
tunnels like cigarette burns
veining through cemented red clay.

Ants pour out like lava.

I make believe you never
gave in and quit smoking;
and I never began this insect-change,
wormholing into midlife.

I conjure a dim cellar, close dive,

where beneath lazy
ceiling fans, in the haze
of circling smoke, I don't
have to share you.

From low clouds,
the sun's searchlight
sweeps off westward.

Summer's on the rise.
Ride with it.

Lunar Eclipse

Hard drinking at the camp house.

Come dusk, we nudge each other
to the pond's edge

where up from the muddy bottom
of twilight
the ruddy moon, a bloated pig,

breaks the choppy surface of the pines.

Netted by mosquitoes,
half-drowned in Cabernet,
woolly-mouthed,

we witness the slow bloodletting.

The moon, diminished,
pale as a communion wafer,
rises.

Our far-gathering shadow,

beastlike, insect-riddled,
swallows it slowly
whole.

DAVID HAVIRD

In Seventh Grade

The door slips from my grasp and slams—
"I hate you, boy" (her textbooks awkwardly cradled)—
on Kit McDonald, a cheerleader known to me
at least by name. Upstairs,

with never a white hair out of place,
Mrs. Culbreath, rumored to drink,
sways against the blackboard, ankles crossed,
legs thin and veiny. Pursing her lips,
she fastens her pink-rimmed eyes
on whom? On *him,* knees locked beneath his desk,
vexed by a sudden erection? Please,
may *she* have a turn at the board

to solve an equation. Downstairs, we're viewing gross-
out films whose mouths and genitals
sport livid chancres. We're getting the facts
of life from Mrs. Chitwood, said to be
an atheist: Adam, as she's disclosed,
was no one, no one man, but Man.
Her uniform a miniskirt
and fitted jacket, Mrs. Chitwood, dark
waves cropped and frosted, boasts a chest
of firm commands . . . while pretty Mrs. White

(blue eyes, blond bangs) in Building *A* declares,
"Yours not to question why,
Yours but to do or die,"
martial law in rhyme, and I forget
to cover my newly wired-tight grin.
"Braces?" I color, having now to smile
for Rebecca and Deedi and Page. When Mrs. White
sheds the round-neck cardigan
and miniskirt and dons a maternity shift,
the apple that reddens her palm

cankers my tongue, and English becomes for us boys
labor in exile. Husks
of harvest, textbooks litter the breezeway.

Downriver with Uncle Paul

Now Winter plants its pickax. Underground
a starburst of deep freeze, and Uncle Paul
clod-cold. I curl in bed

and try to go to sleep. My wristwatch hums,
the wristwatch newly mine;
for Uncle Paul, at 59, is dead.

The Accutron, its luminous green face
emblazoned with a trademark tuning fork,
hums as with light. The dresser top,
that drumhead, amplifies the sound
until the whole dark bedroom glows
behind my shut eyelids an eerie green.
I huddle as within his humming star.

Another sound
augmenting, then diminishing that tone—
outside the house a hum that comes and goes.
Believe in God, and it won't have to come
from any mere transformer; for tonight
sounds carry an eternity. I make

believe it emanates
from God's own tuning fork. Try as it might
to keep the music of the spheres on pitch,
it cannot now; for Uncle Paul,
game-legged Uncle Paul has, lurching, come.

She'd watched him walk across the living room
and fall, Grandmother told me once—
a growing boy whom infantile
paralysis had spilled. My father's baby brother.

Summers I'd spend a week or so with her,
and weekends he'd show up to ride
his horses, motorcycles . . . Bored

on one occasion with his toys, he bought
himself a boat. His plan: we'd motor down
the Saluda River to Lake Murray,
eat catfish at Holiday Shores,
and be back home by dark.

Well, homeward every cove
looked like the river's mouth
until we ventured in and failed to find
the snags that choked it. Night
thickened. The small prop churned the lake
not much. The outboard knocked
against the muffling whine
of midges, while my flashlight bent its beam
to sweep aside the dense bug-haze. At last
the river shut its mouth on us,
and we became the river's word unsaid.

My uncle cut the engine. Anchorless
but caged within unnavigable snags—
from somewhere he fished out a mason jar
of corn, white lightning, killed it, then
pitched over onto seats laid flat for a bed.

Such an eruption then of snores I looked
for that black river, like a dragon's tongue,
to foam with lava. Sparks
or else the gibes of gadflies burned
my ears, elsewhere raised welts,

and less and less I seemed the weightless soul
a body floating feels itself to be
and ever more a beast, the weight
of whose own bitten corpse its burden is.

Meanwhile my uncle's brand new Accutron
was humming its one reconciling note . . .

God hurls his bolt, a father to his child:
Now go to sleep. But Uncle Paul,
who had a thing for watches, hums
a luminous green song of time.

A night of utter cold, a night of sounds
that carry an eternity—tonight

a body ought to rise
upon a call of light, a breath
that quivers with one's secret given name.

But I, sleep's orphan, huddle now
within the drone of gravity itself,
the gravity of a collapsing star
that tugs its neighbors from their certain rounds,
that hum which tunes the orchestra of stars
to its off key.

TERRANCE HAYES

Ode to Big Trend

Pretty soon the Negroes were looking to get paid.
My partner, Big Trend, wiped his ox neck and said

He wasn't going to wait too much longer. You
Know that look your daddy gets before he whups you?

That's how Big Trend looked. There was a pink scar
Middling his forehead. Most people assumed a bear

Like him couldn't read anything but a dollar.
But I'd seen him napping so I knew he held more

Than power in those hands. They could tear
A Bible in two. Sometimes on the walk home I'd hear

Him reciting poems. But come Friday, he was the one
The fellas asked to speak to the boss. He'd go alone,

Usually, and we imagined the boss buckled
Into his shadow because our money always followed.

Palmetto State

Because the word means "little palm"
It reminds me of that that that brats cried
For the flawed merchandise merchants hawked

At the Lexington flea market all day Saturdays.
Terrance Hayes, for example, cried for a cap gun
With no caps. He flopped like a catfish

In his father's clutch and it makes me sigh
What's the use: too soon the Saluda River
Will be mist. South Carolina, you are in love

With cackling, catchphrases, and catastrophes.
I will visit you when snow falls on the north,
I will leave my children tone-deaf and churchless

And return to Main Street, Columbia, as the slaves
And their masters did the morning after Sherman
Burned the city. Legislatures of a magnificent

Malfunctioning manufacturing history. The self
Can't work on the self alone. Other hands are needed.
I am homesick for the motels of Caesars Head.

I want to find someone who has never owned
Nor consumed anything American: a Catawba Indian,
A Goose Creek gypsy. If I say "I love you" more

Than "I hate you," if I say "I love you" several times
A day it will accumulate truth, South Carolina.
Mother, nature, God, father, grade school, bully, pulpit.

Hell's misspelled angles. A place as paradoxical
As chocolate imported from the Congo: South Carolina.
A place the tongues are made of gold, rumor, crabgrass.

I have reliable information from people who are close
To other people. All my teachers are dead.
All my lovers are dead. Terrance Hayes slept in a motel

With a bullet in the gun on his pillow and is dead.
The brand new Bible he found was a black and tender
Leather, but his mother kept saying it should be red.

HASTINGS HENSEL

Jump-Start

Always now I grip the jumper clips
and with the electric neurotic spark
hear again our old mechanic, Sarge,
sitting on a ripped-up, stripped-out
pickup cab-seat at the Phillip's 66,
bark: *Son, you better always remember:*
black for negative nigger, after positive
redneck red. Sometimes the trick is
to forget what's said, don't forgive,
but now, remember, Sarge is dead,
and gone the shell-shocked limp,
the chubby bald head, the charges
fired at his lackey, Wild Bill Colpini,
who, shirtless and lean as a fan belt,
drank himself to sleep each night
in a Plymouth minivan propped up
on cinderblocks behind the garage.
To forgive what's said, that's the trick,
but don't forget, remembering now
how not to get shocked bringing back
the dead. I bend in the hood-shade
just like I did in the tire-pillar shadow
when Sarge and Wild Bill worked
two afternoons on my father's Ford,
hoisting the engine with a chain-lift
from a live oak—*just like a lynching,*
they agreed, and who could forget
the sight of the car's heart dripping
with grease in the heat of the sun?
And who would forgive the dead
for all that they've said and done?

The Rope in the Motor

Scissor-kicking, knife-wielding, I sawed
the ski-rope snarled in the inboard prop,

then rose to a dock of family bystanders
broadcasting their panic like newstalk,

so dove down again among the underwater
glass-green, the distant engine insect-sound,

where filaments frayed, skeins of ski-rope
tore away, but each out-of-breath rise

was met with the tantalizing inquiries
of "You got it yet?" and "How bad is it?"

It was bad. A problem, partly, of guilt:
rope thrown over stern, boat in reverse,

and only I felt how tightly it hugged
the motor, only I knew how long it'd take

to undo my mistake. It took the whole hour
it would take with the therapist or priest.

Hour of anger in sunlight and lake-light,
hour I confessed shallow, terrible things

beneath the surface while cutting at it—
litanies of illicit sex, the misuse of funds

from the family trust, the fact I thought
my wife a bitch. Down there it felt good

for my words to be misunderstood—
bubbles, garbling up, to where they stood.

Filet

The thin blade bends
in fish skin
saws along the shoulder,
fins, extends
through belly and breast,
comes clean out
the other side, swept
in air where
the eye has hardened
to a marble
and then entrails then
spill, the guts
erupt, and gray lungs
plunge out
then the slippery rip-
riding of spine,
each blade-stroke flat
in one direction
over the smaller bones
like fretwork—
pulling skin, pushing
the knife ahead
to hold, then, the limp
flimsy filet
free, but dully limpid
like memory,
or ice. Then the stray
shards of bone
discarded, the blood-
flecks washed
away from the smooth
grooves of vein.

RON HOUCHIN

Meanwhile

We don't understand all that leaves do,
and cannot actually translate one bird's song—
right now the late July peas harden
in their pods, and my hemorrhoids swell, too;
since April, a fungus has turned the lawn
white so the kids have to stay on the walk—
hard rain last month softened our peach trees
at their trunks; and I can hardly talk,

my every other tooth is loose—then this
on the news: most of our DNA floats
about in space from all of those
bits of skin, hair, and nails we slough, the piss
and shit that evaporate. Mostly I sweat
the problems we don't know we have yet.

Outhouse

I understood rooms for several and for none,
as bedrooms for twins or the guest who may come.
I knew there were sheds and outbuildings that stood
away from others as if outcast or shunned.

I noticed how indoor bathrooms felt personal,
but not ours or our cousin's outdoor ones.
I was never ready for traffic of flies bumping
my face on the way out and in. Sunlight hung

in bright strips like meat on a smokehouse wall.
Most of our children will not believe how many
of their ancestors shat in places like this, all
inside air at once fetid and fecund.

The Broken Eye

As if one of the gods didn't like a fan
running in winter, a blade flew out,
tearing through the plastic frame,
slicing into my left ocular cavity.

"Why *cavity,* Doc? It implies a lack,
something missing." The world had
wavered then flickered, light guttering
like a wick falling into waxy darkness.

When I returned, the faucet still
dripped directly down the open drain
and into the throat of the trap. Now,
I liked the clear, musical tone

of the little water striking the big—
otherwise, I presumed, everything
had changed as half the world
lay under a white bandage.

The next drop froze in place,
light stiffening into porcelain—
it reminded me
of the earth beneath snow.

REBECCA GAYLE HOWELL

No One Was Born Here

Across the white highway, dogs drift unmoored.
Silver-tipped seagrass, but no cactus. An offing
of shopping plazas, their harsh light and low roofs.
That's the way with drought; first dissent,
a worm belief that one place could be another.
I bet it feels good to twist a head of cotton
clean from the stem's fat and browning boll.
I bet it feels good to stand in irrigated rows.
Most people smile around town. Big, too.
We're so pleased to meet you. But we met last week.
Days, gone with a handshake. The thing about dogs is
they actually need us. Otherwise they're half-animals,
scabbed raw with mange, scared of the noonday sun.
As for me, I came here to keep my mouth shut.
Did I mention the dust?

We're on a Need to Know Basis

The kid is riding his bike, Fibonacci spiral
in a cement lot. It's hot. I'm in one of the parked
cars, idling. I don't know where to go.
A man with a star inked on his neck crosses
the street toward us. Five points and American
blue. He's alone, the kid. He knows better.
Drink water, but don't drink the water here,
his mother could have said. Above us, birds
charge the west along abacus wires strung tight
to—what? We are not held by this sky, or anyone.
No one counts our living sins.

The Quick and the Dead

The fire ant, his red dirt turret; my bare hands.
The fire ant, his sugar load. The moonlight in pieces
on little backs, slipping through the world's split
then gone and, just like that, a hot place is getting
cold. I have nothing worth return. On the walk
a cigarette stub lottery, floss toothpicks, scutch
grass fighting to spread. Fried wings chewed
to the tendon, left to decompose. This is today.
A war must be over, for all the damned noise.

DAVID HUDDLE

Even Then I Knew

for Lisa Fay Coutley

Our mother was often desperate
because of my brothers and me—once

she threw the dish drainer at Charles,
slapped the back of Bill's head so that

his face plopped down into his spaghetti
and what did she get for that? More boy

guffaws in our victory over her self-control.
Our mother wore little mascara, served her sentence

of three sons in a house at the end of a dirt road
in a time of no post-it notes, two channels on TV,

no shrinks, no antidepressants, and her only role model
was Mrs. Perkins who one afternoon rode Toby's bicycle

down Church Hill, skirts fluttering over her thighs,
to buy a six-pack of Pabst Blue Ribbon. Decorum

meant everything to our mother, and if someone had told
my brothers and me that mothers can drive away,

that would have frozen us in place like a game
of statues before Charles would have said *Oh yeah,*

and where would she go? and Bill would have said *Maybe*
down to the Post Office? And me? I'd have been

scared, because I loved her way more than my Roy Rogers
silver cap pistols with their white fringed holsters,

but finally I'd have found something real
funny to say.

Evidence Contributing to a Late Illumination

1

Photo of my father, wire-rimmed glasses,
only son, nerd prince—his mother, grandmother,
tighten his tie, pat his jacket, comb his hair,
advise him not to marry Mary Frances.

Photo of my mother, age maybe sixteen,
lace collared polka dot dress so proper
but still showing the source of her power
over those old ladies—she can have babies—

and how they must have loathed the child! Her arm
around my mother's waist, Great Grandma Lawson—
complainer and snuff dipper—might smile if
only she could push this brat bride off a cliff.

My mother's face shows she knows it and won't
run from rage wrapped in manners like a present.

2

Though she lived only minutes our oldest
sister was named after her grandmothers,
who detested each other. Her stone offers
one date for the birth and death of Ida Grace.

Mother was seventeen then. Last year moved
by desire, this year it had to be something else.
The rest of her life she woke to loss, then got
sent to bed at night with its bitter kiss.

Charles came along and stayed alive, two years
later there I was, then Bill. Never another
girl, just boy, boy, boy. The later pictures
show her as still proud but a little forlorn—

Photos of a face concealing how much it hurt
wanting a daughter, a lifetime half thwarted.

Trotlines

New River's muddy bottom feeds catfish
that hook themselves on biscuit dough bait dropped
by men using flat-bottom boats to set
trotlines they check just before dinner time.
New River feeds Deetum Dunford, my
first-grade classmate who never learned to read
and who cares for me just about as much
as I care for catfish, which is to say
only in the abstract—if I talk to him
very long, I see Deetum start to hate
me in a bored kind of way.

His cousins
Joe and Charles, twins and my classmates
through fifth grade, were smart boys I played with
until they drowned in New River. That day
they helped George Cary and Pig Clemons
break the chain that tethered a boat to a tree,
four of them in a craft made for two people
and a mess of fish. When it sank, the big boys
made it back to shallow water, while Joe
and Charles in their overalls and high top
shoes were pulled down into the mud.

Hours
later men in Rescue Squad boats dropped cords
with dragging hooks, found them, pulled their bodies up,
then other men in white coveralls
loaded my friends into white trucks that screamed
away—even though along the river
bank we'd seen how Joe and Charles had blue-white
skin so we all knew they'd turned cold as deep
river current.

I can't count how many times
I've told this story and written it out,
each time living it again and thinking
finally I've gotten it right, just to see
whatever truth I think I've fixed in place
start dissolving and sifting right out

of the words, and a few years later, there
I'll be, trying to write it again. Here's
what I can tell you—this is true as I can
make it, and it's still not right. How do I
know that? Just close my eyes and see the Lord
of the River, Deetum, shaking his head,
sucking his teeth. We know I'm lying again.

ANDREW HUDGINS

The Names of the Lost

The nights burned all night long that Freedom Summer—
ninety-four at midnight, eighty at dawn. Late June,
a high-speed chase. Goodman, Chaney, Schwerner

rammed off the road and hustled from their car.
Wayne Roberts asked, "Are that nigger-lover?"
The nights burned all night long that Freedom Summer.

"I know exactly how you're feeling, sir,"
said Schwerner. Roberts shot him in the heart.
They shot them all: Goodman, Chaney, Schwerner.

"You didn't leave me nothing but a nigger,"
Jim Jordan griped. "But at least I killed me one."
The nights burned all night long that Freedom Summer.

Ray Killen prayed a funeral prayer. The preacher
beseeched God's mercy on these communists,
these agitators—Goodman, Chaney, Schwerner—

before they buried them, using a bulldozer.
The murderers, old men now, still walk the town.
The nights burned all night long that Freedom Summer.
Ask Andrew Goodman, James Chaney, Michael Schwerner.

My Daughter

After midnight, I dragged carpet padding
from a trash bin and spread it on the asphalt
between the wall and dumpster. Screened from sleet,
I pulled carpet remnants over me, and that night
I married, raised a family, and outlived everyone
except a daughter—a teacher—and her two children,
one damaged. I woke when a bread truck scraped the bin.
From under damp carpet, I watched punctilious men

sign invoices, sweep, hose down the docks. A boy
in a bloody butcher's smock leaned against the wall
and smoked through bloody fingers.
                                        At night, I search
and sometimes find my daughter. "I make good money now,"
I tell her. "Let me take Teresa home with me.
I can buy the help she needs." My daughter smiles
asks how I'm doing, and I lose the moment
to my wife, my job, my actual
family, as the thick-faced infant bucks in her arms
or beats her forehead hard and almost musically
against the table. When I clench her to my belly,
she screams, red faced and rigid. "Hush, hush, hush,"
I serenade her. "O unhushable baby, hush."

In

When we first heard from blocks away
the fog truck's blustery roar,
we dropped our toys, leapt from our meals,
and scrambled out the door

into an evening briefly fuzzy.
We yearned to be transformed—
translated past confining flesh
to disembodied spirit. We swarmed

in thick smoke, taking human form
before we blurred again,
turned vague and then invisible,
in temporary heaven.

Freed of bodies by the fog,
we laughed, we sang, we shouted.
We were our voices, nothing else.
Voice was all we wanted.

The white clouds tumbled down our streets
pursued by spellbound children
who chased the most distorting clouds,
ecstatic in the poison.

Out

My father cinched the rope,
a noose around my waist,
and lowered me into
the darkness. I could taste
my fear. It tasted first
of dark, then earth, then rot.
I swung and struck my head
and at that moment got
another then: then blood,
which spiked my mouth with iron.
Hand over hand my father
dropped me from then to then:
then water. Then wet fur,
which I hugged to my chest.
I shouted. Daddy hauled
the wet rope. I gagged, and pressed
my neighbor's missing dog
against me. I held its death
and rose up to my father.
Then light. Then hands. Then breath.

T. R. HUMMER

Slow Train through Georgia

The mist that rises from this river solidifies the air
Underneath the rusty trestle where a train has come and gone.
It is the precipitate of the chemical morning, dumped
Unceremoniously into the clear solution of a summer night.
Hours earlier, the midnight freight detonated under starlight
Three hours late and thundering toward Birmingham, the red glow
Of the steel mills, the tincture of that constant dawn.
But now the air shuts down. Now the distant whistles of the morning shift
Into the throats of mockingbirds, and the sun works
Its electrolytic clarity from the top down, starting with the ozone.
The mist rising off the muddy little river curves south beyond the bridge.
It follows the water, of which you might be tempted to imagine
It is the astral body, downstream toward the Gulf—
Because you want to believe in the soul of the river, don't you,
You want a name and a positive destination
For this ghostly swath like a scar between banks of new-leafed oaks,
As if the world had a center and you were standing in it,
As if everything turning were your own self-evident revolution.
But watch this scene long enough and the sun
Will defeat you, the beautiful obscurity of the mist
Will dilute and disappear. Already the revelation is working
Its inevitable way toward you from the upper atmosphere. Soon
The oil-scummed image of the surface of the river will superimpose
Its visionary dreariness on what you can see of the earth:
Red clay, a distant cotton field, the tin roof of a tenant house
Where morning touches a mirror and moves at the constant speed of light
To touch the face of the sleeping man who stirs and touches his wife
Who is awake already, worrying over breakfast, remembering
The deep-night noise of the train that stopped
Whatever dream she might have had, the double blackness
Of coal-heaped gondolas hours after midnight, the anonymous steel
Of wheels against greased rails, inhuman, turning—like everything she knows
About God and politics—against her, going nowhere.

The Antichrist in Arkansas

At the edge of town, day lilies the gold of old whiskey
Move tonelessly. At the margin of the courthouse shadow,
A little sky gives off its one unchanging line.
It is written in the Gnostic Gospel of Truth that life is nightmare,
As if people were murdering them, though there is no one
Even pursuing them, or they themselves are killing
Their neighbors, for they have been stained with their blood.
Let there be a little clarity here, let the light arrive
The way the dynamite train rolls in from Arkadelphia:
An overwhelming ablution, a scheduled breakdown.
In the crib behind the cotton gin, three of them are gathered.
In the alley off Jefferson Street, they are giving secret signs.
Who are they? Call them the Brotherhood of Darkness.
Give them emblems: khaki workshirts, Prince Albert in a can.
They worship at the Synagogues of the Flesh of the Holy Pig.
Mornings, hours before sunrise, they kneel at the open flame;
Past midnight, if you wake in an impure sweat, you can hear
Their pentatonic psalms sift through the veils of the juke joints.
You who are uninitiate, you who walk the sunlit bricks
Of the Main Street sidewalk past the bank to the hotel café,
You of the regimental necktie, you who render
Unto Woodrow Wilson, live in the obvious houses,
Drive Fords, dance to "Arkansas Traveler"—Brotherhood of Light,
You think the fields at least are innocent, gathered without
The rhetoric of pastoral, the flat farmland, the plows
Moving in the middle distance; you believe at least
In the trees, gone in their green brooding. But in 1919,
83 bodies were given to druid oaks on the fringes
Of these blesséd little cities: Conway, Fort Smith, Fayetteville,
West Memphis, El Dorado, Pine Bluff, forest City,
The mecca of Hot Springs. How many know
The ritual formula that exorcises unclean flesh?
How many have learned the arcana, the knotting
And unknotting of hemp? So it has been written
In The Paraphrase of Shem, and quoted
In The Little Rock Gazette: Nature turned her dark vagina
And cast from her the power of fire, which was in

From the beginning, through the practice of darkness.
Look: already the evening brightens, already the locomotive
Crosses the valley in a shimmer of pure entropic heat.
Everything in the flesh converges. In a moment it will be too late.
Gather them up, believer. Put them on the backs of mules.
Take them where the wind completes its broken sentence
Of damnation against the elder, against the ash.
The secret is simplicity: pray to me, the spirit who steals
The breath of the one whose feet no longer touch
The ground; make sacrifice to the god who silences him
Whose testicles bleed in his own unsanctified mouth.

Greek

Hard now to remember those winters, snow scabbing the stones
Outside Gettysburg ten years after the names sank in with the carcasses.
What did I know about the unities? It was freezing, we had nothing,
We'd eaten the mules, the wheatfields were scattered with salt.
I hunched in the seminary balancing the leatherbound Euclid
Against the Homer my father had scribbled his name in once, a boy
Like me, still ignorant and alive. Outside, Pennsylvania was a hellish
Polygon of ice. The opposite sides and angles of a parallelogram
Are equal to one another, and the diagonal bisects it; that is, divides it
Into equal parts. I imagined him repeating these things
Twenty-five years ago in a body smaller than mine.
I imagined him in the ground, the ground bisected, two worlds
Divided, the line drawn between him and me.
Things which are equal to the same thing are equal to one another.
I would take up the ministry that laid him down. I would speak the Word
That choked him. His body after ten years under was less than mine,
A volume of icy grit surrounding a Minié ball. We were learning. I knew
History was doing the same things others had done, being born,
Sweating, fighting, saying axioms by rote. I drew the geometry
Of fields in early spring, dead men at the plows,
Forty acres of ground chiseled and harrowed, laid out naked in the sun.
I know now they died of everything you can think of: Evisceration, shock,
Peritonitis, gangrene, malnutrition, incompetence, deceit,
Every conceivable loss. Then, I knew only what we copied
From the poet and translated: The spear in his heart
Was stuck fast, but the heart was panting still and beating

To shake the butt end of the spear. In the freezing house, my mother
Was sewing trousers, running her ruined fingers over the parallel lines of a bolt
Of corduroy, burning her hands on linen, stitching, shivering,
A conventional emblem of loss. If equals be taken from equals,
The remainders are equal. How could she weave him back? She had no loom.
She made uniforms for soldiers. They taught me to say these things:
My father in the underworld is bloodless, wanting nothing.
What is a nation to him? What is a son? There are rivers, stinking fires,
Ghostly pain like the pressure of starlight, emptiness, illusion,
There are six hundred thousand souls repeating their indifference every second
In the Hades of the Brothers' War. He is a citizen of that polis now,
And I hate him in the language of the dead I am still learning slowly
For the sake of his memory, sign by inevitable sign.

TJ JARRETT

Of Late, I Have Been Thinking about Despair

its ruthless syntax, and the ease with which it interjects
itself into our days. I thought how best to explain this—

this dark winter, but that wasn't it, or beds unshared
but that isn't exactly it either, until I remembered

Saturday afternoons spent with my father in the garage
and those broken cars one after another. At the time,

that's what we could afford. Broken things. Saturdays,
there was always a game on the radio and I'd stand

beside him or lie under the engine, oil cascading from
the oilpan. Daddy would curse wildly, sometimes

about the car, sometimes about the game. Sometimes
Mama called for one or the other of us from upstairs and

I'd trudge up to see what she wanted with a sigh.
We sighed so much then. Funny. If you asked us

if we were happy, we'd say: *Families. They are happy.*
There's a solace in broke-down cars: you can find what

is broken. You can make it whole again. I'd pop the hood,
peer into the sooty inside and Daddy would pass me parts

for my small hands to tender to each need. Daddy
scrambled into the front seat, turned a key and a roar

came out that would be cause for rejoicing. But time came,
(this is the inevitable part) when he would draw the white

handkerchief to his head in surrender. I would always ask
if we could just try harder. *Baby girl,* he'd say. *She's gone.*

Late That Summer

That summer night, we gathered again around the table,
drinking with all the bugs that lit up and some that didn't.
When Mike said: *I wonder how my ex-wife is doing,*

we looked down at our phones which glowed like
all those fireflies, and we looked up old loves. Except me.
I remembered I crossed a city in winter once,

scaled a steep snowy stair to a man farther from me
than distance. He could not love me. Not then.
The betrayal, he said, *is just too much.* Then he

closed that door and latched it resolutely. Anyway.
One woman found her ex married again;
he held a child in a picture captioned: *This is the best*

it's ever been. She bent her head and wept.
One shouted*: Look, look. Look how fat she is,*
but even so something crossed his face like weather.

The woman in the picture was smiling as if she
swallowed some joy so great it could split the skin.
Oh look, I said, *see how happy they are without us.*

The wind was cool and soft, and insects drawn to fire
fell into hot wax never to escape. I thought on that
in long days after. I've thought on it a good long time.

Meridian, MS, 1978: Miss Polly Attends the Altar at Mt. Zion

I want to be moved, to forgive, to let forgiveness bear away
memory: you spitting in my face, saying *you are dead,*

dead. Nigger, you are dead. But already it is welling up in me,
this thing called forgiveness, and I reach up to your head

to bring you down, to make the metaphor apparent. You kneel.
You are on your knees now. You came for this. We let you come

into the house of the Lord for this. You have spread your arms
in a gesture of the Christ to say *forgive me. I come in peace.*

Forgive me.
And I want to be moved. For so long, I was stone.
For you, I was stone. Oh Lord, move me. I want to be moved.

RODNEY JONES

The Power of the Quote

1965

For Maurice and Amanda

The day Portis was assigned
the free paper he saw
three things that interested him:
a hawk carrying a snake,
a letter John Keats wrote
to John Hamilton Reynolds
from Scotland in 1818,
and a woman in
the outhouse behind the church,
peeing standing up.

Then he went, as ordered
by his grandmother,
to help collect rent
from the Ledbetters
and waited with
his granddaddy
on the porch. A long time.

A pig ran out the door
and then three chickens.
A wasp got after him,
and all the time,
the smell from inside
made a racket. "Cat,"
thought Portis,
not pig or chicken,
and sure enough,
out sauntered a little
towheaded girl dragging
a kitty by its ears.

Then the old lady, Rosellen,
who always got
his grandaddy's goat,
emerged, studied him
a piece, cackled, tousled
the young'n's hair, and said,
"Annky, thay oddam."
And when that didn't bite,
paused and cackled,
then said it again,
"Annky, thay oddam."

"Mizz Ledbetter,"
said Portis's granddaddy,
"if you'll be
so polite as to get shed
of that snuff,
I'll try and consider
precisely
what you're meaning."

And then she did, she
spat, if spitting
is not a pit or coop,
but a cathedral: a swallow
that gathered an insweep
to a cleansing hawk
that squeaked the springs
and set the red wad
flying between them
to resolve against
a rusty sheet of tin.

Whereon Mizz Ledbetter repeated,
but this time cleaner,
"Nancy," and rubbed
the little girl's tow head,
"Say goddam for these
nice gentymen," and when
the little girl complied,
the old lady smiled,
winked at Portis's granddaddy,
raised her dress,

blew her nose on the hem,
and cackled again.

A funny thing
occurred to Portis then,
with darkness over it,
the madness of an old man
and an old woman who
might have kissed long
ago at a Christmas
party under mistletoe,
and maybe it went farther.

In any event, there would be no rent,
there never was, and
grandma Portis didn't like it.
And mumbled as she fried
their tongue. Then sat a spell
in solitary, and dragged
a ball and chain of silence
to the organ and pumped on
"Softly and Tenderly, Jesus Is Calling"
for a little more than an hour.
Then was restored herself again.

But back to the paper
Portis had intended to write.
In bed, he thought about it,
and two parts stirred:
not the hawk and snake
that D. H. Lawrence might handle;
or the Keats letter,
which sounded like Mark Twain;
or what occult ecclesiastical
hygiene might warrant
a Christian woman peeing standing up.

More what was meant by free?
And if it was, he felt
the spiders in those marks he hated,
that hung there in the air,
stung what people said,
and spun the web around it.
And felt the secret labor

press upon the paper.
A rainy night. He was alone.
And tried on words like shirts.
And scratched the loneliness of the burden.

Then went down to the kitchen
to make himself some coffee
and saw the words
all shining in the cupboard.
Some waited for company
that never came. Mainly
these stayed clean.
But others rattled against the ice
and woke him late at night.
This was the goddam south.
Some words
he'd need to put
in other people's mouths.

JUDY JORDAN

From *Pete's Lake*

For Pete Allen, ?–1863

All that summer fire followed us.

Air bitter with burn:
beds, couches, and cracked wiring,

and the breath-strangling stink of singed hair and centuries,
breath-strangling stink of cotton dust and sweat
all bored into those dusk-colored rough-cut
plank walls.

Air turned oily and opaque with gas station drinking glasses,
Alpine Cigarette stamp-bought pots and pans, my father's WWII medals

and the final blood-pooled gasps
of Preacher Marvin Rushing who'd lived there
before us and had drowned in his own breath,
a black bloom across the kitchen's floorboards,
a palimpsest for the steel band of tuberculosis
and its germs, germs
my mother believed soaked each lint and dust-laced wall
germs which would kill
us all.

In the end, he lost so much weight as each blood-wracked cough
hacked out fat and muscle and his disease-scoured bones grew porous,
grew hollow as a wren's, the old woman
who walked two miles every day from her unpainted clapboard
flustered room to room, pulling shut windows,
worried about those gaps of sky, worried
a strong wind would lift him,

as if he were a scrap paper kite and float him toward the evening's smolder
of smoke.

He was another ghost story my brothers scratched from the skirled sky.
He was what I believed in just as I believed in our cow pasture,

fine-grained, drought-shrunk, full of its dead
with its tombstones and spinney of trees
whose buckled roots cradled the scratched creek rock
hammered with names and death dates

so that my dreams were stitched bone,
each step a tangled bridge, hands slipped in ribs,
babies the size of mice curled in the nests
of their mothers' pelvises. All that I believed in.
Not tuberculosis.

Not my mother's superstitions. Not her fear of germs.

Not her conviction that we were all going to catch tuberculosis.

My mother hated that house with its uninsulated walls,

rattling ghosts,
germs and layers of cotton dust.

By the time the fire engine clanged down the driveway
our house was pulsing embers,
dull eyes glowing beneath a collapsed tin roof.

✦

Some heavy thing, a dark curse, lay across the land
though I was too young to understand
how easily someone could disappear,
bodies dumped and bodies buried,
graves hastily dug, lives swallowed in swamps and quicksand.

My brother swore an early settler made some slinking,
ill-fated deal, that cursed the land

but he feared calling evil down on himself
and wouldn't say which settler it was
though that day we were lugging water to the workers

in the cotton field, their hoes jabbing at the earth's scabbed crust,
he pointed out the black snake, thick as my thigh,
writhed up the trunk of the thorn tree
that seemed to burst from Mr. Allen's chest buried
there beneath that marble stone.

My brothers said, Mr. Allen leapt from his grave each night,
skinny, pale, and naked, and raced the dogs
to the bridge and back to the hill in our cow pasture

where he eased himself back into the earth beneath his cracked gravestone
and the photo of himself, wild-eyed and straggly bearded,
glass-encased, just above the chiseled ache of his name.

✦

House on fire. Fire in the fields. Fire in the front yards. Crosses of fire.
Hay bales forked open. The spin of a match
through the star-charred sky. Furious debris hurling
explosions that silence the frog-spun night.

Fire in my stomach. Fire in my spine. Head full of fire.
Purple and stiff, I lay in a bed of ice. Screams split
through my skin. Screams split through flame
as I rose from myself, as I hovered over the crisp beds,
as the doctors said *meningitis,* as the doctors
said, *sorry,* said, *there was nothing more we could do,*

said, *dead. Dead,* the doctors said.
I bumped along the ceiling and down the corridors
smelling of bleach and piss, floated down the hall
as mama fell to the floor, screamed out to God
and offered anything in my place: *The farm,* she said. *Me*

she said. *Take me instead* is what I heard my mama,
who would die a few short years later, say,
so that all these years later still I wonder who listens,
wonder who trades, who keeps count

though then I knew only that I was sucked
through the double doors
into the glittery parking lot which teemed
with peacocks strolling between cars, straining
their jeweled heads to preen in side mirrors,
pecking at the reflections of themselves,
their long tails dragging behind them.

No tunnel. No light. Just the impossible
in those rolling hills of the Piedmont:
jagged snow-crowned mountains against
a sky curtained red and green, a roiling river,
orange-headed, jewel-winged parakeets
and a woods edge where there should have been a highway
toward which I felt myself drawn

when the peacocks all turned and stretched their blue necks
skyward, then lifted and spread their tails and displayed,
flashing each feather's end coins of blue and copper,
coins flipping through my chance at the extraordinary,
my chance at becoming one of my brothers' ghosts stories
as I was dragged toward infinity above a parking lot
full of big-finned cars and box-nosed trucks

as the peacocks joined all the other noises:
eighteen-wheelers on the highway gearing down for the hairpin curve,
cicadas, those rusty trumpets fingering their oilless keys,
and mama's screams which had followed me all that way
and all the noises formed a chorus of cries that jerked me,
as if from sleep, and told me I had a decision to make
and I turned back through the grease smudged doors
to bump back down the hospital corridor
and stare at myself there on the hospital gurney

already stiff and waxy, already discolored
as blood pooled in my veins.

✦

Children of fire, children who stumble their way
through the finger-smudged doors of eternity,

children of spark and fizzle, children who smolder and smoke,
children who slip their skin, who swim through a cloudless sky

until the whole world begins to ring, a loud chiming
of engines and insects, bird calls and men shouting,

strange, slit-eyed, sheet-wearing men, shouting as they work
their way through the streets of downtown Monroe,

and these children, these children, they shatter.

TERRY L. KENNEDY

Concerning the Hunt

The entire morning was misery.
The killing, more so. Plus
the cold: the air, of course;
the river, intended for refuge—
a place to sleep amongst
the stars—slowly soaking
my worn and tired boots.
Also, the thunder of the shotguns—
their acrid smoke drifting toward us,
through us—and laughter to match.
You counseled *patience.* You promised *beauty.*
And like magic, one, three,
then five drakes glinting
in dawn's glow—their calls
an echoed chorus to the balloon
of daybreak until the others
quick on their reels, brought them
home. What of this did you want me
to witness? The guides upriver
loading the now-empty duck crates
into their trucks? The ruby-red blood
dripping from the corners of the drakes'
open eyes? Or the fathers and sons
grinning for pictures with their hard-won bounty?

Concerning the Puppies

These ones, in the cedar, we'll find homes for.
The others—drown in the river, she said.
"The others," being those who arrive too small,
aren't fed by the mother. *It's nature's way,*
she added. Only then, the unstoppable
hum and heat in the ears that arise

with unwanted reminders
of what it means to pass whole, into,
and out of, this world. What aversion
the body shows when faced with what is,
ultimately, only a truth—but a truth
the heart won't, or can't, admit to.
What I'm trying to say is this:
we spent the afternoon in the sun
on the bank of river; we spent
the afternoon trying to give comfort—
a sense of release. But to whom?

YUSEF KOMUNYAKAA

From *Requiem*

& already *The Book of the Dead*
unfolded pages, & water rose
to leaf through the before
& after, the benedictions
& prayers spoken in tongues
rising in the tide of flotsam
& debris of fallen churches
across the Lower Ninth, slush
working its way up clapboard
& slave-brick walls of houses
tilted in a dirge, up the last rung
of the ladder, up to the voices
caught in an attic, & then stopped
in midair like a hundred washing
machines churning, & already
cries from a domed purgatory
broke from the storm within
where proxy armies clashed
on weekends, & for a moment,
as if we aren't here, demons ride
the shoulders of outlaw angels
through streets of the antiworld
where thieves of bread & milk
are clubbed to the sidewalks,
but here on earth, the levee's
uncorked boom drowns the solo
of Bolden's cornet driving a note
up the river of rivers, saying,
I'm the mama & papa of ragtime,
& already an unearthly hush
was returning to the people
trapped behind barred windows
& waterlines measuring the sag
in the dragline as bottom fish
floated up, lost in the Big Muddy

unburying the wormy compost
of days rotting in the darkness,
& a wind-up toy inching along
crawfish mud & bloody slag,
& already they're turning pages
of the uncharted old lost seasons
footnoted in the abridged maps
warning of man-eating savages,
to Jean Baptiste's flotilla of six ships
bringing six carpenters & thirty convicts
to rip out miles & miles of saw vines
& dig trenches, born to erect makeshift
shelters of raw sappy wood & speculate
on their stolen dreams, the engineer
Pierre Blond de la Tour saying, No,
not here, the river will never stop trying
to reclaim what's taken from her, even if
we build earthen walls to block her reach
because she will go around, under, or over,
& already the spine of their logbook
of calculations was broken & splayed
as newcomers hailed from the far-reaches
as pirates, woodsmen, & moneychangers,
(all hard men) ready to claim coffin-girls
sent by high churches of France,
& already a thick vein of ink
widens into midnight, into daybreak,
the wind walking Audubon's ghost
through the almost gone, straggly
grass, out into the oily marsh bog
where disappearing land begs no footprint,
out to where hard evidence rainbows
up, leaving thousands hurting to be
counted as nothing more than sea turtle,
eel, brown pelican, egret, mud puppy, crab,
& already water wounds everything
into uncountable small deaths moored
in cypress, stinking up Springtime
with a pestilence back to the dark ages
on harbors where boats sway in shifting light,
the dead talking to us from a lost masterpiece,
asking, Where is this, somewhere we are

forbidden to remember, where scavengers
are defeated by what they devour?
& already from a mile down plumes
keep rising up through weeks & months,
animal cries & the language of robots
where diving machines moon-walk,
surging & falling like drowned shadows
of carrier pigeons clouding the waves . . .

The White Handkerchief

The stage was fenced off with chicken wire
    when Amédé Ardoin sang a high-pitched
  gutbucket blues at the Basile club.

Cajuns hooted their invectives
    at creoles, riding a sweaty nocturne,
  before they hurled beer bottles.

They danced when they didn't wish,
    dragged drunken images into the deep,
  back to their half-broken farms,

& swore never again to go
    hear those jumpy birds hidden
  in this black man's accordion lit by chrome

& ivory buttons. But they always returned.
    If only to call him lazy, if only to see him
  shading beneath an oak beside the canebrake,

they still lost themselves in his croppy
    dirges. Hadn't he stolen up north
  to cut that recording in '34?

When he climbed up on the stage
    he was two players, his wide hat cocked.
  Their boots struck the wooden planks,

& a hugged sway tilted the hourglass.
    For a moment he was a lion caged,
  & they ghosts of crows on a fence.

One night, sweat & the one-five stomp
bled together, & he said, Please,
somebody, throw me a clean rag.

Mr. Marcantel's daughter plucked
a lace handkerchief from her bodice
& stepped up to wipe his brow,

& by the third verse of "Valse de Opelousas"
two half-drunken men in a corner
nodded their heads to cast his fate.

The night unhealed & tangled up
two-steps, his fingers dancing all over
the box with its nine lives inside.

When the car rolled to the edge
of the farm, Amédé said, Thanks,
I'll walk from here. The memory

of her slow perfume was on his face,
& leaves crackled under brogans.
He shifted his small frame to ease

the twenty-five-pound flour sack
holding his infamous squeezebox.
The two men waited beside a live oak,

a bullfrog croaked in the grassy ditch
along the path, & the raw feeling
of a new song was on his tongue

when punches & wild kicks tore open
the night, & he called out again & again
to the whippoorwill, to a ragged bloom

on a dogwood. He was left dead
in the ditch, but as he crawled home
a trail of black ants followed him

to the doorsteps of the farmhouse
where horses limped for years to come,
& the dogs begged for bread with his cry.

His fingers on the keys, the bellows
breathing in & out, those wild kicks
took hold again, & Amédé ended up

at Pineville mumbling to phantoms,
    unable to ask for bread or a drink
  of water, unable to ever again taste lemon.

Augury at Sunset

The albino family on the other side
of the bean field—one son black
as his father, two daughters & another
son pale as their mother—all six
hugged around an upturned cable-stool
in the backyard beneath a chinaberry.

In that four-room brick-sided house,
what did it mean to close one's eyes
& see country laughter a half mile,
how it rises up & shimmies the air
till a bullfrog answers a goatsucker
from a muddy patch of cattails?

Maybe they talked old remedies
African as their faces, saying,
If you wish a cure try a handful
of gum moss, a thimble of anise seed,
a handful of corn shucks, & steep
in a quart of rain. Drink at sunrise.

Back then thrashers wounded maypop.
The hounds barked. A crow on a fencepost
told us how to keep a cat at home
by feeding her sugar at seven o'clock
before rubbing grease on her paws
& bending her face to kiss a mirror.

Their affection thick as molasses,
the aroma of collards, green tomatoes,
chicken, cornbread, & peach ice cream
at dusk. I could hear them singing
names of the dead before they rose
to walk the night into pine woods.

JOHN LANE

The Day Andy Griffith Died

If you cross me, or make a shallow scratch,
a Dixie dirt farmer emerges as when
that asshole New Yorker came up behind
doing 90 on The New York State Thruway.

In that Audi I saw my doppelganger of place,
a man whose DNA flourished ghetto to barrio,
'hood to Upper Westside for as many generations
as I claim allegiance to rural plots. That man drove

like he knows this century's all about city speed
but did not understand the last one was still
barely about the slow country life living on in
men like me, clodhoppers, squash fryers, hoarders

of seeds for the right pole beans, the wide ones
my six aunts served at farm dinners, Monday through
Saturday, outside Wilson, NC. This all comes back
like gall soon after we hear on the radio,

between Albany and Speculator, that Andy Griffith's
dead. We stop for lunch and the pretty Adirondack
waitress says, "Oh, Andy, that's sad," and heads back
to the kitchen to tell the tattooed biker boy cutting

our strawberry-rhubarb pie. TV shows don't have
themes you whistle anymore. No one names a character
Ernest T. Bass or Opie, Goober, or Gomer. Vanishing
are the farm clichés, chickens crossing the road,

geese laying a golden egg, wild oats sewn, no
more oats. No more seeds, or making hay while
the sun shines, or furrowed brows, or bad eggs;
certainly no more raisins in the sun or wood shedding;

and thrown out is the plough, the back forty,
tossed down is any reference to the milk
maid, or Farmer John; no one's bought the farm
in a decade, or waits for the cows to come home,

gets up with the chickens, eats like a pig, or goes
to a feather bed tired as a mule. But I think Tobacco Row,
Peachoid, South of the Border, Alligator Alley, Graceland,
the Gourd Museum, the Y'all Line, Lil' Abner,

Cracker Barrel, Nashvegas, and a state university
in the Delta whose mascot, I swear, is a fighting okra
with boxing gloves. And in less than a half-mile
on New York Rt. 30 we passed the "World's Largest

Lumberjack" and the "Adirondack Moouse Hair Salon"
spelled with two Os so passers-by will get the joke.
Maybe bad humor is universal, like communication
and weather. Now cease this poetic bullshit. There

is no Mayberry, no Andy, no Aunt Bee, and Gomer's
simply standing on the corner of Commerce
and Pop Culture waiting for a bus bound for Hollywood
not Siler City. Opie went on to direct *Grand Theft Auto,*

Willow, Backdraft, and *Apollo 13,* lives seasonally
in a condo at Hilton Head. Andy left Helen Crump
at the church dance, slipping on *Matlock* like a loose
suit of Sunday clothes. Andy's dead and why the hell pine

on for that small town life of Mayberry? It never existed,
only lived like a wisp of smoke up somebody's fake
chimney, a chiffarobe made out of cardboard painted
dark like rich mahogany and set in the corner for a shot

or two. Where are all those black faces I knew on the town's
edge, across the tracks, never in jail with Otis for specter
crimes made up by the sheriff? After all, that was 1960
when the show came on, beamed like sit-ins into every

home with a TV, and the cast was bleached white
like the grits on my breakfast table. So I haul
my imagination on home from New York to South Carolina,
give up that conjured driven dude in the Audi and settle

for a future stripped of greed and the heady exhaust
of the city rising up behind us both like Oz or Columbia
before Sherman burned it down. Now I carry Andy
with me like a carved peach pit pressed

in the pocket of my only suit. I've picked this cultural
plot of all available cotton, I've ginned the icons, the images.
The green beans have cooked for hours, as my aunts said,
"from scratch," until the bright green bled from them

like a shadow and the pot boiled and bubbled
and waited on the stove for us to come in from the fields
to watch TV, to tune in, to take our place in
the national dream that we all drive forward even today.

Tony Dorsett and His Band

Here you are, drunk again, and me
on a voluntary visit from Virginia,
stewing in your breath soon as I breach
the front door.
The house sways in it, this sodden dance
you choose for a week each month—
the old console stereo up so loud and hostile
that the neighbors think I've never left.

But this is not some New Wave band
or a smack of Dylan's "Homesick Blues"
riding on a needle blunt as a spool
It's the same two smooth black albums
with dust covers somewhere filling out with dust
among paperbacks and unavoidable bills,
that tightened my throat through high school
in the middle of nights
when I would finally lose you and the world
in what resembled sleep.

Those nights Hank Williams crooned
"Hey Good-looking" to the peeling walls,
to your face and arms bruised from falling
when you forgot your partner wasn't real.

That was pure night music, played late and warm,
the Bayou yodel and sexual tremor of old Hank
floating out on a voice rich with grease
of late-night flop houses, easy women,
and hard living.

You knew all the words and got them
right sooner or usually later than the music.
A yodel caught in your throat and broke
higher than a child's voice.
Your song floated you above all the pain
of rented houses, a husband's suicide, and years
of low-pay, workday weeks.

Now on this morning, as I return home
one more time, the other album
cracks the glass of my fatigue—
the crisp morning music,
a brass section swings in pleated-skirt,
seamed hose, dark-haired style you lost
too soon to a cotton mill shift.
In the past year, my sister says you've taken
to calling this one Tony Dorsett and his Band.
You cheer "do it Tony!" in drunken enthusiasm
like he sees a hole he could walk
his big band through—then you fill
the air with the release of your stupored body
falling through collapsible end tables,
prepared and wobbled in cases of repeat performances.

Without applause, I take you I my arms
and drag you in a slow dance we both remember
from other years and houses,
through trumpets and alto sax,
through reams of smoking air
to your bedroom to sleep off this dream week
of music one more time—
my mama, myself in the wrong light.

Wreckage

For Uncle Bobby

You beer-breathed oracle of quick moves
and lost friends, how did you find hours—
    laying off from mill work?—to stack

boxes, beds, TV, and couch in two tight-hipped
'62 Chevy trucks to shuttle us back across town
always one last time?

I never hoped to look kindly on a childhood
of rented five room houses, a mother
with a chronic hang-over, and roaches
not only in each greasy kitchen, but bedrooms,
halls, dens and baths. I count back
one by one until finally the peeling wood face
of each house fills out and floats, embodied
by some particular in all the
of neighborhoods sloughed off each year.

In Arkwright, a fig tree with ripe
fruit, bulbed and sexual for two summers.
On Ash Street, a cousin's warm breasts exposed
in the attic, taking them full-bodied
in the flushed palms of my hands.
And Uncle, they always said you two twins
grew up fast, loose, and hungry, but at only twelve
I watched the truth in the back bedroom of a neighbor's
house, warm and wet and churning.

In then years moving I found
freedom has nothing to do with motion.
Staying in a house three years
to see my best friend out-grow his Sunday
suit, the one I might get in hand-me-downs,
beat the hell out of boredom born
in the full bed of your pickup
stacked high with the same scarred bureaus.

Every move, unsure of mama's
choice of low-rent, short-term housing,
you jerked the skids out from the rounded edges
of my fragile childhood sense of place—

"If you don't like the neighborhood, boy,
sit back, keep your motor running, and
it'll change again."

Where are you now Uncle Bobby?
It's ten years since you prayed off beer

to sign on with a wife, a bank mortgage, a trailer
and a low-haul rig in a park of aluminum houses
on the growing end of a cotton mill town.
Then, out of nothing, you called
last week from DC where weekly you haul
two runs from South Carolina on eighteen wheels.
Your voice seemed richer
back then, when beer-breathed stories
held me fixed to the floor.
Through a vibrating distance
of phone lines, a thousand empty rooms,
a few salvaged lives, I listened as you stammered
through your best Southern
monotone, unsure of words to use on a boy
you'd last seen seven years past
at his last family reunion before college.

Good-bye, Bobby. I know it wasn't
a ride home you offered passing through
Virginia on your weekly haul north. But I know
whatever motivation, it was deep-seated and—
my number straight from mama, stuck in your throat
as the operator returned your dime, completing the call.
It was purely that connection of kin, that twist
of the genes deeper than place or proximity,
a slow skip of sparks across distances.
You'd say a myth-sized face from my past
and a small child's shadow
was what held us there on long distance
for more than the two minutes we talked.
It was a blood-course, you're right,
and a past too large to fit,
as we stumbled through a language
the wreckage of which could not fill
any distance between us.

I should have told you things that night.
I should pressed the ragged arc
of my life into the receiver, into some raw song
you once understood. I could have said these days
I roar head-on down those same roads where you
left your beer and pickup cooling,
traded in the last duck-tail in Spartanburg

for a Sunday suit and lace shoes,
got on your knees and prayed for the fire to burn
you salt clean of all itinerant girls' thighs,
all the cold cans of beer, all the squeezed
shift knobs popped in your palm for speed.

I've looked like you did for something
so fast and perfect I could lose all sense
and bearing. I spent four years searching
solely for that sustaining speed.
I want to come full circle in a world
of endless departures and returns, to call
this place something more than tomorrow or years.

Uncle, between you and me,
I'd chew nails to stop from shitting regular,
break my back to keep from standing still.
Your hope's to look around at fifty
and pray nothing changed for half your life.
Mine's to call up the past and back off from nothing.
At 25 I trail the ashes of 15 houses
and a million miles of telephone poles,
call up trains and jets and buses.

You ride your long-haul rig
in the same tight circle twice a week.
I still ride around books and women
like fingers around cans of beer.
We both might arrive empty.

NATON LESLIE

Completion

It's a place to call your very own.
Smuggler's Notch brochure

My uncle was an Allegheny hustler,
hill-haunt, stump jumper,
ridge runner, dusk poacher,
coal thief, Am-Vetter, late night
devotee of beer lights
and back-lit bottles.

He was someone whispering
rebellion, a crow on a barstool
cackling ideas, explaining how

to shoot a deer at night with one shot,
there and gone in the warden's ear,
how to steal potatoes.

Can it be that simple?
I might grow a facsimile
of his single crosshair moustache,
a gift of Gable, and follow
the pulse lent him by whiskey

and smoke. It all mattered at the end.
He even smuggled bottles
into the veteran's hospital.
It made the world vivid,

worth stalking across mountaintops,
howling to the skies
when you are dying
the same way you lived.

Country

You are from around here,
and I am not. You grew up
in a forest of older brothers
who teased you, kept you running
after goats in the fields

and I can see that young girl
when something softly takes you
and you whistle an Eddy Arnold
tune—or was it Eddie Albert?
Sometimes Patsy Cline.
When you idly make music,
I can see you, half-combed hair,
a wild child full of questions,
peaches or blackberries,
your mother simply wanting
you to survive her.

When I was twelve my parents bought
something we thought purely marvelous:
a *stereophonic hi-fi record player.*
We would turn one knob off to hear
which instrument or voice inhabited
the separate speakers, the miracle
of discrimination. They bought one
record, country and western songs
from the forties and fifties.
We played it until it was ground
down to a thin series of hiccups.

As you whistle I hear that record,
and could sing along, dancing
in the basement with my sister,
hear one of those songs,
I don't remember which, one
by Jim Reeves maybe, my father's
favorite, or Hank Williams singing:
Please release me, let me go.

ED MADDEN

Inferno

rice field, Cowlake, Arkansas, 1979

Hell appeared when Greg sat on the levee,
and the outer darkness opened up behind him.
Before then, it did not exist, or existed

only as the story of a rich man, thirsty,
wanting a poor man to dip the tip
of his finger in water and cool his tongue.

Some summers before, I stumbled up
when the church sang my name—*o sinner*—
up for the dunking, preventative, like dipping sheep,

or dogs. Dogs licked the poor man's sores.
O taste and see, says the psalm—meaning
the tongue is how we know the world—

and then God with his footbaths and sheep dip,
God with his crop dusters, sowing love
and death, the bitter grains of it trickling

down my shirt, burning, God with his levees
and me with my shovel, digging a spillway
in the levee for the water to come later,

and Greg sitting there, his jeans ripped
at the knees, the crotch, watching me,
the darkness opening up behind him. The rice

was coming up all over, like a green
fuzz, like hair. I didn't look. I did.
There will be weeping and gnashing of teeth.

The fire is not quenched, the worm does not die.
The tongue is also a fire. It defiles
the whole body. The crop dusters are flying

over. Greg is not a metaphor. The field
is hot. There's a water jug in the truck.
Oh, that he would dip the tip of his finger

in water and cool my tongue.

AL MAGINNES

Pornography

How would I have come to it but through the damp pages
 of old Playboys stashed in the woods behind Greg Dial's house,
tiny circles of mildew like decayed stars marking the bodies
 we gawked and gawked at? So maybe
the confusion started there, the wondering whether
 this was a sacred vessel we stared at or something to cast aside
once the need was done. My computer screen fills
 with offers for time shares, lower mortgage rates, invitations
to Brandi and Tiffany's web-cammed dorm room
 where all major credit cards are accepted, where
a glassed-in passion mocks the fever that opened
 those damp magazines, portals that offered the first
inkling of what might be though the pleasure they extended lay
 so distant no rank and futile dreaming could touch it.

But that is not what I'm talking about. Nor am I speaking
 of flesh suddenly real, of the first time my fingers brushed
through rough hair and curled to touch what folded
 underneath, those mute regions hidden so long
I could have doubted their existence, could have believed them
 one more horny legend, like mountain oysters or men
and boys who coupled with goats, if I had not seen
 the glossed and airbrushed pictures that proved
the truth behind rumors of that long-sought delta. So when
 Dallas Mangum gave his nuts a hoist and promised
to wear out some split-tail tonight, I believed, even though I knew
 he would end the night passed out in his car, sleeping
in the shadow of the closed-down pool hall. And I believed again
 when the first girl who let me in surged beneath me.

Pleasure so short-lived may deserve only the passive face,
 the stilled half-smile practiced by the motionless women
in photographs. Yet mine was the face clamped silent
 as her breathing and her voice dredged forth a language
buried in the oldest valleys and tides the body holds,
 something no snapshot coyness or cottony movie clip

made me ready for. Once I looked in the window
of a novelty shop festooned with rubber and plastic devices
that make parody or ritual from our need for other bodies,
that, like the techniques men's magazines offer
in clinical detail, reduce all passion to manipulation,
a progression to a desired result. The masks
staring from the walls, black leather sacks designed
to make us faceless, erased my gaze.

If we are anything more than vehicles for body parts
dependent on friction, it comes from our ability
to construct the face behind the mask, the fluid wince
and grimace the model's pose denies. These nights
I walk upstairs to sleep beside a woman who is
my life's good fortune. And if, once or twice, I followed
the computer's pointed finger to Brandi and Tiffany's room,
isn't curiosity the unextinguished part of desire?
Worse to me now are the times I rose and dressed
for my own vanity, times I was steered not by affection
but by icy appetite and the need to add to some hidden tally
that wanted nothing to do with the first open-eyed gazing,
the spear-thrust of a desire that believed in the beloved
grace of every breathing body I would touch.

Firefly Gospel

Because we have made them the intermediaries
of the stars and, by extension, the planets,

we endow them with an existence larger
than the glimmer of one night

or one season, their summer bloom and flicker
one constant of our time-fogged span.

We know or believe we know how brief
a firefly's span, since they die

so easily once captured, but the fire hovering
green-gold and planetary

in the emptiness between trees might be
the same glow that cast its lamps

over a back yard in Alabama forty years ago,
glow I ran through the dark to capture.

Each morning the bodies were shriveled and smelled
of dead copper, but the hot, burning dimes

of stars always surfaced and were echoed by
the weaving ballet of fireflies, more light

than anyone could capture. Now I have learned
those lights, like human voices, are signals,

go-betweens for bodies tired of being told
they will die, a beckoning

to the oldest orbit bodies know, but I see them
exactly as I have always wished to see them,

small, stark missionaries descended
to deliver night's gospel of fire.

Music from Small Towns

No one is nearby to give lessons, but boys willing
to needle L-O-V-E and H-A-T-E into their knuckles long before

they sniff the damp walls of a jail cell would not listen
if there were. Drummers learn rhythm by chopping wood,

guitar players find a few chords and sniff nail polish
or glue before practice. Since they have nothing

to sing about, that is what they sing. The secret is playing
long enough to allow the houses where they sleep, the stores

where they buy magazines and gum, the parking lots where fathers
or brothers ground them in the harmonies of pedal

and clutch, all to find room to breathe inside that nothing.
The ones who have not driven those streets hear

red lights and blood, car wrecks, crazy sisters, the cost
of living a life you know you will never understand.

Dust and pollen film windshields, a tire sighs flat.
Imperfection might prove one form of salvation.

On the sidewalk, a bird that broke its neck
    flying into a window washed too clean.

Empty chords ring out, called for
    by natives and strangers when the runaway sons

glare and play their version of a place
    that didn't know it had a name before it became a song.

JEFF MANN

A Brief Christian Visit; or, The Butch Bottom Sends Old Ladies Packing

For JW and Geri

In the face of such talcum-dusted aggression,
it's taken me decades to become this blunt.
"Is this a Christian visit?" I ask the two old ladies
standing on my stoop with Bibles clutched like
sinister infants in their arms. "I'm sorry, ma'am"
(that intro being what's left of Southern manners),
"but I'm a homosexual and a pagan and I really want
nothing to do with your religion." They look up at
the man I've become, my bulky, muscled frame,
my smooth-shaved head and camo cargo shorts,
my bearded frown. How much do they see, how
much do they comprehend? My left arm's entirely
ink-sleeved: C.S.A., a Mars symbol, a pentagram,
the face of the Horned God, a bear paw, thorns
and thistles, a flaming sword. From the sides
of my wife-beater spill chest hair and the purple
bruises of a damned fine pec caning to match
the flogging welts across my back. Really,
whose world do they think this is? Off they go,
scuttling down the front walk, past the flower
beds brimful of poppies and peonies my handsome
husbear's planted. Sweet, silvery ladies, wives
of a long dead god, my body will do as it pleases.

The Shepherdstown Sweetshop

For Eddy Pendarvis

Moulder Hall—One of many buildings in down town Shepherdstown that were used as hospitals when casualties *"filled every building and overflowed into the country round . . ."* Moulder Hall was used for amputations. Currently the building is used as a bakery and restaurant.

The Historical Marker Database

It is, without question, the most profoundly
delicious Bavarian-cream-filled doughnut
I have ever greedily, lipsmackingly devoured.

The sheer weight of it's a marvel, heavy with
that heart luxuriant of sugar, egg, milk, vanilla.
I lap chocolate, tongue-probe cream, chew and sigh,

roll my eyes with rapture, while Antietam's wounded
are gasping all around me, upstairs and down.
My Rebels thrash and sob and bleed beneath

the Shepherdstown Sweet Shop's coffee bar,
beneath éclairs, bear claws, cookies, cupcakes,
beneath my feet. The doctor pulls out his bone saw,

his tourniquet. This black-bearded soldier's only
eighteen, from the same Virginia mountains as I,
his thigh shattered by grapeshot. Chloroform's

run out in the great battle's aftermath, so I rock him
in my arms, tip whiskey to his lips. He gulps and gulps
and grins; he grips my hand, grits a stick I slip

between his teeth. I wipe black powder from his face,
squeeze his shoulder, smooth his sweaty hair. When he nods,
I help three others hold him down so the doctor may begin.

JEFF DANIEL MARION

Hand-Me-Down Days

Girl in the backrow
    whose only gift for Christmas
        is a pencil box,

empty, its sole treasure
    your name crayoned in letters
        stark as winter trees:

you linger in the doorway—
    far away your father rocks
        in some dark corner of a tarpaper

shack, curses the wind whistling
    through cracks. Near the river
        your mother's new grave glistens.

Late afternoon light slants
    across our desks.
        We huddle by the stove

to read the lines of your hands
    hovering above the fire,
        scrubbed raw

on ridges of washboards.
    Wind skirls across rocky fields
        whipping you all the way home.

Orpha

she came daily
past us
to rusting mailboxes
lined like loaves

the bitter bread
no word, no letter
from distant kin

inside, warmed
we watched
while the sky spit
snow

that winter
she died
they brought her son home
from the state
penitentiary

what memory restores
to us
a grave, mound of earth,
loaf,
our daily bead

Winter Watch

So it comes to this, then:
backward toward a time when
memory is a scar cross-
stitching pain to joy, grief to loss
across a darkening valley where
already the horned owl waits,
perched in the larch for nightwatch,
his lantern eyes scanning the stillness
of abandoned home, woven tuft of weed
& matted hair nestling in the sycamore's crotch.
So begins the trilling of first cold,
crisp October whose blue clarity is
a lullaby to settle the cornshocked field
before winter locks in, setting its
teeth on edge & every eave:
wherever water seeks to run,

the hard cold fact glistens:
here winter nails us in
between hearth and dark
corners where already
our stories grow too dark to tell.

LINDA PARSONS MARION

Chicken Pickin'

Mighty good wage for wartime, five dollars
a Saturday, half that after school, back of Fudge's
store farmboys hauled in crates, pullets stuffed
beak to tail, fryers and roasters bound for fine
eating, Herbert at the cleaver, me and Ma Fudge
swinging them squawking birds.

Hickory flamed, vat roiling, my father led
the fiery dipping, earth's marrow shed of feather
and quill, pink as babies slapped into being,
his own hands their instrument of devilry,
their slow-browned redemption in milk gravy.

And how did you feel, I ask, wrung to your elbows
in entrails, bloody chickenshit, bringer of winged
apocalypse, how did you button your collar,
thread your laces after even one day of chicken
pickin', deafened surely by life's hue and cry?

Why, I felt nothing, those bills burned a hole
in my pocket, way more than Daddy's Navy pay.
Mother couldn't speak for the pride. A boy twelve,
stoking a man's sweat, washed in woodsmoke and lye,
I heaped dollars like collard greens on the table,
I come clean as the snow-white dove.

My Stepmother Takes Me to the Fair

Give me again your upturned wrists that night
at the Tennessee Valley fair. Our green car wheeled
over knotted crowds and lakes, the Midway

a sequined collar, carnies' shout: *guess your weight,*
your weight for a quarter. Swoop and twitter of bullbats,
our world topsy, the Scrambler twirled like sugary scarves

in the cotton candy machine. Now our heads thrown
back, wrist to wrist under the canopy, grinding
the last of September into sawdust. We could live

in the straw with the prize lambs, crawl down
the calliope pipes, travel to Chicago with the Bearded
Lady. I could leave my brother alone in the crib,

my mother's house of mirrors I stumble through.
Foaming out of the hallway, she and my stepfather
naked, rank with beer, her head slammed in the wall

like a ball at the stacked bottles rigged to never
collapse, never win a rhinestone hat or bowl of goldfish.
Turn the whites of your wrists to me again, spin off

higher than anyone can see, drunk in the seat
of big-shouldered trees, burst of chrysanthemums
pounding our hair, our surrendered faces.

Repossessed

The chaise floated on hot gravel, my mother
in short-shorts, turned to the stare of Sunday sun.
A sweaty Pabst cooled her copper thigh, then cheek,
then brow. She lounged next to my stepfather's
baby-blue De Ville, tailfins and power windows
I had never seen the likes of.

That day I jumped from the preacher's car, afire
with the Savior and life eternal. Brother Clyde
said I was a wanderer no more, but had strapped on
Jesus' sword, dipped in His precious blood. Heat
glanced off the grand and sinful Caddy, off
my mother's oiled legs. In the gospel light
she covered what she could of her shame.

That handsome man dragged her down, she always
claimed, down the unrighteous path. Their glory
road outshone even memory's shattered remains:
a man revving his passions, one day the Cadillac
burning rubber; the next, repossessed by the bank.

Did I see you get saved? she asks now. No,
but you were there when my head went back,
immersed in the Father, when temptation sucked us
both under—mine few and uncomplicated,
yours seared beyond blame or repentance—
when my robe rippled to the surface,
nigh as the wayward lamb to deliverance.

CHRISTOPHER MARTIN

Parable of the Carolina Chickadee

You can't sit still in this place, breathe for a moment,
without consuming spirits. High on Little Kennesaw's rocks,
sprawled as a dead man, gneiss cool against my back, I swig
whiskey from a flask, flick ladybugs from my shirt, creatures
gathered on this summit like a benevolent plague.

Chickadees chatter from stunted oaks not yet in leaves,
though red flowering weeds in the path foretell the green
to come. One bird descends to a boulder, shaggy with moss,
and disappears. I rise, specters already flowing my bloodstream
from the strenuous hike, stagger to stone, find a foothold,
lift myself to see water droplets fuming from fissure,
the chickadee wallowing, beating wings in a leaf-strewn pool,
drinking the reckoning of rock and a season of rain.

When the bird spots me, spooked, it flees, reoccupies
its post, banters my presence from a nearby branch.
I cup my hands like a camped Rebel, immerse them,
break the leaf mold surface, salvage water from silt,
set the freshness to my lips. I return to my lookout,
form my pack to a pillow with one last sour mash sip,
lie down to sleep, the last lights flickering, dusk diffusing
over interstate, strip malls, and munitions plants,
the Shermans of the world below making their plans.

Visiting Wildman's Civil War Surplus and Herb Shop

We were boys, knew something
about the place was wrong, sick, but still
we walked into Wildman's door.

Dressed in mockery of the man
who claims to be Stonewall Jackson's reincarnation,
we wore thrift store overalls, no shirts underneath,
camouflage caps, stems of grass in our teeth.

Past a *White History Year* sign, the hanging
Stars and Bars, a rack of T-shirts emblazoned
with Klansmen images, burning crosses,
captions that read *The Original Boys in the Hood,*
we saw him soon after—wiry, wild-bearded,
a man one might take for an old hippie
but for the .45's at his hips, the matching guns
screen-printed on his shirt framed by the phrase
It's the law in Kennesaw.

We nodded at him, tried to conceal smirks,
browsed his crypt of Confederate ephemera
and Civil War memorabilia, much of it cheap
though strewn among relics quite real.

Sitting at his counter, behind junk piles,
old documents recalling some lost cause,
he watched unmoved, saw through
our satire, knew exactly why we had come.

In smugness covered only by costume,
I looked upon jars of cotton balls labeled
Niglet Repellant
and thought I was the enlightened one.
When I saw the drawings of black people
swinging from trees like monkeys,
I thought I was forward-thinking.
I knew I was no racist, no remnant
of some backward time: I shopped
at the mall, did well in school,
played for the basketball team,
could even quote Martin Luther King,
assumed the irony of my presence enough.

In the back, near the racks of herbal remedies,
we passed a Klansman mannequin, hooded,
draped in a musty robe, nearly yellow,

holding a length of rope and a noose.
Any meaning the joke might have had
disappeared, shrouded in my silence.

We hurried out as Wildman waved,
smiled, though it did not strike me then
that such nooses as the one we saw
were once held by living hands—
not motionless, not as ornaments
in the back of some racist's shop,
not symbols in a young man's mind
raising some time left to history,
standing in for the hate of a single man,
but were flung over limbs, tightened
around necks in nearby woods.

Even when Wildman rests like Stonewall
under the shade of the trees,
even as his shop rots into the ground,
shades of the clearcuts outside the old walls
will remember those who dwelled
in this place once forested, will recall
human beings hanging whether we do or not,
whether or not we know their names
or speak for them at all.

CHRIS MATTINGLY

No 'Count

Though I can't smell it
Any more, I know
This house still smells of
Menthol and mothballs.

I been living here
Since my grandpa died
Two months ago. His
Imprint light on the

Mattress where he went.
If I'd have something
When I go, it'd be
The palimpsests left

Like circus posters
After the show's done
Gone: hair brush of worn
Down bristles, the sweat-

Stained fedora and
Boots with foot stamped soles.
Now and then an aunt
Or cousin drops in

For keepsakes. The lace
Curtains, roll-top desk
And oak wardrobe are
Now gone. But his brown

Pants still hang from the
Glass doorknob from the
Last time he took them
Off. Sometimes I stand

In the hall, looking
Down at the paths worn
Into the carpet
Where he'd stumble, fall,

And grope for Mamaw
Gone years before him.
Today, my sister
Come by. I sat at

The table watching
Her cigarette burn
As she rummaged through
Rooms while talking on

The phone. In fifteen
Minutes she had all
She needed: duct tape,
A box of trash bags,

Dish soap, aluminum
Foil, every last roll
Of toilet paper,
Some coat hangers, even.

Summertime

The deadliest weather
In Louisville history.

What grass hadn't died,
What shrubs and trees

Could still breathe,
We were meant to manage.

Minimum wage,
And if the day slow,

To the big man's house
We go to clean his pool,

Paint his portico,
Or drag stones

From the dry creek
And stack into sections

Of wall meant to mimic
Bucolic Kentucky ruins.

Between us we had one diploma,
Two pair white shoes

Stained lime green
With grass, and half

A ham biscuit
We'd end up splitting

In the broke-ass shade
Of a tree we'd be hauling

Away by noon. To be honest,
Me and this fifty-something

Would creep into the blue
Bottoms of every property

We could and sleep
The hottest parts away.

Sometimes, this man
Would get me to army crawl

Under a house to lay
On bellies in the spider cool

Silt and sand. Can you imagine,
Hiding like a mutt

With a man your father's age?
A man you once heard

Called "boy?"
Maybe you're from

The kind of place
Where it's common

To call a man "boy."
Maybe you come from

A place where you don't
Have to know where

You're from, think it's nothing
To hear a man address his help

In the dizzying heat
Of the deadliest week

In Louisville history: “Boy,
Don’t be going in

My pool house for water.
You’ll turn my dogs loose—

I don’t want them exposed
To this kind of heat.”

MICHAEL MCFEE

Yaller

My stringy step-cousin was a gullet with legs:
he was never not eating
but what he liked best was a mustard sandwich,

two slices of white bread
slathered with yellowest French's, all condiment,
no meat. He'd lick the knife

then slap the halves together and devour it
in quarters, four big bites
followed by four bigger gulps and faint grunting.

Terry smeared Duke's mayo
on the left side "for lubrication," he said the time
I tried one of his sandwiches,

hoping to impress him with my own appetite,
choking before chasing
that dry wad with cold milk whiter than the bread.

He broke my left arm once,
tripping me with a low rope stretched taut across
the top step of our front porch:

he ran away for days, hiding in unlocked garages
until the cops found him
and his dad's belt delivered its familiar lesson.

Years later, Terry killed himself
alone in his car at my sister's house, who knows why,
gun pressed to head, a dull pop

behind rolled-up windows. He was never not doing
something with his hands,
those nailbit hands, those always-famished hands

making a "yaller sandwich"
and swiftly taking it into his body while standing,
squeezing a little of the filling

around his stuffed mouth, that sour gold bright
as a road's double center line
or signs on the shoulder warning trouble ahead.

Breaks

Work was something we did between breaks,
those fifteen-minute vacations twice a shift

when we stopped stomping the wide foot pedals
that sent our massive machines into their cycles

of bending or pressing or welding or trimming
the steel pipes that required quick human hands

to position and turn and lift and package them
in that long-gone auto parts plant in Arden.

We'd hustle down the narrow concrete aisles
to a low room under the bosses' platform

where the machines we really wanted to touch
were waiting, humming quietly, glowing—

the ones that wouldn't slice or crush our fingers,
the ones that gave us drinks and snacks and smokes

in exchange for the warm coins in our pockets,
the silver circles dirtied by our touch.

Lunch was a longer breather halfway home
when most of us drifted outside to eat,

away from the heat and din and oily stink,
but it was the other breaks that kept us going:

those quarter-hours included our walking time
to and from that official Concession Area,

even if it took seven minutes each way
and only left us sixty frantic seconds

to gulp a coke and choke down a few nabs
and take some puffs on a fresh cigarette

before grinding it out and heading back
to our distant stations in that factory,

fueled for the next few hours of doing
the same job our mindless bodies always did,

resuming the manufacture of tailpipes
designed to fit under machines like the ones

we drove to work that and every other day,
already looking forward to our first break.

Cottonmouth

At first, I thought it was a dirt bike tire
somebody had dumped way out in the woods

(though why go to so much trouble,
to haul that spent radial into a remote thicket?)

and then it stirred, slowly uncoiling itself,
straightening its dark thick muscle of a body

long as I was tall, aiming straight at me,
the unslick tread of its skin gaining traction

as my skinnier-than-a-water-moccasin legs
unfroze and sped my upright paleness away

from that cold-blooded heat-seeking snake,
my cotton mouth wide open but, for once, mute.

RAY MCMANUS

Dog Box

I

I can tell when it's lunch
by squinting at the sun
and standing against the base
of a tree with an ax in my hand.
The foreman yells *shave it.*

This time I won't fall in love
with the sound bark makes
as it flips in chunks
across the lawn. I won't pay
attention to sap or sand or imagine
I'm in the top of the tree
screaming that I'll jump
if I have to. This time I'll get
lucky and won't stand in a bed
of ants or a nest of yellow jackets,
won't hear what sloshes in the tank,
won't feel the saw on my knee.

II

The foreman leans in to say
the numbers like it was bad
news about his mother.
Sometimes he looks both ways
first, sometimes he never lifts
his eyes. I like that, imagine
someday us riding in the cab,
doesn't matter who's driving,
and when static settles on
the radio and whatever song
begins to play, he'll say
what he always says—*you know*
all songs are really about fucking.

We keep the ropes in the dog
box, all the rigging, and mixed
tools. The foreman tells me to
learn the names, but if I ask,
he yells at the weather as if
he always wants it to rain,
and I'll know not to ask why
because I like being up front.

III

Lunch won't be here
for another hour, so
when the rain comes
it is welcomed and we
sit on empty buckets
under a tin overhang
with our boots soaked
and watch the bull-rope
take water. It's not my
turn to get it, but I'm
told to anyway.

IV

When the hitch breaks
and the trailer sags, we weld
it back where we can,
and the foreman yells
flash burn and tells me
not to stare at the arc,
and of course I try
to see how long I can
stare without blinking
for Darvocet, for blisters,
for an early trip home,
but I'm not going anywhere,
not with these kinds of promises.

So bad eye closed, mouth shut,
and no muscle I learn
the difference between friction
and tension, the hold that slips
when the tree comes down.

At the stump, the foreman
yells *shave it,* and this time
I won't fall in love
with the sound of grunt
and grind, the leaf in the wind
before the ax in the chipper.

Disturbing Remains

The easiest way to put a truck in
a ditch is to ignore broken fences.

Sometimes the crash is too hard,
and the headstones get buried.

The older the stone, the better
the chances, ask the cotton field.

Ask a salesman about the hosepipe.
Ask Sid about the bottom of his boot.

These are the things we eat to remember,
our dust-mouth, the pig in us, rooting.

Staying in the Truck

Sleight of Hand
They say Jesus could talk
from the cross because
a gypsy ran off
with the last spike.

Twist of Fate
It takes two to pick
a peach, no time
to stand there
with your mouth open.

On a Bed of Nails
I'll ring the bell.
Cut the blacktop
with kerosene.
Let me do the talking.

THORPE MOECKEL

Spittoono Lily

Copenhagen, Kodiak, Grizzly, Skoal—
Lily dipped them all, loved the brown shreds of leaf
as they swashed against her tongue, escapees
from the den of lip & gum,

and it was nearly as meaningful
when she was young, stealing pinches in the corner,
training the gut to handle reflux & burn
so she could get away

with it in Algebra One, where Mrs. Rowland
never taught nicotine or the brain's strange charity,
how multiplied they equal calm, focus,
and ill, being a rebel

at that straitjacket of a school. Later,
so she could find the freshest tin, Lily moved
to Nashville where the finest, Copenhagen,
is made. That moist softness

between index and thumb, feeling her face
purse like old fruit in hot sun, nearly rivals sex, Lily said
on our last date, and, anyway, she clipped, since
everyone knows life's

hazardous to health, isn't addiction
synonymous with love. Lily's drained gallons
of saliva since that contest in Clemson—
Spittoono, they called it

(she won)—but if she gets to its cousin
in Charleston, I hope she doesn't spit anymore
gently or discreetly, but enjoys the motions
of dancers as that other dance

tunes the dark orchestras of her blood.

Cold Range, Hot Range

We're at the Potts Mountain Shooting Range
on a hot day in March, blowing ammo,
hosing the shale. Submachine, .357,
Glock. And to pepper fine holes

in the paper target, an assault shotgun
that holds eight shells. It's wild
as fire to play with fire. I like it.
Pressure thick in the gut, tremors

ear to marrow. Each cone of flame,
the burnt powder's sweetness & stench.
Down the line a man sights in
a .50 caliber muzzleloader,

all smoke & ear protection. Cold range,
the .22 shooter shouts, questioning.
Cold range, we reply, and check again
the guy with the .308, the bald one

with the aught six, before heading
to gather, change targets, boots
crunching brass. It's the velocity
I like, perfectly invisible & close,

more timeless than timelessness.
And the potency—almost innocent—
of one gentle finger squeeze.
And how each time the dust flies,

thirty rounds of nine mil out
the MP5, I'm amazed to be
breathing still. Out there I tell
my demons to dance. I don't ask

for final words. This is serious.
Lucky, crazy. And maybe
some of us are aiming less
at the target's inner circle,

strange whirlpool, than at the itch—
everywhere, nowhere—to hold the barrel
to the mouth's gummy roof. If
suicide's the only serious question,

as someone very serious once said,
what of murder, what of the bullet
worming red tunnels in flesh?
It's not that I want to carry one,

though sometimes it seems crazy not to,
it's that I can't ignore the gleam—
like birdsong—of light on the barrel,
and on my friend, taste it, her smile.

Living by Water

How many times can a man go to the river,
dip his hands in, touch them to his face,

face the wind, the sun, then touch the rocks
so as not to fall stepping across,

scrambling to a certain beach or grotto
where in going, in arriving, in every breath

between, the heart sheds foul layers—
greed, vanity—as if shale, the flakes

worked by gravity to sand, mineral—
water he spits, water he thirsts for;

how many before he's holding the hands
of children, keeping them from falling in,

knowing they must, as a river must
not make a circle nor a man too easily believe

in rivers, no matter droughts known,
obscenities of flood, choking trout,

bloated fawns; no matter how many boats
pushed off in—boats of sin,

redemption-boats—or bodies explored,
campsites slept with sounds of water

tucking behind every rock burst against;
how many before he must be carried there,

perhaps by a stranger, perhaps he's the stranger now,
but not to the birds, beasts, flowers because

he's forgotten their names, knows they were
never grateful of his awe, less of his pity.

ROBERT MORGAN

Manure Pile

Heaped gold and powerful behind the barn.
The crust, faded by weather, almost
never freezes, steaming off snow with fever
of its inner work. Birds worry
the seeds exposed by rain.
Black chemistry of the core
nurses weeds on the baked hide
while the yard is frost-dead. Once
a little chick peeped from its straw
in January, hatched by the warmth.
The matter dug from its side for fields
is too strong even for worms to live in,
sealed years by the ammonia.
Haunted in the hot months by a genie
of flies, it jewels the downwind.
Sundays the many purple butterflies
that suck its inks, shiver off into the sky
where carillons of convection ring.

The Gift of Tongues

The whole church got hot and vivid
with the rush of unhuman chatter
above the congregation,
and I saw my father looking at
the altar as though electrocuted.
It was a voice I'd never heard
but knew as from other centuries.
It was the voice of an awful fire.
"What's he saying?" Ronald hissed
and jabbed my arm. "Probably Hebrew."
The preacher called out another
hymn, and the glissade came again,

high syllables not from my father's
lips but elsewhere, the flare of
higher language, sentences of light.
And we sang and sang again, but
no one rose as if from sleep to
be interpreter, explain the writing
on the air that still shone there like
blindness. None volunteered a gloss
or translation or receiver
of the message. My hands hurt
when pulled from the pew's varnish
they'd gripped and sweated to. Later,
standing under the high and plain-
sung pines on the mountain, I clenched
my jaws like pliers, holding in
and savoring the gift of silence.

Man and Machine

Besides drinking and telling lies,
nothing interested my cousin Luther
like working with the tractor.
Astride that bright and smelly beast
he was a man inspired.
Revving and tearing the stubble
of early spring he cussed
the metal like a favorite mule,
parrying any stallout with the shift.
In too big a hurry to turn
at the end of a row he jammed
in a brake and spun around,
lowered the harrows
into the winter-bleached field
and blasted off for yon end.
Barely able to read, he took
dusters and bush hogs and diesel movements
apart with the skill of a surgeon,
hollering on the phone for parts
as far away as Charlotte or Atlanta.
Would stay on his ass at the filling station

or country store for weeks
while wife and kids and parents
picked in the heat the crops he'd
drive to market. Neither storm-threat
or overripening could move him
to join their labor. Until time
for dusting with the homemade blower
mounted on a jeep. Or after the vines
were cut he'd windlass in the long wires.
Winter Luther lived only for his truck,
banging down the dirt road to Chestnut Springs
for booze and women. But that was just
occasional. Most days he'd brag at the store
about his pickup, or be trading for another
with even thicker tires, more horsepower
and chrome, a gunrack in the window.
At home he'd maybe tune a little,
oil the plates of the planter.
But off the machine he was just
another stocky hoojer, yelling
to make up for his lack of size
and self-esteem, adding fat and blood
pressure. Late February breaking time
transformed him. He leapt on the big
diesel and burned out its winter farts
all the way to the bottoms, whipping
the animal until it glowed, became
his legs and voice and shoulders.
To children and himself he tore up ground
like a centaur. Plowing with the lights on
all night in the river fields
he circled more times than any race driver,
shouting in the settling damp while
we slept hearing the distant fury.
And by morning the fields were new.

RICARDO NAZARIO Y COLÓN

Mi Nuevo Hogar: Kentucky

In my new
Kentucky home, the sun still shines
even though the new
darkies speak Spanish
and everyone is gay
about the mayor's skittle rainbow.

Salsa music trails
up and down Appalachian spines
like the smoke of tightly rolled cigars,
dipped in blueberry
or apple Mountain Dew.

Mi Nuevo Hogar:
Kentucky donde

Bare feet *Garifuna*
women beat on woodchip floors
when they dance on
Rowan county hill legs. There
are always hard times when
ICE comes a-knocking.

Sling blades
hablan un español de enamorados around
tobacco leave
torsos. Pronouncing accents illegal
for tongues
unable to undulate the sound of T and H.

Mi Nuevo Hogar:
Kentucky donde

Halfbloods are
not taught how to answer the question
"What are you?"
and little boys

try to make sense of their long hair by
proclaiming it's part of their
Puerto Rican/Spanish Heritage.

Is no longer
stained with early morning brown or drive
through mulch.
It is *mi sitio* of contradiction, *de un aliento*
anonimo and a *deseo* without prejudice.

TARA POWELL

Watching *Deliverance* with My Students

Breath still snags on my heart like teeth
when Drew gasps, "I'm lost," his laugh
drifting up to the banjo boy's inscrutable perch,
and then, Ronny Cox showing his own teeth to sky,
the glint of leaf and sun in his eyes, before
the camera curves back into the trees
and dark frames close around the film like bars,
that's the moment I remember every river bend
of my own travels, his face like your faces now,
ringed around this heavy seminar table,
oak polished to mirrors. You don't know
what a red shirt is, don't fathom what happens
down the river of their discontent as the closed
dark frames bore you, their beer bores you,
the stringing of the bow, the owl howling
in the dark wood, the teeth of the forest
clacking in hunger while you are sleeping,
you who have seen all this before.
And the moment when it comes and refuses
to pass, but goes on and on in our dark room
in our honors college, pictures reflecting
from the screen to the golden table
like sun on cypress water, squeal
like a pig, squeal like a pig, pig, pig,
even then you don't imagine your own
bellies fanning the damp leaves,
the scent that will stay with you always,
that moment your parents stopped the clumsy
pressing of their bodies to watch, not watch,
but feel something tilt at the malaise
of sex and war and being young—
you, there, back of the class, head bowed weeping
with Bobby in the leaves and sweat and dark
before the lights go on and we all ride
down to the neon world again,

you have seen the thing itself alone,
even as you clench your eyes in terror
against the lesson, the television,
the sleeping bodies warm beside you,
the table holds the memory tightly
of your wet hands straining to hold on.

RON RASH

The Skeleton in the Dogwood

Watauga County, 1895

Two lovers out walking found
more than spring's promised blessing
on new beginnings hanging
in a dogwood tree's branches.

No friend or kin claimed those bones.
The high sheriff came. Foul play
he was sure, but how or why
he found no answers, so stayed

to help break the ground, help haul
a flat rock out of the creek,
sprinkle some dirt, some God words,
then left for more recent crimes.

The lovers wed that winter.
On their marriage night they dreamed
of bouquets of spring flowers
blooming in a dead man's hand.

Winter Lightning

When lightning struck the big oak, cracked
and splintered Curt's deer stand, he ignored
the old hunters back at camp
who spoke of winter lightning as if more
than natural and swore it best
seen as a sign more ominous
than an owl at noon. The oak was now cursed,
bad enough to touch it, much less
spend time perched high in its limbs.
Curt rebuilt his stand the next morning,

and stayed up there despite the warning,
until he fell and broke his neck.
The man who found him closed his eyes,
then left to notify his kin.
An accident, some said, although
none climbed the tree to fetch his gun.

Animal Hides

As if in flight they ascend
on barn-back, shed-side: bobcat
and fox, raccoon and black bear,
limbs splayed as if gliding on
wind-lift as coats dry and tan
to become somehow more than
brag of well-hid trap, true aim,
a poor man's taxidermy—
for they remain when weathered
into fur-scrap, pelt-shadow
ghosting across graying boards,
as though their death-hurriers
kenned animal once meant soul,
like those first hunters believe
some essence may yet linger,
must be earth-freed, giving wing.

JANISSE RAY

Land of Milk and Honey

An Homage

1. milk

the moon a pond of magnolia
petals. porcelain moonflowers
twining bleached bones
of deer. china saucers scraping
the whitewashed cupboard.
enamel pan. white-hot water singing
against the lacy skull of milch cow.
milkweed fluff tugged from its pod
by seven white horses of wind. breasts
beneath cotton gowns of ibis-winged
women. panting of the women.
cirrus throats of sparrows.
panther claw scratching
at a parchment window. moth papers.
hairs of my grandmother
cupping white eggs of doves.
powdery ashes of white oak, sifted
through the moon's cheesecloth.
fog of the morning of every
twig's birth and winter child's
breath tatting tiny flowers.
dew on gardenias like buttermilk.
meringue on a frothy creek.
tablecloth clattering its teeth.
the evening star hissing through
faded arms of white sycamore.

2. honey

slant of October sun on tupelo
hives. saddlebags of worker bees
spilling gunpowder to Sunday.
drone of barred owls.

catacombs of fertile eggs
from rusty chickens. iron bolts.
wagon tongues groaning
with the weight of coming night.
feathers of crowing cocks.
tannic Ten Mile Creek pouring
toward the golden river, morning
of the river. humps of cypress.
poplar hand-hewn into table,
axe-handle and bowl. sumac.
the hawk's red tail dripping
gallberry. wildflower fire
inside a brick chimney above
a thousand chipping sparrows.
thunder-showers of longleaf burrs,
early fall on red clay.
rainwater funneling toward
the branch, past stone crockery
filled with brown eggs.
outside the window, dun fields
of clover, millet, sorghum.
warm bread and an open jar.

PAUL RUFFIN

Frozen Over

In Mississippi I recall only once
how the cold came down like a lid of iron,
clamping the landscape, stilling the trees,
and all the ponds froze over: not
just a skim for crashing rocks through,
but thick and hard enough to walk on.

The gravel pit where we swam in summer
spanged and creaked as I edged out
toward the gray, awful middle where,
if I went through, no one could reach.
I moved like a bird coming to terms
with glass, sliding one foot, then
the other, holding back my weight
and breath until they had to come.

I could see, beyond the far shore,
cars moving on the highway, slowing,
faces in the window ringed with frost,
the little ones waving, pointing
to that child walking on water.

Circling

"When you are lost in night woods,"
my father said, pointing about us,
"you can't just guess at a line:
one leg's shorter, you'll circle.

You must walk in a set direction,
picking a tree, one farther on,
and on, until you have strung out
tree after tree in a straight line
to some place better than where you are."

"But in the dark?" I questioned him.

"There's always enough light for that,
but don't you trust the stars and moon:
they move." He asked if I understood.
I nodded and looked at the dark trees.

"Then find your way back to the truck."

"But it's getting late, I'm hungry,
I don't know what direction to start."

"That is the direction. Now go."

He pointed to the wall of woods.
I lunged into the underbrush
in the direction he had pointed,
forgetting utterly his advice,
no tree different from another,
crashed and plunged until I knew
that I was lost and circling.

I could see nothing but dark trees,
hear nothing but my terrified run
and the thrashing of my heart.

The stars spun wildly overhead,
the moon bounced across the sky.

He let me wander, stumbling, calling
his name until the woods stilled

and I crouched wet and cold,
like some wild abandoned thing
waiting for him to find me.

"You did not pick a tree," he said
as I followed him out of the woods,
"you did not hold a direction."

I stepped in his mooncast shadow,
long leg, short leg, resisting the circle
until the stars fell into place
and the rising moon stood still.

Gigging Frogs

There are some things on this earth
that may be fooled by two moons,
one still as a stone in the sky,
the other dancing. Not these frogs.
A moonlit night is not a night
for going after frogs. When your light
joins the moon, their clatter stops,
the pond goes dead: they are not fooled.

It must be done on a dark and dooming night
when yours will be the only light above
the rim of the pond. You must move
with the stealth of winter with your moon,
as slow as a stone sliding across the sky.

Then, as you see the eyes take life in
a seeming joy, moonstruck, you steady
the light, aim the deadly gig, and jab
the prongs through belly or head,
swift and sure as a cottonmouth.
When you have taken all you want, you
must ice them down for the trip home,
first cutting the hind legs, still joined,
from the upper torso, skinning them
like removing tootight jeans
and laying them side by side
in the ice of your cooler,
the legs of so many lovely girls
collected by a moonstruck man
who slew them for his joy.

Sawdust Pile

A pile, they say,
will burn for twenty years,
seething with deep heat
those long years out,
cool enough on top
for weeds and barefoot boys.

Like early ice it lures
the unwary up a greening slope
firm to the foot, firm
and cool up to the very peak,
where the crust sags, gives way,
and legs, torso, and head
sink to the fierce core.

There are the tales:
Bo Simpson's horse, a pack
of pureblood coon hounds,
Sarah Potter's little girl-
all gone to a quick hell.

Out here the rattler warns, lightning
strikes from a growling sky:
each terror is given a tongue.
But the fire lies quiet in this pile,
a coiled thing, tongueless and waiting,
beneath the devil's cool shell.

STEVE SCAFIDI

To Whoever Set My Truck on Fire

But let us be friends awhile and understand our differences
are small and that they float like dust in sunny rooms
and let us settle into the good work of being strangers
simply who have something to say in the middle of the night
for you have said something that interests me—something of flames,

footsteps and the hard heavy charge of an engine gunning away
into the June cool of four in the morning here in West Virginia
where last night I woke to the sound of a door slamming,
five or six fading footsteps, and through the window saw
my impossible truck bright orange like a maverick sun and

ran—I did—panicked in my underwear bobbling the dumb
extinguisher too complex it seemed for putting out fires
and so grabbed a skillet and jumped about like one
needing to piss while the faucet like honey issued its slow
sweet water and you I noticed then were watching

from your idling car far enough away I could not make
your plate number but you could see me—half naked
figuring out the puzzle of a fire thirty seconds from
a dream never to be remembered while the local chaos
of a growing fire crackled through the books and boots

burning in my truck, you bastard, you watched as I sprayed
finally the flames with a gardenhose under the moon
and yes I cut what was surely a ridiculous figure there
and worsened it later that morning after the bored police
drove home lazily and I stalked the road in front of my house

with an ax in my hand and walked into the road after
every car to memorize the plates of who might have done this:
LB 7329, NT 7663, and you may have passed by—
I don't know—you may have passed by as I committed
the innocent numbers of neighbors to memory and maybe

you were miles away and I, like the woodsman of fairy tales,
threatened all with my bright ax shining with the evil

joy of vengeance and mad hunger to bring harm—heavy
harm—to the coward who did this and if I find you,
my friend, I promise you I will lay the sharp blade deep

into your body until the humid grabbing hands of what must be
death have mercy and take you away from the constant
murderous swinging my mind makes my words make
swinging down on your body and may your children
weep a thousand tears at your small and bewildered grave.

The West Virginia Copper-Wing

An apple falls through the branches of the tree
  and a green snake rises up flying
    with little wings iridescent

as the evening begins in the orchard
  on the edge of town. Three deer
    whisper grazing in the lane.

You could be eleven or twelve
  standing with a stillness you have
    never before known, a halo

of gnats around your head and this
  could be any year in recorded history
    of human life. No one

ever exactly remembers this moment
  or the next. We find ourselves
    in a royal pause and then we go on

asking what's next. We fall
  toward sorrow and we forget.
    Someone captures the miraculous

green snake with a net—
  pins it to a board. Someone
    sharpens a knife at the center

of the earth and it sounds like a wheel.
  Houses appear. Thousands
    of windows twinkle suddenly in

the settling dark. Stillness,
  which was the god of being
      eleven or twelve on the edge of town

just before someone you love
  calls you home and home being
      the god of this place, disappears.

All of it disappears and you are left
  lost in the majestic green clockwork
      that is next

The Hillbilly Break-Dance and the Talking Crow

So the school bus skids around the mountain and kills
my friend's dog almost instantly and Lester in the back seat
sticks his face out the window to say "Don't eat that dog,
he's dead meat" and laughs and that was long ago and Lester

lives in the mountain ghetto where the rich have not yet
ruined the land with their paper mansions and he is hillbilly
wild as a teenager and learns to break-dance and locks
and pops and turns and rocks like a robot on summer nights

drunk under the Christmas lights of his back porch where
we watch as Lester works through his routine and once
he moon-walked right off the edge and dropped down
hard into the honeysuckle and the blue rocks of the place

and sprung back to his feet and said I'm alright god dammit
and shinnied back up to move some more and so it is not
hard to believe Lester banged out of his house last week
bored on a Sunday afternoon in August and wandered in

the woods of the mountain as if through some cathedral
so dark with leaves and fiddlehead ferns that light only
reaches the ground through a thousand little tunnels and
suddenly at his feet hop-hop-hopping along comes a crow

who says *alright then, alright, how are you?* and Lester
stops. *Alright then, how are you?* says the crow again and

cocks its head and looks up with its beady eye at Lester
who looks away. Trucks rumble down the mountain hard

in the distance and an airplane starts to make a sharp curve
a mile above but they don't know anymore about the world
for a minute, Lester and the crow talking awhile, he says just
shooting the breeze. He says that crow knew the names of his

father and his grandfather and "all kinds of personal shit"
and it said *Lester, Look at you. You've grown middle aged*
and fat but I like you anyways and flew back into the trees
just to let him think about it. And six other people have

talked to this crow and now it is legend and that is why
I am sitting in the Mount Hebron cemetery with a picnic
lunch and waiting while the story does its thing I guess
flying from tree to tree chasing owls maybe looking

for something shiny which is why I have lined up ten
dimes and a safety pin on the stonewall. To attract some
magic, to call down the blessing of an impossible thing.
Alright then. It is getting darker. Let the new life begin.

JAMES SEAY

It All Comes Together Outside the Restroom in Hogansville

It was the hole for looking in
only I looked out
in daylight that broadened
as I brought my eye closer.
First there was a '55 Chevy
shaved and decked like old times
but waiting on high-jacker shocks.
Then a sign that said J. D. Hines Garage.
In J. D.'s door was an empty Plymouth
with the windows down and the radio on.
A black woman was singing in Detroit
in a voice that brushed against the face
like the scarf
turning up in the wrong suitcase
long ago after everything came to grief.
What was inside we can only imagine—
men I guess trying to figure what would make it
work again. Beyond them
beyond the cracked engine blocks and thrown pistons
beyond that failed restroom
etched with our acids beyond that American Oil Station
beyond the oil on the ground
the mobile homes all over Hogansville
beyond our longing
all Georgia was green.
I'd had two for the road
a cheap enough thrill
and I wanted to think
I could take only what aroused me.
The interstate to Atlanta was wide open.
I wanted a different life.
So did J. D. Hines. So did the voice on the radio.
So did the man or woman

who made the hole in the window.
The way it works is this:
we devote ourselves to an image
we can't live with and try to kill
anything that suggests it could be otherwise.

Kelly Dug a Hole

I set the stakes, stretched the twine,
told my labor crew
how deep, how wide to go,
told them not to twist
or bend their holes,
not to bring them
to a point or flare
because we'd have
to have the bottoms
square and flat
to pour the footings
where a building
would finally stand.
Other workers flared,
caved in the walls,
or bent theirs
out of shape,
but Kelly dug
and kept his straight,
dug fifteen feet
into a hill
the dozer missed.
When Kelly got on grade
I dropped the plumb
to check his hole.
At the top
I held the string
three inches from the edge;
down below
the plumb bob
ceased its swing

three inches from the wall
and told me
Kelly's hole was true.
We built in ice and heat;
we built a building
five stories high
in Oxford, Mississippi.
The walls and floors
are spider-cracked in places
from some slight shifting,
but the building stands
and if any part will hold
when things begin
to slide and fall
that part will be
where Kelly dug his hole.

DAVE SMITH

How to Get to Green Springs

Nobody knows exactly when it fell off the map
or what the pressures were on its flooding river.
The hedge, the tottering mailbox, were gone. That dimple
of light from the bicycle that raised itself to creak
at noon across a clattering bridge names my father.
His blood silent as a surging wish drags this town
lost through my body, a place I can get back to only
by hunch and a train whistle that was right on time.

But time and trains were never right in Green Springs,
West Virginia. What color could map the coal's grime,
shacks shored against the river every March, mail
left to rot because no one answered to occupant?
Farmers low on sugar cursed the heat and left bad cigars
boys would puff back to clouds where they dreamed
of girls naked as their hands under outfield flies.
Scores were low. There were no springs for the sick.
Women lined their walls with the Sears catalog, but
the only fur they ever had was a warbled rabbit.
To get here think of dirt, think of night leaking,
the tick of waterbugs, a train held in Pittsburgh.

In the Yard, Late Summer

In the yard, the plum tree, wild
with a late summer wind,
shakes its thousand planets
of sweet flesh.
Does it mean to resist
this gush that drops
one order of things
into another? It keels,
leaning at forces we can't

see, can't know the edge of.
Its memory keeps only two
commands: this lives, this
dies from the licking sun.
There is no metaphor
to reveal what it has known
in its brooding years.
We watch the purple fruit fall
as leaves shear and snap
and nail themselves to light.
Between us the wind
is a word seeking a shape,
hovering in passion
and risen from the ground
of memory clenched
in roots and long tendrils.
Hearing that, knowing ourselves
wingless and bestial, we wait
for the sun to blow out,
for the return of that first
morning of pink blossoms
when we saw the dark stains
of our feet printing
what we were on that
dew-bed of the world.
The tree, too, waits
in its old unraveling
toward a naked silence,
its language wild and shocked.

The Tire Hangs in the Yard

for Robert Penn Warren

1

First it was the secret place where I went to dream, end
of the childhood road, deep-tracked, the dark
behind my best friend's house, blackberry
thickets of darkness, and later
where we stared, with our girls, into the sky.

Past the hedgerow and the house-stolen field, past
the wing-shooting of crow remembered, I drive
bathed by green dashlight and the sun's
blood glinting on leaves just parted, then see

again the dead end, the dying woods, that stillness still
ticking like throat-rattle—and Jesus Christ
look at the beer cans, the traffic, even
hung on a berry vine somebody's rubber,

and wouldn't you know it that tire still hangs.

2

In the Churchland Baptist Church the hot ivy hung, smelling
of dust, all mouths lifting their black holes
like a tire I kept dreaming. Clenched
by mother and father who stank sweetly in sweat,

I sang and sang until the black ceiling
of our house seemed to bellow with storm
and the tire skulled against my eyes
in time with the great clock in the far hall.

Hanging in darkness, like genitals, it made me listen.

3

Years pass and memory's pendulum swings to changeless shame:
one summer night I came to fistfight Jim Jenrett,
whose house she came to and she no more now
than a frail hand on my cheek, and I
am beer-brave and near wild with all
the dozen piling from cars. Jesus,
look at us in the ghost-flare of headlights,
pissing, taunting, boy-shadows all right,
and me in the tire spinning my childish words.

We pass also, and are blind, into the years like trees
holding their scars, half-healed, the dark where Jim,
dunned by our words, goes out
near dawn and steps in the tire
and shies up the electric extension cord, noosed,
by the rope whose tire, burdened, ticks slowly.

4

Ghost-heart of this place, of dreams, I give you a shove
and sure enough I hear the tick and all that was
is, and a girl straightening her skirt walks
smack against you and screams. You know
who laughs, smoking in the dark, don't you?

There are no headlights now, only the arc of blackness
gathering the hung world in its gullet. Blink
and maybe he's there, his great feet jammed
halfway in the hole of your heart,
gone halfway.

5

Where do they go who once were with us on this dream road,
who flung themselves like seed under berry-
black nights, the faces black-clustered,
who could lean down and tell us
what love is and mercy and why now

I imagine a girl, mouth open in the sexual O, her hair
gone dull as soap scum, the husband grunting
as his fist smacks again, the scream
not out yet, nor the promise
she could never love anyone else.

I climb in the tire, swinging like a secret in the dark
woods surrounded by the homelights of strangers.
She swore she loved me best.

In the church I imagined this place left forever behind
but it's with me as I try to see the road begin.
Blackberries on both sides blackly hang.
Tall trees, in blackness, lean back at me.
When will they come, the headlights washing
over me like revelation, in cars
ticking and swirling?

Once when my mother could not find me, they came here.
Said "So this is it, the place." It was dark,
or nearly, and they said I might have died.

I asked them what being dead was like.
Like going blind or flying at night.

I shove my foot at the dirt and swing in absolute black.
The whine of the rope is like a distant scream.
I think, so this is it. Really it.

R. T. SMITH

A Local Doc, over Rocky Lunchtime Bourbon, Speaks of Barter and Hopeful Home Remedies

Nostrums? Lordy, I have seen them all.
Alcohol's the favorite. Many a quack's
panacea bottled in a cellar and hawked
from door to door is thriving still.

Bindweed's supposed to heal a bruise.
Cherokee remedies still survive,
and slave recipes—hyssop, juniper salves.
Garçon, freshen my elixir, if you please.

One day a hefty woman who works a loom
down at Pepperell Mills sauntered in
with no appointment and perched herself prim
as an English queen in the waiting room.

What happened next? For a prolapsed
uterus, folk medicine recommends
inserting an Irish potato. It works,
if you can bear the weight, my friends,

a fact. Well, she'd relied on that specific
since winter. We'd hit, you understand, July,
and her complaint, not one smidge shy,
was *Leaves in my Virginia.* Not beatific,

exactly, but she was composed, no maniac,
and it made some sense. What better place
than a protected pocket, warm and moist?
But the spud had sprouted, sent runners amok.

You never know in these backwoods burley
counties if your manual skills will bloom
as sawbones or private gardener. Deftly,
I removed the obstruction and took it home.

I've raised a whole colony in my window box,
and bake, fry or roast, I'm proud as hell
of this year's crop. The woman paid her bill
with eggs and applejack. Life is a paradox.

Now I've got to rush back and tend my flock.
Got appointments at four—a pregnant lassie,
a leg to set, twins to inspect for chicken pox
and Marvin with his routine emergency.

I guess you might say my practice is thriving.
Drop on by, and I'll fry you up some shallot
hash browns in Margie's seasoned skillet,
a flavor I can promise is sure to revive

any ailing soul. Where do I get my onions?
Don't ask. The whole blessed world is a garden.

Horton's Store

Over smashed beam, batten and soffit
the bent tin roofing was rusting in a sorghum
field gone to yellow dock, but I thought
I could raise it—woodstove, scarred counter,
one raconteur warming up to his story:
the man who never . . . the dwarf who nearly. . . .
Where Trestle Rod farmers gathered
for tobacco, Hadacol and yarns, the shack
was a haven, even if hog prices dropped.

Just learning the itch for fiction I listened
to Newt Cooper blowing smoke and vowing
Muscogee ghosts ate a dozing plow horse
down to its bones. Ed Thaxton showing off
the banjo Old Scratch swapped for his soul
drove me under the counter with its jangle.
Cade Seeger whispered about a girl
who bathed in rose honey so she could fly.

Wanting every tale to have the gospel glow,
I was too amazed in the shadows to know
how every story cauled a grief, regrets,

cruel ruin and a world of the darkest scars.
In the lull after the last session's hum,
I dreamed of the long-buried and unspoken,
the way one glazed-over cracker would step up
and reach past facts as his neighbor's faces
strained to catch the tune of soothing untruth.

I wanted the knack, every bittersweet
technique that moved a tongue to utter *amen*.
I yearned to delight and bewilder and bind,
but looking back, I can't resurrect the hour
of cricket chirr and the lighted wicks.
Those evenings of cold Sun Drops, ambeer
and the odor of sweat seem half-hijacked
from Faulkner novels and country clichés.

Tainted myself, I'm just not sure. Licorice
whips and Sen-Sen drops? Yes, but what
of the Talmadge ham lynched from a rafter?
Was it Cy Whitfield or his brother Collis,
killed later by a bucking baler, who swore
a good story was the best part of being
a whole man? Did Hovis say then, "I swan,
it puts me in mind of the time my twill
trousers caught fire for no reason but spite"?

It's all a jigsaw no, a shambles asking
if I can't reach deeper than dock leaves
and rubble, to pull it up—threshold, joists
and ridgepole. To hear the floorboards
creak with human weight and catch Besom
Horton's sorghum voice and his hazel eyes,
I'll have to conjure that rapt Georgia boy
not quite baptized in the waters of story,
only half a man but already ready to lie.
Magic banjo? Rose honey? I'll have to fly.

Dar He

When I am the lone listener to the antiphony of crickets
and the two wild tribes of cicadas and let my mind
wander to its bogs, its sloughs where no endorphins fire,

I will think on occasion how all memory is longing
for the lost energies of innocence, and then one night—
whiskey and the Pleiades, itch from a wasp sting—

I realize it is nearly half a century since that nightmare
in Money, Mississippi, when Emmett Till was dragged
from his uncle Mose Wright's cabin by two strangers

because he might have wolf-whistled at Carolyn Bryant,
a white woman from whom he had bought candy,
or maybe he just whispered "Bye," as the testimony

was confused and jangled by fear. The boy was not local,
and Chicago had taught him minor mischief, but what
he said hardly matters, as he never got to testify,

for the trial was for murder after his remains were dredged
from the Tallahatchie River, his smashed body with one
eye gouged out and a bullet in the brain and lashed

with barbed wire to a cotton gin fan whose vanes
might have to him seemed petals of some metal flower,
had Bobo—as friends called him—ever seen it. And why

this might matter to me tonight is that I was not yet eight
when the news hit and can remember my parents at dinner—
maybe glazed ham, probably hand-whipped potatoes,

iced tea sweeter than candy, as it was high summer—
shaking their heads in passing and saying it was a shame,
but the boy should have been smarter and known never

to step out of his place, especially that far South. Did I
even guess, did I ask how a word or stray note could give birth
to murder? He was fourteen, and on our flickering new TV,

sober anchormen from Atlanta registered their shock,
while we ate our fine dinner and listened to details
from the trial in Sumner, though later everyone learned

the crime occurred in Sunflower County, and snoopy
reporters from up north had also discovered that missing
witnesses—Too Tight Collins among them—could

finger the husband Roy Bryant and his step-brother
named Milam as the men in the truck who asked, "Where
the boy done the talking?" and dragged Emmett Till

into the darkness. His mother Mamie, without whom
it would have all passed in the usual secrecy, requested
an open-casket funeral, so the mourners saw the body

maimed beyond recognition—his uncle had known
the boy only by a signet ring—and *Jet* magazine
then showed photos, working up the general rage

and indignation, so the trial was speedy, five days
with a white jury, which acquitted, the foreman
reporting that the state had not adequately established

the identity of the victim, and I don't know how
my father the cop or his petite wife the Den Mother
took it all, though in their eighties they have no love

for any race darker than a tanned Caucasian. I need
a revelation to lift me from the misery of remembering,
as I get the stigma of such personal history twisted

into the itch of that wasp sting. Milam later told *Life*
he and Bryant were "guilty as sin," and there is some
relief in knowing their town shunned them and drove

Bryant out of business, but what keeps haunting me—
glass empty, the insect chorus fiercer, more shrill—
is the drama played out in my mind like a scene

from some reverse *To Kill a Mockingbird*—or worse,
a courtroom fiasco from a Faulkner novel—when
the prosecutor asked Mr. Wright if he could find

in the room the intruder who snatched his nephew
out of bed that night, and the old man—a great uncle,
really—fought back his sobs and pointed at the accused,

his finger like a pistol aimed for the heart. "Dar he,"
he said, and the syllables yet echo into this raw night
like a poem that won't be silenced, like the choir

of seventeen-year insects, their voices riddling strange
as sleigh bells through the summer air, the horrors
of injustice still simmering, and I now wonder what

that innocence I miss might have been made of—
smoke? rhinestones? gravied potatoes followed
by yellow cake and milk? Back then we called

the insect infestation *ferros,* thinking of Hebrew
captivity in Egypt and believing they were chanting
free us, instead of the *come hither* new science

insists on, but who can dismiss the thought
that some fifty years back their ancestors dinned
a river of sound all night extending lament

to lamentation, and I am shaken by the thought
of how easy it is for me to sit here under sharp
stars which could mark in heaven the graves

of tortured boys and inhale the dregs of expensive
whiskey the color of a fox, how convenient
to admit where no light shows my safe face

that I have been less than innocent this entire
life and never gave a second thought to this:
even the window fan cooling my bedroom

stirs the air with *blades,* and how could anyone
in a civilized nation ever be condemned for
narrowing breath to melody between the teeth,

and if this is an exercise in sham shame I am
feeling, some wish for absolution, then I have to
understand the wave of nausea crossing me,

this conviction that it is not simple irony
making the whir of voices from the pine trees
now seem to say *Dar he, Dar he, Dar he.*

SHERYL ST. GERMAIN

Addiction

in memory of my brother, Jay St. Germain, 1958–1981

The truth is I loved it,
the whole ritual of it,
the way he would fist up his arm, then
hold it out so trusting and bare,
the vein pushed up all blue and throbbing
and wanting to be pierced,
his opposite hand gripped tight as death
around the upper arm,

the way I would try to enter the vein,
almost parallel to the arm,
push lightly but firmly, not
too deep,
you don't want to go through
the vein, just in,
then pull back until you see
blood, then

hold the needle very still, slowly
shoot him with it.
Like that I would enter him,
slowly, slowly, very still,
don't move,
then he would let the fist out,
loosen his grip on the upper arm—

and oh, the movement of his lips
when he asked that I open my arms.
How careful,
how good he was, sliding
the needle silver and slender

so easily into me, as though
my skin and veins were made for it,
and when he had finished, pulled
it out, I would be coming
in my fingers, hands, my ear lobes
were coming, heart, thighs,
tongue, eyes and brain were coming,
thick and brilliant as the last thin match
against a homeless bitter cold.

I even loved the pin-sized bruises,
I would finger them alone in my room
like marks of passion;
by the time they turned yellow,
my dreams were full of needles.

We both took lovers who loved
this entering and being entered,
but when he brought over the
pale-faced girl so full of needle holes
he had to lay her on her back
like a corpse and stick the needle
over and over in her ankle veins
to find one that wasn't weary
of all that joy, I became sick
with it, but

you know, it still stalks my dreams,
and deaths make no difference:
there is only the body's huge wanting.

When I think of my brother
all spilled out on the floor
I say nothing to anyone.
I know what it's like to want joy
at any cost.

Always Wear Clean Underwear, You Never Know When You Might Get in a Car Accident

She always slightly missed the point, my mother, like a woman
who can't tell the difference between lust and love, marries
the one she lusts after, thinks her love affairs trivial—
I never wore underwear, though she gave it to me year
after year, cotton and silk lace panties blue and pink,
white and clean as death.
I'd throw a pair in the dirty clothes every other day
so she'd think I was wearing them, but I never
wore them, no, I was afraid to get
in a car accident if I did, and besides,
if I did get in a car accident
I would want them to find me dead
as I was alive, the wind rushing up my legs under
my skirt, everything open
and frank as the highway,
not smothered and sad by underwear;
I would want them to find me
bare-assed and bleeding,
spread out on the street.

Wild Ones

Three times I have seen the one I love
cuffed and jailed. Arrested ones are always
loved by someone, the way soil
and weather love weeds, offer home
for roots, space and place to flower . . .

The cop throws the one you love against a wall
or door, jerks his arms back—
arms you've caressed, hands you've kissed—
locks the cuffs in place in seconds.
They must train for this, like roping a calf

to see how fast they can do it. In the dark
you watch the car take him away.

And after they lock him up, your dreams
are full of cuffs—metal cuffs, leather cuffs,
invisible cuffs—cuffs upon cuffs that choke
and bruise and crush. There are heads and
hands and arms, but everything is necklaced
with cuffs. The cuffs are like gods, you
have no power over them. And him:
                                                        he is milkweed
and thistle, coneflower and violet, creeping
charlie, crabgrass, flowering dandelion. Neither
cop's cuffs nor your boundless love can save him.

LEON STOKESBURY

To Laura Phelan: 1886–1906

For James Whitehead

Drunk I have been. And drunk I was that night
I lugged your stone across the other graves,
to set you up a hundred yards away.
Flowers I found then. Drunk I have been.
And am, standing here with no moon to spill
on the letters of your name; my loud fingers
feeling them out. The stone is mossed over.
And why must I bring myself in the dark
to stand here among the sour grasses
that stain my white jeans? Drunk I have been.
See, the thick dew slides on the trees, wet weeds,
wetness smears the air; and a vague surf
of wildflowers pushes my feet, slipping
close to my legs. When the thought comes at last
that people fall apart, that the things we do
will not do. Ends. Then, we come to scenes
like this. This scene of you. You apart:
This is not you; and yet, this is where I stand
and close my eyes, and feel the ragged wind
blow red and maul my hair. In the night somewhere,
dandelions foam. This is not you. Drunk
I have been. Across this graveyard, that
is where you are. Yet I stand here. Would ask
things of your name. Would wish. Would not be told
of the stink in the skull. The eye's collapse.
Would be told something new, something unknown.
A mosquito bites my hand. The only sound
is the rough wind. Drunk I have been,
here, at the loam's maw, before this stone
of yours, which is not you. Which is.

Midway

That last night of the Southeast Texas State Fair,
your father refused to go inside
to see the freaks, but waited
outside the sideshow tent while you
wandered in alone to be amazed
by Abdulla, The Assyrian Swordswallower,
and then by The 900 Pound Man,
and then by Melvin The Mule-Faced Boy.

But when the time came for the grand finale,
the star attraction,
The Three-legged Man With Four Feet,
some guy came over and grabbed
your arm; said
the show was over; dragged you
to the exit and pushed you back outside.

In tears, you told your father, and he,
provoked, aroused, incensed and staunch
defender, took you over to the ticket seller
and demanded they let you back in.

Back on the front row, you beheld
the three-legged man shuffle out on stage
trailing clouds of glory,
sit down and begin to explain
the natural nature of things.
He wore a gray special-made suit
with an extra-wide third pants leg,
and then, when he pulled that pants leg up,
dangling worthlessly out, and seemingly
joined to the base of his spine,
was the thinnest third leg in the world,
him wriggling its toes to reveal
just how real.
Amid much applause
he pulled the pants leg up further, up

over his knee, and then—
the entire tent went still.

Coming out of his knee
where the kneecap should be
hung the fourth foot,
six inches long, worm-like
and white, hairless
and limp, with a hole at its end.

Outside again, the thick sweet reek
of old hamburger grease floated on the air.
And across the midway,
the nonstop barker of the *Totally Nude Review*
had ceased his babble and blab.
There, at the edge of the night,
uncostumed men in denim
disassembled the Tilt-a-Whirl,
while a web of wrist-thick electric cables
crisscrossed the ground everywhere.

How quiet it seemed then.
Even today, you can still remember
how nothing was making a sound.
And when you looked up, you still
can recall, you saw no stars in the sky.

RICHARD TILLINGHAST

Lost Cove & the Rose of San Antone

Evening comes on. I put on a clean white shirt
and feel how well it fits me. I pour bourbon,
with spring water from a plastic jug,
and look out sliding glass doors
at green suburban hills blurred with smog.
Two watches lie on the table before me:
one set for now, one telling time in 1938,
their glass faces reflecting the round California sky.

The man I see through the eye of the second watch
sits in a silence too deep for my nerves
and stares out at twilight
fading on trunks of pine and oak.
The black Model-A car rusts into the stream
that runs past his cabin in Lost Cove, Tennessee.
He reaches for the whiskey on the table,
and his sleeve clears a path through pine-needles and dust.

The coal that tumbles out of his hillside
soils the air and brick houses in Nashville.
Words burn in the rain there
from the power of water that runs past his door.
He looks at his watch and turns on the radio.
The music reaches him, all the way from Nashville.
He holds his glass of whiskey up to the light
that is almost gone. Its color suits his thoughts.

The fiddles and autoharp fill up the dark room
and push out through paint-blackened screens
into black oaks that press against the house.
His face hurts me. It doesn't look right.
He goes against the grain
of whiskey he has made himself, and rides
the wire-song of a steel guitar through small towns,
through the bug-crowded air of farm-crossings late at night.

The disembodied, high guitar line swims in his nerves
like a salmon up a flint-rock stream,
falls like a hawk on blood.
The whiskey burns and soothes.
His tongue starts to move to the words of the song:
trains and big woods and bottomless rivers,
hard drinking, broken hearts, and death.
His blood knows whose song this is.

He's never swum in no bottomless river,
or rode that night train to Memphis,
or sat and stared at those thirteen unlucky bars.
But he sees the moon rise, with the Rose of San Antone
tattooed on it in blood.
A waitress in Denver glides toward him with drinks on a tray.
He stumbles, drunk, through strange woods by an airport
and walks out in San Francisco with a gun in his pocket . . .

The moon sets, over hills cold and unfamiliar.
I shut off the radio, and hear the sea-roar of the freeway.
Who is this man I have dreamed up?
I cork the bottle, and get up and lock the door.

Allen's Station: They

For Beverly Travers

The stars cool their fires in the river of night.
The big people sleep.
I step out barefooted onto the dewy, rough-boarded porch
And open my eyes among farm buildings.
Their yellow pine boards and whitewash
Illuminate my way.

Down the kitchen-garden path, through the orchard,
All the way this side of the leaning barn
Where the horses shuffle and snore,
Past a slumbering bull in a meadow,
Past the for-once quiet chickens

I pad over velvet dust,
Through heady stands of ragweed,
Past the cooks' cabin
Where Kate and Aunt Martha
Have lit the morning lamp already
In their sturdy square cabin
Wallpapered with years of the Sunday comics.

Orphan Annie's eyes
Never narrow or squint
Like Aunt Martha's do
And Dick Tracy is forever in profile
And will never look straight at lame, hobbled Martha
who was born a slave
And because even her church is on the property,
Has never left these acres.

And red-headed, Cherokee Kate
Who never has a civil word for no one
But my Uncle Frank—Why is that, I wonder?—
A different kind of uncle;
A cousin more like, if the tree were drawn.

Dagwood blunders across these walls
And will do so in his Bumstead way
Until the paper peels.

And Blondie with her thirties frizz
Is out shopping again
And will again commit the crime of unthrift;
And Major Hoople in his quilted dressing-gown harrumphs,
Fires up his meerschaum pipe
And sums up his opinion of life at Allen's Station:
"Egad!"

George A. and his wife and her sister and her sister's husband
And their three children, and Napoleon,
And a walleyed Indian-looking woman with a corncob pipe,
And some people I don't recognize
Are going to the fields today to chop cotton.

Their blue overalls bleached to the ghost of white,
Their streaming Mason jars of well water,
Their readiness for whatever reason to work twelve hours

In the West Tennessee sun—
People today don't look like them, or talk like them.

The whites of Napoleon's eyes are purple.
Later in the morning, when he feels a little better,
He'll tell me again about the penitentiary
And show me the healed, pink bullet hole in his arm.
I'm seven, the farmer's little cousin from Memphis.

The lug-wheeled John Deere tractor
Strains with its wagonload of people
And follows the sun up and over the raised L & N tracks
That divide our farm from Beverly's father's.

The land surrounds us with its life:
Not the soil only—the oaks and poplars and sycamores
And cotton plants and birds and beasts,
And all of us a part of it:
The people who work it, the farmer who owns it,
The boy who watches.

At the end of August my uncle
Will flag down the L & N
And I'll ride it to Memphis
Through the whitewashed towns and sparse farms
And be met in a car
At the big station built with cotton dollars,
And go back to school
And grow up and move away.

They stay in the fields.
I watch them chop cotton,
Drinking water from their jar—
And them not seeming to mind—

As the dense green cotton leaves burn
And the purple boll explodes into ripeness
And the sun describes its slow arc.
They chop cotton, and stay right where they are.

DENO TRAKAS

End of August, 2005

For MD

Under a smudged and sticky sun
they lounge in chaise,
in bathing suits and shades
with rum and Cokes in plastic cups
on the deck of their new old house.

They're young, poor, and happy,
their dreams as loud and brassy
as trumpets playing the French Quarter
where they love to go, a bus ride
from their blighted hood.

Their dreams rise like nickel moons
above their cluttered view,
above the sunken city, the shrinking wetlands,
the oily Gulf where a spindly hurricane
brushes Miami and turns north.

Their dreams are as big and easy
as their house is cramped and messy,
but at least it has a roof that doesn't leak,
a roof so tight that when the water rises
and they climb into the trusses

of their axeless attic, among the floating
boxes of Christmas decorations,
their noses touching the ridge beam,
they gasp and struggle unable to fathom
that it, they, could end this way.

Walking to Work on a Snowy Morning

I don't have time for winter,
for unpaid leisure, for six inches
of snow with a boss that won't close
the plant where I work on the clock.

This morning roadcrews added a drift
of sand and salt to mix a rough slush,
but still, there's nothing worse than a hard
winter for an old guy with bald tires.

So I walk to work, an angry stubborn
bundle with a thermos of coffee and bourbon,
stomp the pristine unplowed backroads,
don't give a shit for beauty, it's not the time.

I slip on black ice and fall,
bang my hip on the curb and cuss,
then see how stupid I look, scowling,
butt-stuck in snow. I lie back,

wind ticks in the branches, woodsmoke
drifts from chimneys, snow falls,
the world slows until it's still
as forgotten dreams.

I sit up, take a long drink, take my time,
see the mark I've made, no snow angel,
no nothing, just a rut of a fallen man,
say fuck it and head for home.

Disclosure

When Bellocq doesn't like a photograph
he scratches across the plate. But I know
other ways to obscure a face—paint it
with rouge and powder, shades lighter than skin,
don a black velvet mask. I've learned to keep
my face behind the camera, my lens aimed
at a dream of my own making. What power
I find in this transforming what is real—a room flushed
with light, calculated disarray.
Today I tried to capture a redbird
perched on the tall hedge. As my shutter fell,
he lifted in light, a vivid blur above
the clutter just beyond the hedge—garbage,
rats licking the insides of broken eggs.

From "Native Guard"

1865

These are things which must be accounted for:
slaughter under the white flag of surrender—
black massacre at Fort Pillow; our new name,
the Corps d'Afrique—words that take the *native*
from our claim; mossbacks and freedmen—exiles
in their own homeland; the diseased, the maimed,
every lost limb, and what remains: phantom
ache, memory haunting an empty sleeve;
the hog-eaten at Gettysburg, unmarked
in their graves; all the dead letters, unanswered;
untold stories of those that time will render
mute. Beneath battlefields, green again,
the molder—a scaffolding of bone
we tread upon, forgetting. Truth be told.

Dr. Samuel Adolphus Cartwright on Dissecting the White Negro, 1851

To strip from the flesh
the specious skin; to weigh
in the brainpan
seeds of white
pepper; to find in the body
its own diminishment—
blood-deep
and definite; to measure the heft
of lack; to make of the work of faith
the work of science, evidence
the word of God: Canaan
be the *servant of servants;* thus
to know the truth
of this: (this derelict
corpus, a dark compendium, this
atavistic assemblage—flatter
feet, bowed legs, a shorter neck) so
deep the tincture
—see it!—
we still know white from not.

Onlookers Gathered at the Traveling Chair's Arrival

Mississippi, 1940

So many of them
faceless beneath the brims
of their hats: so many

men and women, and always
it seems, children too,
drawn to the spectacle—

some finding the camera,
lifting their faces to history.
Here: two men stunned

  into record, a boy squinting,
one man smiling as if
to leave his mark on the day.

From the bird's-eye view
  you can see the delicate part
  in a girl's hair, the dapple

of shadow on concrete—
leaves of the tree from which
  the photographer must be

shooting. I can't stop finding
  the small wounds limned
  into focus: a tiny dog

in a boy's arms, one leg
dangled—a hook angling
  toward the machine;

  another boy cradling
 a stack of books, his head
cropped by the frame;

a woman resting her hand
on the chair's arm; and how
even the sun, bright

as the flash that whitens
their faces, polishes
  the darker ones like stone.

ADAM VINES

Prologue and Return

The spotlight from a barge
searching for the bend
fidgets along the riverbank.
A heron's tar-gargling cry
recedes into fog
while an armadillo wobbles
through the thicket
like a lost child.
A snapping turtle snatches
the leg of a mallard—wings slap
the water like oars, trying to pull
free from the unseen snag.
In the pit lined with creek stones,
flames gnaw on split hickory,
hawk out sparks like seeds.
Downhill lie the spine and ribs
of my great-grandfather's ferryboat
I once pretended was the carcass
of an alligator gar,
the swivel chair with straps
that harnessed him
while he rowed—his legs
crushed in a dogtrot mine
when he was a boy. His claim:
we were spawned in the sloughs,
in log jams and stump rows,
under hyacinth and cattail,
and that's where we all return,
to be swallowed slowly
with each year's leaf fall and rot.

Mine Rats

They're always behind you
just beyond the light—
hugging the coal rib and cribbing

timbers, squeezing in
and out of cracks, searching
for what's been lost or discarded:

trolley wire, safety tags,
fuses, canary feathers.
Once, in a dynamite box,

a miner found a nest
made of chewed scripture
and company scrip.

A quick turn or yawn
and you might catch one
in your headlamp's glare

on the shaft collar
or tucked in a kerf
sitting back on its haunches,

eyes burning coal,
spit-shining its face
with licked palms.

One old-timer still pitches
pie crust to shadows.
He says the rats

can feel Mary Lee #1
shudder, hear roof chocks
buckling under her weight,

and when it happens
he will follow
dragging tails

and grinding teeth
out of the shadows
down the chosen path.

The Old Salt's Brag

For Frank

> Unequaled as a partner in battle, her reliability borders on relentless. To say she is tough is to speak an understatement of immeasurable proportions. There is nothing casual in her lines or timid in her performance.
>
> *Contender Boats advertisement*

All I need is a rusty hook dangling from my ear.
I'll swim in the buck out to the Dry Tortugas,
braiding a leader out of chest hair.

I'll whittle my pinky finger to the bone
with a seagull beak and hone it with my heel.
I'll slit my belly with it and unravel a length of gut.

I don't need your lily-white war mistress
with waxed galley and perfumed head,
your Boss Magnum TwinDrag reels

with Joint Strike Fighter aluminum
and aerospace-grade stainless-steel bearings,
your Power Butt rods, touch-screen GPS,

and your polypropylene skivvies.
I'd rather pluck out my good eye,
snap a thumb clean, and butterfly the flesh for bait.

I'll make a rattling teaser out of fingernails.
When I lure that blackfin up,
I'll pull her in hand over hand

and hold her lines up to your world.
I'll tuck her in the corner of my maw
and sink to the bottom where we belong.

ELLEN BRYANT VOIGT

Bright Leaf

Like words put to a song, the bunched tobacco leaves
are strung along a stick, the women
standing in the August heat for hours—since first light—
under the pitched tin roof, barefoot, and at their feet
the babies, bare-assed, dirty, eating dirt.
The older children hand the leaves from the slide,
three leaves at a time, stalks upright, three handers
for each stringer, and three more heaped canvas slides
waiting in what little shade there is: it's ten o'clock,
almost dinnertime. They pull the pails of cold lunch
and Mason jars of tea out of the spring
when they see the farmer coming from the field, their men
stripped to the waist, polished by sweat and tired as mules.
By afternoon, the loose cotton dresses, even
the headrags are dark with sweat.
Still their fingers never miss a stitch,
though they're paid not by the stick but by the day,
and the talk—unbroken news of cousins and acquaintances—
unwinding with the ball of twine, a frayed snuff-twig
bouncing on one lip, the string paying out
through their calluses, the piles of wide green leaves
diminishing, until the men appear with the last slide
and clamber up the rafters of the barn
to line the loaded sticks along the tiers. It's Friday:
the farmer pays with a wad of ones and fives,
having turned the mule out to its feed and water,
hung up the stiffened traces and the bit. He checks
again the other barns, already fired, crude ovens
of log and mud where the crop is cured;
in that hot dry acrid air, spreads a yellowing leaf
across his palm, rolls an edge in his fingers,
gauging by its texture and its smell
how high to drive the fire.
His crew is quiet in the pickup truck—do you think

they were singing? They are much too tired to even speak,
can barely lick salt from the back of a hand, brush at flies,
hush a baby with a sugartit. And the man
who owns this land is also tired.
Everyday this week he's meant to bring home pears
from the old tree by the barn, but now he sees
the fruit has fallen, sees the yellow jackets feeding there.
He lights a Lucky, frames a joke for his wife—he'll say
their banker raised a piss-poor field this year.
And she will lean against the doorjamb
while he talks, while he scrubs his hands at the tin basin
with a split lemon and a pumice stone, rubs them raw
trying to cut the gummy resin, that stubborn
black stain within the green.

The Trust

Something was killing sheep
but it was sheep his dog attended on the farm—
a black-and-white border collie, patrolling his fold
like a parish priest. The second time the neighbor came,
claiming to have spotted the dog at night, a crouched figure
slithering toward the pen on the far side of the county,
the farmer let him witness how the dog,
alert and steady, mended the frayed
edge of the flock, the clumped sheep calm
as they drifted together along the stony hill.
But still more sheep across the glen were slaughtered,
and the man returned more confident. This time,
the master called his dog forward,
and stroking the eager head, prized open the mouth to find,
wound around the base of the back teeth—squat molars
the paws can't reach to clean—small coils of wool,
fine and stiff, like threads from his own jacket.
So he took down the rifle from the rack
and shot the dog and buried him,
his best companion in the field for seven years.
Once satisfied, the appetite is never dulled again.
Night after night, its sweet insistent promise

drives the animal under the rail fence and miles away
for a fresh kill; and with guilty cunning brings him back
to his familiar charges, just now stirring in the early light,
brings him home to his proud husbandry.

Cow

end of the day daylight subsiding into the trees lights coming on
in the milking barns as somewhere out in the yard some ants
are tucking in their aphids for the night behind
hydrangea leaves or in their stanchions underground
they have been bred for it the smaller brain

serving the larger brain the cows eat so we will eat we guarantee
digestion is the only work they do heads down tails up
they won't have sex they get some grain some salt
no catamounts no wolves we fertilize the fields
we put up bales of hay we give them names

but again this week one breached the fence the neighbors
stopped to shoo it back a girl held out a handful of grass
calling the cow as you would a dog no dice so what
if she recoiled to see me burst from the house with an axe
I held it by the blade I tapped with the handle where the steaks come from

like the one I serve my friend a water sign who likes to lurk
in the plural solitude of Zen retreat to calm his mind but when it's done
what he needs I think is something truly free of mind a slab of earth
by way of cow by way of fire the surface charred the juices
running pink and red on the white plate

Owl

the sign for making the most of what you have
on the human hand is a thumb at full right angle to the palm
for the owl it's two talons forward two back a flexible foot
that crushes the prey and lifts it to the beak to the eyes
which are legally blind this is why the owl

hunts in the dark in the dusk when nothing is clearly seen
and why the owl's eyes are fixed facing ahead to better focus
so its whole face swivels in each direction like the turret on a tank
the round plates of feathers surrounding the eyes collect the least sound
when it turns the owl is computing by geometry

the exact location of the mouse or snake or songbird
that moves imperceptibly in its nest toward which the owl
sets out from the hole in the tree the burrow the eave of the barn
and crosses the field in utter silence wing-feathers overlapped
to make no sound poor mouse poor rabbit
last night
from the porch obbligato to the brook and the snuffling deer
intent on the gnarled worm-bitten apples we leave on the tree
I heard what must have been a Barred Owl or a Barn Owl
or a Lesser Horned Owl close by not deep in the woods
what I heard was less a call than a cry

a fragment repeating repeating a kind of shudder
which may be why the country people I come from
thought an owl was prescient ill-omen meant to unspool
the threads they'd gathered and wound I was a grown woman
when my father took the key from under the eave

and unlocked the door to the darkened house he had grown up in
and stepped across the threshold and said as he entered the empty room
hello Miss Sally as though his stepmother dead for weeks
were still in her usual chair
in the Medicine Wheel
the emblem for wisdom is the same for gratitude at dusk at dark
the farsighted owl strikes in utter silence when we hear it
from the tree or the barn what it announces
is already finished

G. C. WALDREP

Elberta

You should be so lucky as to make that journey.
Orchards planted when I was a child
are already abandoned else uprooted, too old
to bear the market's weight. Outside Inman,
east of Greer packing sheds lean into the future
the same way trees do, gnarled, low to the ground
as if gravity were a defense for children,
a child's game really, requisite
sing-song adumbration. Stein was right, heaven
is the place where we finally have the leisure
to speak the truth to objects
in proper sequence, functions of the body
or of the mind irredentive to that order.
The signs read PEACHES. The signs read
FIREWORKS, CIGARETTES, LAST CHANCE!
either side of the four-lane piled high
with pruned branches, whole trees bare now
in the March sun, good for nothing but burning.
Heading north the exits tick backward
from the singularity of the border, a wide space,
another sign. Faint blur of blue smoke:
it's the sweetness we can't do without,
that sets us planting again, seedlings wrapped
in white tape against late frost. Come June
we'll buy a bushel from some roadside stand
off Route 11 where we used to drive when we wanted
to feel the world suspended for our benefit.
The past answers itself in its own range—
dogs hear it, same as they do those tin whistles.
They understand love, tails wagging at our feet
while we let the juice run down
our chins in some sandy lot. Never minding
that it stains. Never minding that the dogs

aren't ours, just some farmer's curs kept around
to keep the coons at bay. We'll drive on,
night will fall and those dogs will howl at the moon
as if it had a number. They're lonely for us
though all we are by now to them is a smell.
Around us branches whisper in the June dark.
We're the fire they didn't see coming.
Relent: from the Latin, *re* plus *lentare,*
to bend again. Now turn left. Here, trust me.
Your touch will let us know where we are.

Vertigo

Shaft-mouth one is aware of that drawing, gut-clench in which presence
 at the lip implies presence at a greater depth, therefore velocity

With its spectral shift, lush green of periwinkle and honeysuckle
 running down to black against red clay, infinitesimal Doppler
 modulation of the bees that descend

In search of one more sucrose extrusion. We see: iron bedstead, ragged
 upholstery of a couch snagged where the first lateral tunnel

Recapitulated this dispensation in terms of earth and ore. Appliance
 skeletons. Not a stable place, one picks one's way

Through briars and scrub elm with care as if a heavy tread could
 dislodge some internal synchronicity, the way it did once at New
 Straitsville, the miners free in that moment

To see their earth on fire; or at Centralia, the surface withdrawing like
 the shoreline of a dead sea, pulling

More tightly in upon itself in smoking temblors. Here the prize was
 copper which melts but does not burn, and for a few years only—

No town, company shacks long ago collapsed into punk-board or else
 carted off for timber. Sun-dapple, drone of the bees as they rise
 and fall

And rise again, programmed toward hidden hives. What we would call
 a quiet place. Sweat-itch at collar and sole:

No one goes there, said the woman at the end of the road, *except they have something they want to get rid of.* Not affective in the same sense; a scandent

Twilight. Lifting sweetness this time from a single string. And the forms more various. Licit we should come so far.

Sustainable Agriculture

Thaw-days, earth-smell, at hand the question
of setting out a garden this year, no mere protocol,
rather an investment in the future of this habitation
whether I stay or no. The soil, cleared in this patch
less than a decade, is still the raw red
that sends pines to the mills, scant corn
to the silo or the table. A winter's worth of manure
waits outside the barn's south door, already
a few blades finding the light, experimenting with it
in the new factories of each cell, drawing life
from that rich accumulation. But I am tired
and the wind is wrong, and though it brings a green scent
my heart is stubborn, it will not let itself
be drawn again into the rhythm of the season.
A light rain falls. I had the best intentions.
Without me, nightshade and thistle and the ghost vines
of the melons whose seeds and sweet rinds
we tossed against the hardpan last August, innocent
of endeavor and therefore plunder as well.

FRANK X WALKER

Spell to Give the Woman a Head

Rewind to a civil war bruised Kentucky, circa 1979
when a middle aged white woman dropped her trench coat
and walked barefoot and naked to the center of the room.
Separate your shame from your fear, your art from your life.

Turn down the volume on your mother's voice
recanting the stories of Emmett Till and strange fruits.
Give yourself permission to ignore American history,
unspoken Dixie rules and social norms.

Pick up your sketching tools, relax, examine the model
address your easel, take another look, only this time
stare . . . stare at her long enough to actually see her face.
See it attached to a head and that head attached to a body.

See her on the page, whole, then ask yourself which is darker:
decapitation, eyeball rape and mob rule, or the charcoal in your hands.

How to Swallow an Elephant

Place an old photo of your father
face up in a saucer of milk.

Make a list
of all the mistakes you own.

Tattoo it in red ink
across both wrists.

Count the times you screamed
yourself awake behind the wheel

or left an emergency room
with only stitches.

Your father's absence
fuels your passion to be present.

Put it at the beginning of a list
of gifts from him.

Take your own children home
to the projects.

Let them play in the dirt
where your anger was born.

Make the longer journey
to his perfect front lawn.

Introduce him as their grandfather.
Stay long enough for one of you to touch.

Cure to Eliminate the N-Word

Gather all wanna be gangster rappers
in groups of seven. Confiscate their designer clothes
and shoes. Dress them in confederate uniforms.

Remove every song they've ever heard
from their tongues with a knife.
Let the first new sound they hear rise up
from the belly of a slave ship.

Replace the jewelry around their necks and wrists
with chains of strong hemp tied in suffocating knots.
Fill their jean pockets with rice, cotton and tobacco.
Give them a reason to sag.

While Dixie is playing in the background
rub burnt cork on their faces, paint their lips bright red.
Stand them like lawn jockeys beside Gus
from *Birth of a Nation,* Amos & Andy and Step 'N Fetchit.

Order them to dance. Order them to stop.
Order them to bend over.

Let the next new sound they hear be a chain gang work song
followed by a tribe of hammers striking railroad spikes.
Let the vibrations mend their backbones and raise them
to their full height again.

Invite them to wade in the water. Baptize them in the name
of Claude McKay, Margaret Walker, Nina Simone,
Curtis Mayfield, Mavis Staples, Gil Scott-Heron,
Gordon Parks, Sonia Sanchez and the Last Poets.

Teach them to read. Teach them to write
music. Teach them a second language.

Dare them to play something other than the radio.
Let them feel the difference between gospel and the blues.
Help them taste the many moods of Miles. Tattoo Adinkra symbols
and Egyptian hieroglyphics in even rows on the bottom of their feet.

Lead them to separate water fountains.
Pray they drink from the one marked Kings & Queens.
Take a deep breath. Let the last sound they hear be, Amen.

ROBERT WEST

Mountaintop Removal

The coal king thinks we owe him thanks
for jobs and fuel we think we need;
he calls us hypocrites and cranks
too quick to gripe about his greed.

He blights the old familiar heights
and taints our water and our air.
But we stay warm most winter nights.
The cost of comfort is despair.

Cornfield

A crow's dark
remark
shadows these
skeletons.

JAMES WHITEHEAD

A Local Man Remembers Betty Fuller

Betty Fuller cried and said, Hit me.
I did. Which made her good and passionate
But Betty Fuller never came. Fate
Decreed that Betty Fuller would not see
The generosity a lively house
And loyal husband bring. She lost her mind
In Mendenhall. She got herself defined
As absolutely mad. A single mouse
Caused her to run exactly down the line
Of a wide road, running both north and south
With execrations pouring from her mouth.

She's out at Whitfield doing crazy time
And she can't possibly remember me
Among the rest. I'm satisfied she can't.

The Alabama Man Remembers All He Can about the Battered Children and the Woman with Almost Perfect Skin in Mobile Seven Years Ago

Mostly the fat one remains inside my head
Because he was most bloody of them all
And was afflicted in his mind.
                                        My dread
Of what his people mean is terrible.

A damaged sister beat upon the door
I was involved behind.
                                Forgive me, Lord,
Those children crying got me off the floor
Whereon sweet love had almost shot us dead.

Continuing—I'm there for normal sin
With a woman with almost perfect skin.
She said, "We'll drive them to Emergency,"
Who were no kin to her or kin to me.

Above the pines the simple moon was bright.
After they were stitched, we said goodnight.

AMY WRIGHT

In That Place

To paint one rose equals a life in that place.
Fanny Howe, "Goodbye Post Office Square"

I

Backhoe operator shaves
a beard of snow with a bucket razor.
The one of several
state employees who leaves
the cleanest neckline, trims
hoary hairs in a cleft chin,
misses nothing—no grizzled dimple,
no icy washboard. A tender develops
tenderness for the land, his jackdaw body
singing in the cab.
When a plot comes up for sale,
he purchases it, pulls an articulated arm
through the dirt, breaking ground. Looks inside
her hills.

II

The Cambrian Earth
populated the ocean
with a sophisticated visual system
of some fifteen thousand lenses
in a single eye. Trilobites saw depth of field
through stone, calcite inner cells of their scopes
visible in a CT scan—magnified—a diamond-
shaped photoreceptor surrounded by petals,
a fossilized flower before the terrestrial world
had flowers. For over 270 million years
they proliferated, evolving eye stalks
to see above mud, shades for light-dappled
trawlers. A long love

doing with the sea what sex does,
antennae diddling the floor.

III

A radiologist scrutinizes the internal
borders on silver-impregnated films,
is paid handsomely for differentiating
pre-invasive lesions from ground-glass
nodules, lives on the same dirt
road as the backhoe operator,
throws up a hand when they pass door
to handled door, eyes in the same meeting place
on their faces.

IV

Horsetail lines the neighborhood
stream, living fossil, the only remaining member
of the genus *Equisetum.* Silicates on bristles,
scouring-rush for tin cups, the understory of Paleozoic
forests. Their moisture-sensitive springs
disperse spores instead of seed
when the sack splits like a hose full of silt
half-buried in the garden
duct tape raveling around its toffee
mouth.

V

Blighted chestnuts come back
on suburban lawns.
Sheep's legs taper
pencil point wicks
in the cool tallow of alfalfa,
blood moon nails
over an oil pan.

CHARLES WRIGHT

Driving through Tennessee

It's strange what the past brings back.
Our parents, for instance, how ardently they still loom
In the brief and flushed
Fleshtones of memory, one foot in front of the next
Even in retrospect, and so unimpeachable.

And towns that we lived in once,
And who we were then, the roads we went back and forth on
Returning ahead of us like rime
In the moonlight's fall, and Jesus returning, and Stephen Martyr
And St. Paul of the Sword . . .

—I am their music,
Mothers and fathers and places we hurried through in the night:
I put my mouth to the dust and sing their song.
Remember us, Galeoto, and whistle our tune, when the time comes,
For charity's sake.

Lost Bodies

Last night I thought of Torri del Benaco again,
Its almond trees in blossom,
                                        its cypresses clothed in their dark fire,

And the words carved on that concrete cross

I passed each day of my life
In Kingsport going to town
                    GET RIGHT WITH GOD / JESUS IS COMING SOON.

If I had it all to do over again
                                        I'd be a medievalist.
I'd thoroughly purge my own floor.

Something's for sure in the clouds, but it's not for me,

Though all the while that light tips the fast-moving water,
East wind in a rush through the almond trees.

✦

The cross was opposite Fleenor's Cabins below the hill
On U.S. 11W.
Harold Shipley told me, when I was twelve,
he'd seen a woman undressed

In the back seat of a Buick, between two men,
her cunt shaven clean,
In front of the motel office.
They gave him a dollar, he said, to stick his finger up there.
What can you say to that?
everything Jesus promised

(My five senses waiting apart in their grey hoods,
Touching their beads,
licking the ashes that stained their lips)

And someone to tell it to.

✦

Torri del Benaco, on the east side of Lake Garda,
Was north past Peschiera and San Vigilio,
under the Bardalino hills.
I seldom went there, and remember it poorly.
One Sunday, I drove through town on my way to Riva at the top of the lake.

An east wind was blowing out across the water,

Down through the vineyards, and down through the trees at the lake's edge.

I remember the cypress nods in its warm breath.
I remember the almond blossoms
floating out on the waves, west to Salò.
I remember the way they looked there,
a small flotilla of matches.

I remember their flash in the sun's flare.

✦

You've got to sign your name to something, it seems to me.
And so we rephrase the questions
Endlessly,
hoping the answer might somehow change.

Still, a piece of his heart is not a piece of your heart,
Sweet Jesus, and never will be, but stays
A little window into the past,
                                        increasingly licked transparent
And out of shape.

When you die, you fall down,
                                        you don't rise up
Like a scrap of burnt paper into the everlasting.
Each morning we learn this painfully,
                    pulling our bodies up by the roots from their deep sleep.

✦

Nobody takes that road now.
                                        The tourist cabins are gone,
And Harold, and Rose Dials
Who lived in a tarpaper shack just off the highway,
Nailed hard to the mountainside.
                                              And the two men and the Buick too,
Long gone down the Interstate
And the satellites that have taken us all from town.

Only the cross is still there, sunk deeper into the red clay
Than anyone could have set it.

And the luminous, nameless body whose flesh takes on
The mottoes we say we live by . . .

✦

Of all the places around the lake,
                                              I've loved Sirmione best,
Its brilliant winks in the sun
And glassy exceptions like a trace in the mind.

Others stay in the memory like pieces of songs
You think you remember but don't,
                                                only a phrase here and there
Surfacing as it should, and in tune.

Gardone and Desenzano are like that, and Torri del Benaco.

Mostly what I remember is one garden, outside the town of Garda,
Between the lake's edge and the road:
Corn and beans, it looked like, and squash and finocchio.

✦

All things that come to him come under his feet
In a glorious body,
                                        they say. And why not?
It beats the alternative, the mighty working
Set to subdue the celestial flesh.

And does so, letting the grass go stiff, and the needles brown,

Letting the dirt take over. This is as far as it goes,
Where deer browse the understory and jays
                                                                                                    leap through the trees,

Where chainsaws
Whittle away at the darkness, and diesel rigs
Carry our deaths all night through the endless rain.

WILLIAM WRIGHT

Trumpet Creeper

1

June light comes again
and again without remorse:
Pollen rummages the scalps
of spent deciduous hour after hour
until two sycamores puffed open by the wind bend
over the creek in twin green flames. Lacertilian armies
raze the garden and the yard's fringes,
flares for ruby-throats, bees.

Around the bowed trunks the loam shoots forth
lush feelers, sprung broad then clustered,
pink star-trails drooped at the stalk
and bursting
now to hum a song I almost hear.

✦

Coiled red mouths, they bloom beyond the shed
into unhinged greenness,
brighten, pump, swell through everything,
fall flaccid,
foiling their own morphology.

All spines suffer their histories, blossom-lattices
formed from water
in microfossil plumes,
when great black smokers
billowed up, kelp-like shifts,
fields of ducts, white worms, smokestacks—
a trillion trillion cellular divinities.

Preglacial, they shift into woods and out again,
coil and articulate
deciduous nooks, flaunt the seasonal genesis:
vast gasps of light and air,
power of galaxies held forever in the lungs.

✦

After June rain, I turn my back to the animals, the hush-hush
metaphors, abandon a green too brilliant
and face the black interstices of the tree-wall.

I feel the imminent collapse, the mass,
vibrissa crowding the ribcage,
my skeleton transformed under
the leaf-kiss, deep earth
watered down,
gourd unwrapped like a gift.

✦

Heaven is neither lamb nor lion: Heaven
is symmetry's absence,
a trumpet creeper's seedpod
drained down the dead man's throat.

Strands and stalks expand
beyond order, uncontainable,
pierce thistle and stone:

Whittled to hair and bone,
the beast rolls its leaf-lobed head,
howls new identities.

2

Summer sky an old onion.
Over the fence flares of pink trumpets.
Bees wheel about their coral bells, fly off.

✦

I am meat, salt, water.
In my skull hums
a three pound sentient chunk.
When I kiss my mother's hair,
a sleeping giant's heart blooms, collapses.

He shifts in his sleep and smiles,
mica flashing.

One day he'll look me in the eye.

✦

A fleet of cumuli leans away.
Freighted with rain, bees drop
to the freshened grass,
red clover.

3

My great uncle Basil died when he was five years old
on a farmhouse floor in Iredell County, North Carolina,
half his face boiled from his skull.

Quilts and winter storms
broke my great-grandmother
to bone and a scorched gown,
pre-dawn dimness on a copper cauldron
that held the lye he tipped and spilled,
his little fingers charred,
hard as rust.

✦

Sleeves of corn stalks flapped and clattered,
ash in the chimney flue, plum jelly's bright jar.

My grandfather turned in
his mother's darkness, eyes fusing.

✦

As the calyx
unsheathes a petal,

as the hand holds
the scalded hand,

furled leaf,
heat to breathe and bear.

As water scars deep grain,
cottonmouths uncurl

over roots that twine kin
to smilax and larkspur:

the stream's clear coil.

Rabid Cat

Rags of cheek sagged from the jawbone's white.
The sick mouth snarled, pocked throat
frothing half-rattle, half-growl.
When it dragged death's pong along the yard,
my father rigged a trap of chicken, wire,
and a stone meant to break its scabrous back,
which worked: Since madness shook the squirrel heart
in its gut, the crazed mouth brave
enough to clink the latch trigger.
As if the bludgeon wasn't plenty,
my father aimed the gun and sprayed
the cat red onto the porch-wall.

Into morning, with gloves, bleach, and scalding soap-water,
we crouched into that pale gore, our sinuses torched
raw, hair steam-wilted, scooping jelly viscera into bags.
Pre-dawn lit the bed I'd lie sleepless in, that demon
eyeing my dream's door, as my father, dog-tired,
hefted the skull bits to the trees.

Triptych for the Days before Her Passage

1

We walked into the valley of dark, our sight

                    pinned to the ember of the single star the falcate moon
could not douse. That was the dusk we learned the blue bowl of air

          had tipped and littered the valley with grass, delicate as hair
and changeable as water for the shuttered eye (changeable as stone,

rhythmic as blood-crux in the salamander or goat,
rhythmic as the green-core of moss or elm).

✦

For years my mother smelled of sour bread.
I'd carry her down the mountain in the blue dark

on my back near the swale where we'd build a fire
in the summer cold.

The bones behind her face had sunken, and I saw her pulse
tick shallow in the shadow of her throat.

Her voice was no more
than leaf-crackle,
no more than kindling.

2

What she remembers:

That in the summer of her seventh year,
storms slanted in and engorged the rivers
and creeks until all waters buckled high,

shattered the levies and bit to the quicks of berms:
Houses that did not kneel and drift away moldered.
They moved the whole town eight miles north—

That in her ninth year she came back to the creek
then in drought and walked barefoot
the dry bed's limb-trash and alabaster—

✦

That something in the slim sun-spears made
her look up into the unshackling of April
and witness a horse skeleton, brown-white

as the soles of her feet and silty hands.
She looked long at how vines twined its brisket,
at the strange philodendron head, drained

of flesh, brainless and almost comical in
its stillness, staid and smiling long with gothic
joy at the sheer oddness of how the Earth had reined it.

✦

That the winter of her thirteenth year
in the frigid mineral-scent of dusk, the Harman
boy breathed warmth on the small hairs of her neck,

the whiskey on his child's breath, how they leaned
into one another in the blindness and purity
of the killed grass beside the creek, the water frozen

pure to the floor, where stunned curves
of minnows flashed tinny and motionless
under the stars' arc-light.

That the thaw snapped and pocked the air like gunshots
so that in the first hint of spring the Harman brother
slew the boy she kissed and dragged his kin down into the gorge.

3

What she cannot foresee:

That centuries the warped door of the moon will open,
house roofs will crumble as the horse bones gripped
in the long-fallen oak will fall themselves, then grind

down with years, fold as dust and meld with the specks
kept there of the murdered boy, millennia-old, both
now in the earth proper, slack and laggard slow.

JAKE ADAM YORK

Collect

> . . . in a way, all of us are responsible for Bo's death, because we've let people like those killers have their way, and decent people have just sat by.
>
> *Mamie Till, "Mamie [Till] Bradley's Untold Story," 1956*

Morning wraps the stars and the dark
that will come again

and so is a promise,
an envelope

in which some dark may be folded
like a list of names,

so first light on the Tallahatchie
is a prayer that light

may be shoaled
by some arm or shoulder

as a pane of light will smoke
until the swollen face emerges

and morning on a magazine's spread
burns into the retinas

the letters of a prayer for the river
and the pine box and the boxcar

on which some light no one will ever remember
has already laid its blessing

and a prayer for Mamie Till
for looking when they told her not to,

for leaving the casket open
so everyone could see

what hatred can do to a body,
what color can do,

so Chicago's breath could settle
through the glass and the suit and into the wounds

to be taken back into the lungs,
a gauze to blot astonishment,

so Mississippi's breath, stolen north,
could swathe him too

then gather like river in our lungs
and keep some part of breath

from entering there again
and so become a prayer

for the breath we did not take
for the words we did not say,

the missing part of breath that makes a silence
in which a body can break the water's calm,

in which everything can be heard,
light peeling from the wounds of the stars

and distant birds that sing like glass,
a clot in the tissue of the sky.

Self-Portrait in a Plate-Glass Window

Selma

Steam rises from my plate,
        chicken and greens and black-eyed peas,

and in the window where I can look
        beneath the honeydew rind or sliver moon of scalp

through my own reflected eyes
        to the sidewalk and the lot beyond

then back to the dim interior where the owner
        turns from his TV mystery back to me.

It's the right address
        though the name has changed,

and he must be asking, as I am,
    am I where I'm supposed to be?

A few doors up—I can almost see it—
    a plaque remembers

James Reeb, the reverend, who'd come to march
    and last ate in this café.

It was Walker's, then.
    Klansmen watched across the street,

waiting for the collar, for the face to emerge—
    three of them, maybe four,

with pipes and bats in the door of the grocery
    someone demolished years ago.

Eyes down, I'm working to the blank plate
    and the questions that have to follow—

Where you from? What you after?—
    even if no one says a thing.

The quiet holds them the way
    dark will hold all color

and one memory will look like another
    and staying will seem stranger than having come.

We'll rise, then, the glass between us,
    one in the dusk, one inside,

close enough to feel the café's warmth
    radiating into the town

and the cool March evening
    reaching into the room.

We'll walk toward the door
    and become one

and slide off the glass,
    leaving on the window

with its inscription
    of moonlight and clouds

tomorrow will rub
    almost entirely away.

Letter Written on a Hundred Dollar Bill

To Howlin' Wolf, from Mississippi

Did your right hand itch when I transcribed your *O*
don't you hear me cryin? phrase I'd pay a hundred dollars
to raise my voice into, cause you got money for sure,
not like Son House in the nightclub film, drunk
as a goat glutted with rotten apples and waving a sawbuck
like a flag, but stacking up in a New York office
like a locomotive's chimney if I keep this going
and then I imagine raining down into the world below
or uncurling on a magnolia only you know
how to find, my hundred plucked, still crisp,
then rolled up in your pocket as you walk again
from White Station and West Point to Grenada,
Ruleville, Rosedale with a guitar on your back,
where you meet Charley Patton again.
You pull out the bankroll and count off a Cadillac
so y'all can cruise to Memphis, St. Louis, Chicago,
unpack at the 708 or Silvio's and maybe House
is already there at the bar, rediscovered
and thirsty for oblivion, when Sumlin walks in
with Dixon and you're ready to pitch it again,
and the microphones are humming so you can invent
rock-and-roll or whatever it is Eric Clapton
tries to play in that London session when you take over,
showing him that music is a kind of language,
you just say this, you just call roosters and cats
and airplane pilots into the club, the whole
Wang Dang Doodle of the afterlife catching your notes
like undampered pianos and sounding long after
you've gone down the blue highways back to Jackson,
Nashville, Lebanon where your girl stands in the door
of the house you kept together as peaceful and bright
as the day you met, you're gathering everyone you know
and rolling down to Natchez where the fire
hasn't ashed the Rhythm Club and the whole town's

waiting for you to take the stage, maybe costumed
like an engineer or busking like a janitor,
the mic taped to a broom handle, the sheet-metal walls
shaking when you let out your *O,*
O there is no sound like this in the world above
except the one you engraved in the great disc of the night
that spins above us, through the hole of which
every C-note floats to bud from that one magnolia
somewhere in east Mississippi where this sound was born.
When you walk down the dirt roads each night,
when you pull your hands from your pockets, the lint
turns everything first-Spring green,
and when you open your song you light the underworld
with a throat and a mouth full of gold.

Inscription for Air

John Earl Reese, shot while dancing in a café
in Mayflower, Texas, October 22, 1955

Not for the wound, not for the bullet,
        power's pale cowardice, but
for you, for the three full syllables
        of your name we hold whole
as a newborn by the feet, and so
        for the cry, the first note, the key
of every word to follow, the timbre,
        the tone, the voice that could sing
Nat King Cole's "If I May," and slow-
        dance the flip-side, the blossoms
fallen like a verdict to the jury's lips,
        not to the blood or the broken
glass or the spiders silking juke-
        box wires in a junk-man's shed,
but the fingers' heat still on the dime
        when it slides to the switch,
the lamp on the platter, the groove
        that tells the needle what to say,
and the pine boards of the café floor
        once moved by the locusts' moan

now warm as a guitar's wood, revived
        with all the prayers of song, *Amens*
that flame when a blues turns bright,
        not for what was lost, but what
was lived, what is written here,
        in the night, in vinyl, in the air,
for the bead of sweat at the hair's deckle,
        the evening star in the trees,
sodapop sugar wild on your tongue and
        for the tongue telling Saturday night
something of Sunday morning, fluent
        as a mockingbird, and for the hand
that opens as if in praise, as if in prayer,
        asking for another to fill it there,
for the smile and for the smile of skin
        behind the ear where love might lip its name,
for you, if we may, pull back the arm
        and start this music once again.

CONTRIBUTORS

Betty Adcock is the author of six books of poetry, including *Intervale: New and Selected Poems* and *The Difficult Wheel.* Her poems "Penumbra" and "Little Song," both first published in *Shenandoah,* were awarded the Pushcart Prize. She is a former writer-in-residence at Meredith College in Raleigh, North Carolina, and teaches in the Warren Wilson MFA Program for Writers. Her newest book, *Slantwise,* was published in 2008. Adcock is also a winner of the Poet's Prize and the North Carolina Medal for Literature, and she is a member of the Fellowship of Southern Writers.

Dan Albergotti is the author of *The Boatloads* (2008), selected by Edward Hirsch as the winner of the 2007 A. Poulin, Jr. Poetry Prize, and *The Use of the World* (2013). His collection *Millennial Teeth* won the Crab Orchard Series Open Competition in 2013 and was published in 2014. Albergotti's poems have appeared in the *Cincinnati Review, Five Points, Southern Review, Virginia Quarterly Review,* and *The Pushcart Prize 33* as well as other journals and anthologies. A graduate of the MFA program at the University of North Carolina at Greensboro and former poetry editor of the *Greensboro Review,* he is an associate professor at Coastal Carolina University, where he teaches literature and writing courses and edits *Waccamaw.*

Paul Allen retired in 2010 as professor emeritus after thirty-six years teaching poetry writing and writing song lyrics at the College of Charleston, Charleston, South Carolina. He relinquished his apartment; gave his furniture to his daughters, his books and CDs to his students, clothes and appliances to Goodwill; and has been living on the road in a twenty-foot camper, which has just enough room for a dozen books, computer and printer and writing desk, and his guitars. He stops at state welcome centers, grabs brochures, and determines how long he'll hang out with which landscape, historical area, or city, playing an open mic or two in some towns. He is working on a collection with the tentative title "Recalculating: New Poems from the Road." His "career poetry" includes *American Crawl* (Vassar Miller Poetry Prize, 1997); a chapbook, *His Longing: The Small Penis Oratorio* (2003); and *Ground Forces* (2008). He has received a Pushcart Prize (2008), a South Carolina Arts Commission individual artist fellowship in poetry (twice), the John Williams Andrews Narrative Poetry Prize from *Poet Lore,* the Mary Roberts Rinehart Award from George Mason University, and the Distinguished Research Award from the College of Charleston.

Brian Barker is the author of *The Animal Gospels* (2006) and *The Black Ocean* (2011), winner of the Crab Orchard Open Competition. His poems, reviews, and interviews have appeared or are forthcoming in such journals as *Poetry, American Poetry Review, Kenyon Review Online, Indiana Review, Ploughshares, TriQuarterly, Writer's Chronicle, Washington Post, Cincinnati Review, Blackbird,* and *Pleiades.* He teaches at the University of Colorado Denver.

Coleman Barks was born in Chattanooga in 1937. He is best known for his collaboration with various scholars of the Persian language (most notably, John Moyne) to translate into American free verse the poetry of the thirteenth-century mystic Jelaluddin Rumi. This work has resulted in twenty-one volumes, including the bestselling *Essential Rumi* in 1995 and, most recently, *Rumi: The Big Red Book* (2010). He has also published eight volumes of his own poetry, including *Winter Sky: New and Selected Poems, 1968–2008* and *Hummingbird Sleep, Poems 2009–2011.* In March 2005 the U.S. Department of State sent him to Afghanistan as the first visiting speaker there in twenty-five years. In May 2006 he was awarded an honorary doctorate by the University of Tehran. He is now retired professor emeritus at the University of Georgia in Athens. He has two grown sons and five grandchildren, all of whom live near him in Athens.

Jack B. Bedell is a professor of English and coordinator of creative writing at Southeastern Louisiana University, where he also edits *Louisiana Literature,* a nationally recognized literary journal, and directs the Louisiana Literature Press. His latest collections are *Bone-Hollow, True: New and Selected Poems; Call and Response; Come Rain, Come Shine; What Passes for Love;* and *At the Bonehouse,* all published by Texas Review Press (a member of the Texas A&M Press Consortium). His recent work has appeared in the *Southern Review, Hudson Review, Connecticut Review, Paterson Literary Review, Texas Review, Southern Quarterly,* and other journals. He and his wife, Beth, have three children, Jack Jr., Samuel Eli, and Emma Louise.

Destiny O. Birdsong is a native of Shreveport, Louisiana, and is currently a lecturer at Vanderbilt University, where she received her MFA in poetry in 2009 and her PhD in English in 2012. Her work has either appeared or is forthcoming in *Rattle, Southern Women's Review, Cave Canem Anthology XII 2008–2009, Handful of Dust,* and other publications.

David Bottoms's first book, *Shooting Rats at the Bibb County Dump,* was chosen by Robert Penn Warren as winner of the 1979 Walt Whitman Award of the Academy of American Poets. His poems have appeared widely in magazines such as the *Atlantic Monthly, New Yorker, Harper's, Poetry,* and the *Paris Review,* as well as in numerous anthologies. He is the author of seven other books of poetry, two novels, and a book of essays and interviews. His newest book of poems is *We Almost Disappear.*

Besmilr Brigham (1913–2000), raised by farmers in the Rio Grande Valley, studied at a women's Baptist college; married a linotype operator, Roy Brigham, with whom she raised a daughter, Heloise; and began writing seriously in Arkadelphia, Arkansas, under the influence of John Gould Fletcher and the disappearance of her brother in World War II. She traveled alone by freighter in 1948 to Europe, where she wrote her first novel, *KATH: the wicked saint.* From 1950 to the mid-1970s, she traveled widely by car and lived in Nicaragua, Nova Scotia, Alaska, Honduras, Guatemala, and Mexico, returning to the United States to work. Brigham wrote prolifically, on her own terms, publishing nothing until the influential bilingual journal *El Corno Emplumado* requested her poem "Yaqui Deer" in 1966, followed by a decade of concentrated publishing efforts and solicitation. In 1972 she published *Heaved from the Earth.* Her final decades in rural Arkansas were dedicated to isolated, conclusive labor over her life's work. A volume of her shorter poems, *Run through Rock*, selected and edited by C. D. Wright, was published posthumously in 2000.

KATHRYN STRIPLING BYER, a native of southwest Georgia, has lived in the Blue Ridge Mountains of North Carolina since 1968. She served as North Carolina's first woman poet laureate. Her blog, *Here, Where I Am,* was named one of the thirty best poetry blogs for 2009. Byer's work has appeared in numerous anthologies and journals, including *Atlantic Monthly, Poetry, Georgia Review,* and *American Scholar.* Her first book, *The Girl in the Midst of the Harvest,* was an Associated Writing Programs Finalist, chosen by John F. Nims, and published by Texas Tech University Press in 1986. LSU Press published subsequent books, including *Wildwood Flower,* the Academy of American Poets Lamont Selection in 1992; *Black Shawl,* chosen by Billy Collins for the Brockman-Campbell Award; and *Catching Light,* the Southern Independent Booksellers Alliance Best Book of Poetry in 2002. Her most recent book, *Coming to Rest,* received the Hanes Prize for Poetry from the Fellowship of Southern Writers in 2007.

Author of many books, FRED CHAPPELL received the Sir Walter Raleigh Prize (1973), the North Carolina Award for Literature (1980), Yale University Library's Bollingen Prize in poetry (1985), a literature award from the National Academy of Arts and Letters (1968), the best foreign book prize from the Académie française (1972), and the Aiken Taylor Award in poetry (1996). His works of fiction include *I Am One of You Forever* and *Brighten the Corner Where You Are,* and his most recent volume of poetry, *Shadow Box,* was published in 2009.

KELLY CHERRY is the author of nineteen books of fiction (novels, short stories), poetry, and nonfiction (memoir, essay, criticism), eight chapbooks, and translations of two classical plays. Her most recently published titles are *The Retreats of Thought: Poems* and *Girl in a Library: On Women Writers and the Writing Life.* Her short fiction has been reprinted in the annual *Best American Short Stories,* O. Henry Award, Pushcart Prize, and *New Stories from the South* anthologies and has won three PEN/Syndicated Fiction Awards. In 2000 her collection *The Society of Friends: Stories,* received the Dictionary of Literary Biography Award for the best volume of short stories published in 1999. She was the first recipient of the Hanes Prize for Poetry given by the Fellowship of Southern Writers for a body of work. Other awards include fellowships from the National Endowment for the Arts and the Rockefeller Foundation, the Bradley Major

Achievement (Lifetime) Award, a Distinguished Alumnus Award, three Wisconsin Arts Board fellowships and two New Work awards, an Arts America Speaker Award (the Philippines), and selection as a Wisconsin Notable Author.

MICHAEL CHITWOOD is a freelance writer and teaches at the University of North Carolina at Chapel Hill. His poetry and fiction have appeared in the *Atlantic Monthly, Poetry, New Republic, Threepenny Review, Virginia Quarterly Review, Field, Georgia Review,* and numerous other journals. He has published *Salt Works* (1992) and *Whet* (1995), and his third book, *The Weave Room* (1998), was part of the Phoenix Poets series. His collection of essays *Hitting below the Bible Belt* was published in 1998. *Gospel Road Going,* a collection of poems about his native Appalachia, was published in 2002 and was awarded the 2003 Roanoke-Chowan Prize for Poetry. In 2006 he published a collection of essays and short stories called *Finishing Touches.* His collection of poetry *From Whence* was released in March 2007. His book *Spill* (2007) was named as a finalist for *ForeWard* magazine's poetry book of the year and won the 2008 Roanoke-Chowan Prize. Tupelo Press also published his book *Poor-Mouth Jubilee* in 2010.

JIM CLARK was born in Byrdstown, Tennessee, and educated at Vanderbilt University, the University of North Carolina at Greensboro, and the University of Denver. He is the Elizabeth H. Jordan Professor of Southern Literature and chair of the Department of English, Modern Languages, Religion, and Philosophy at Barton College in Wilson, North Carolina. His books include *Notions: A Jim Clark Miscellany* and two collections of poetry, *Dancing on Canaan's Ruins* and *Handiwork.* He also edited *Fable in the Blood: The Selected Poems of Byron Herbert Reece.* His work has appeared in the *Georgia Review, Prairie Schooner, Denver Quarterly, Greensboro Review,* and *Asheville Poetry Review.* He has released two solo CDs, *Buried Land* and *The Service of Song,* and three CDs with his band the Near Myths: *Wilson, Words to Burn,* and *. . . and into the flow.*

ALLISON ADELLE HEDGE COKE's roots are as diverse as the routes her life and poetic career have taken. She carries in her blood a mix of Huron, Metis, Cherokee, Creek, French Canadian, Portuguese, Irish, Scot, and English ancestry. She was raised in the South, with years spent in North Carolina and Texas, but also in Canada and the Great Plains. She returned to her native North Carolina, taking jobs as a fieldworker and construction worker and attending North Carolina State University. She earned her AFAW in creative writing from the Institute for American Indian Arts and an MFA from Vermont College. Her publications include the chapbook *Year of the Rat* (1996), the poetry collections *Dog Road Woman* (1997), *Off-Season City Pipe* (2005), and *Blood Run* (2006), and the memoir *Rock, Ghost, Willow, Deer* (2004). She is associate professor of poetry and creative writing at the University of Nebraska at Kearney.

DANIEL CORRIE lives on a farm in Tift County, Georgia. He has received the *Southwest Review*'s first-place Morton Marr Prize presented by the *Southwest Review.* Other of his poems have appeared in the *American Scholar, Hudson Review, New Criterion, Southern Review,* and *Virginia Quarterly Review,* among others.

Kate Daniels was educated at the University of Virginia (B.A. and M.A. in English literature) and Columbia University (M.F.A., School of the Arts). Her teaching career has taken her to the University of Virginia, the University of Massachusetts Amherst, Louisiana State University, Wake Forest University, Bennington College, and Vanderbilt University, where she is an associate professor of English and chair of the Vanderbilt Visiting Writers Series. Her first book of poetry, *The White Wave* (1984), won the Agnes Lynch Starrett Poetry Prize. Her second volume, *The Niobe Poems* (1988), received honorable mention for the Paterson Poetry Prize. *Four Testimonies* (1998), her third volume, was one of Dave Smith's selections for his Southern Messenger Series. Her fourth volume is titled *A Walk in Victoria's Secret.* Daniels was named the winner of the 2011 Hanes Prize for Poetry by the Fellowship of Southern Writers for her work to date.

Kwame Dawes's eighteenth collection of verse, *Duppy Conqueror*, appeared in 2013. His awards include the Hollis Summers Prize, the Forward Poetry Prize, a Guggenheim Fellowship, and two Pushcart Prizes. He is Glenna Luschei Editor of *Prairie Schooner* and Chancellor's Professor at the University of Nebraska. He also teaches in the Pacific MFA Program.

James Dickey received the National Book Award for *Buckdancer's Choice* in 1966 and served as a consultant in poetry to the Library of Congress (a position later to be known as poet laureate) from 1966 to 1968. He then became a faculty member at the University of South Carolina and remained there until his death. Dickey authored the novel *Deliverance,* as well as several other volumes of poetry, novels, books of criticism, and children's books. He became a member of the National Institute of Arts and Letters in 1972 and was elected to the American Academy of Arts and Letters in 1987. *The Complete Poems of James Dickey* (University of South Carolina Press), edited by Ward Briggs, was published in 2013.

R. H. W. Dillard is the Susan Gager Jackson Professor of Creative Writing at the Jackson Center for Creative Writing at Hollins University. A native Virginian, he is the author of novels, short stories, critical essays and monographs, translations, and eight volumes of poetry, most recently *Not Ideas,* published in 2014. He is also the manager of a small but teeming wildlife habitat that includes among its inhabitants deer and many fat, healthy groundhogs.

Born and raised in Chatham, Virginia, Claudia Emerson studied writing at the University of North Carolina at Greensboro. Emerson's several volumes of poetry include *Pharaoh, Pharaoh* (1997); *Pinion: An Elegy* (2002); *Late Wife* (2005), which won the Pulitzer Prize; and *Figure Studies: Poems* (2008). Her honors include two additional Pulitzer Prize nominations as well as fellowships from the Library of Congress, the Virginia Commission for the Arts, and the National Endowment for the Arts. In 2008 she was appointed poet laureate of Virginia, a two-year role. Emerson has been poetry editor for the *Greensboro Review* and a contributing editor for *Shenandoah.* She has taught at Washington and Lee University, Randolph-Macon Women's College, and the University of Mary Washington.

Born in Brooklyn and raised in west Texas, TARFIA FAIZULLAH is the Pushcart Prize–winning author of *Seam* (2014), which also won the 2012 Crab Orchard Series in Poetry First Book Award. Her poems have appeared in *American Poetry Review, Oxford American, jubilat,* and *New England Review* and have been anthologized in *Poems of Devotion, Excuse This Poem: 100 Poems for the Next Generation, The Book of Scented Things,* and *Best New Poets 2014*. Honors include scholarships and fellowships from Kundiman, the Fulbright Foundation, Bread Loaf, Sewanee, Kenyon Review Writers Workshop, and Vermont Studio Center. She has collaborated with rapper and emcee Brooklyn Shanti, composer Jacob Cooper, and photographer Elizabeth Herman. She is the Nicholas Delbanco Visiting Professor of Creative Writing in Poetry at the University of Michigan Helen Zell Writers' Program and codirects the Organic Weapon Arts Chapbook Press & Video Series with Jamaal May.

FORREST GANDER has degrees in geology and English literature. His recent books include the novel *As a Friend,* the book of poems and *haibun, Core Samples from the World,* and the translation *Firefly under the Tongue: Selected Poems of Coral Bracho* (PEN Translation Prize finalist). A United States Artists Rockefeller Fellow, Gander is recipient of fellowships from the NEA and the Guggenheim, Howard, and Whiting Foundations.

GEORGE GARRETT (1929–2008) was a highly prolific and accomplished writer in an array of genres, publishing eight poetry collections, eleven novels, eight collections of short stories, and three plays, in addition to numerous nonfiction books and screenplays. Garrett taught at Bennington College, Hollins University, the University of Michigan, and the University of Virginia, where he was Henry Hoyns Professor of Creative Writing. He served as the Poet Laureate of the Commonwealth of Virginia (2002–2004) and was honored with many awards, including a Guggenheim Fellowship (1974), the T. S. Eliot Award (1989), and the Aiken Taylor Award for Modern American Poetry (1999). Garrett was a founding member of the Fellowship of Southern Writers and of the board of directors for the Association of Writers and Writing Programs.

JESSE GRAVES grew up in Sharps Chapel, Tennessee, the community where his ancestors settled in the 1780s. He is an assistant professor of English at East Tennessee State University, where he was granted the 2012 New Faculty Award from the College of Arts and Sciences. Graves's first collection of poems, *Tennessee Landscape with Blighted Pine,* won the 2012 Weatherford Award in Poetry and the Poetry Book of the Year Award from the Appalachian Writers' Association. His second book, *Basin Ghosts,* was published in 2013 by Texas Review Press.

JEFF HARDIN, originally from Savannah, Tennessee, is an eighth-generation descendant of the founder of Hardin County. He holds degrees from Austin Peay State University and the University of Alabama. A professor of English at Columbia State Community College in Columbia, Tennessee, he is the author of two chapbooks and two collections: *Fall Sanctuary,* recipient of the 2004 Nicholas Roerich Prize, and *Notes for a Praise Book*. His poems have appeared in the *Southern Review, Hudson Review, Gettysburg*

Review, North American Review, Southwest Review, New Republic, Poetry Northwest, Measure, Tar River Poetry, Meridian, Poet Lore, and many others. His work has also been featured on *Verse Daily, Poetry Daily,* and Garrison Keillor's "Writer's Almanac."

ASHLEY MACE HAVIRD's book of poems *The Garden of the Fugitives* (Texas Review Press, 2014) won the 2013 X. J. Kennedy Prize. Her chapbook *Dirt Eaters* (2009) won the South Carolina Poetry Initiative Series Prize; a second chapbook, *Sleeping with Animals* (2013), was published by Yellow Flag Press of Lafayette, Louisiana. Her poems and short stories have appeared in many journals, including *Shenandoah, Southern Poetry Review, Southern Review,* and the *Virginia Quarterly Review.* In 2002 she was awarded a Louisiana Division of the Arts Fellowship in Literature. She lives with her husband, the poet David Havird, in Shreveport, Louisiana.

DAVID HAVIRD is the author of two collections of poems: *Map Home* (2013) and *Penelope's Design* (2010). His poems and articles on such southern writers as James Dickey, Flannery O'Connor, and Elizabeth Spencer have appeared in many periodicals, including *Agni, Mississippi Quarterly,* the *New Yorker, Poetry, Sewanee Review, Southwest Review, Southern Literary Journal, Virginia Quarterly Review,* and *Yale Review.* A native of South Carolina and a graduate of the University of Virginia, he teaches English at Centenary College of Louisiana.

TERRANCE HAYES was born in Columbia, South Carolina. He is the author of four poetry collections, including *Lighthead,* winner of the 2010 National Book Award, and is a professor at the University of Pittsburgh. His fifth book, *How to Be Drawn,* was published in April 2015.

HASTINGS HENSEL is the author of *Winter Inlet,* winner of the 2014–2015 Unicorn Press First Book Prize, and the chapbook *Control Burn,* winner of the Iron Horse Literary Review 2011 Single-Author Contest. The 2014–2015 South Carolina Arts Commission Fellow in Poetry, he lives in Murrells Inlet, South Carolina and teaches in the English department at Coastal Carolina University.

RON HOUCHIN, a West Virginia native, lives on the banks of the Ohio River. Before retirement he taught public school for thirty years. He has read his work at Bewley's International Café, Dublin; the Ypsilan Theater, Prague; the Hemingway Days Festival, Key West; and many other venues. He has appeared in anthologies in the United States and Ireland. His poems have recently appeared or will soon appear in *Five Points, Birmingham Poetry Review, James Dickey Review, Valparaiso Poetry Review, drafthorse, STILL,* and the *Hampden-Sydney Poetry Review.* His seventh volume of poems, *The Man Who Saws Us in Half,* was published as part of the Southern Messenger Poetry Series in 2013.

REBECCA GAYLE HOWELL is the author of *Render/An Apocalypse* (2013), which was selected by Nick Flynn for the Cleveland State University First Book Prize and was a 2014 finalist for *ForeWord Review's* Book of the Year. She is also the translator of Amal al-Jubouri's *Hagar before the Occupation/Hagar after the Occupation* (2011). Among her awards are two fellowships from the Fine Arts Work Center and a Pushcart Prize. A native of Kentucky, Howell is the poetry editor at *Oxford American.*

David Huddle grew up in Ivanhoe, Virginia, taught at the University of Vermont for thirty-eight years, and currently is the Visiting Distinguished Professor of Creative Writing at Hollins University. He is the author of sixteen books of poetry, fiction, and essays, including *Paper Boy, Only the Little Bone, The Writing Habit, La Tour Dreams of the Wolf Girl,* and *Glory River.* His work has appeared in recent issues of *Appalachian Heritage, Redivider, Michigan Quarterly Review,* and the *New Yorker.*

Andrew Hudgins attended high school, college, and graduate school in Alabama. He is now Humanities Distinguished Professor in English at the Ohio State University. His first book, *Saints and Strangers,* was a finalist for the Pulitzer Prize. He has published nine books of poetry, most recently *American Rendering: New and Selected Poems* and *A Clown at Midnight.* His memoir, *The Joker,* was published in 2013.

T. R. Hummer's eleventh book of poems, *Skandalon,* has just appeared; his second book of essays, *Available Surfaces,* was published in the University of Michigan's Poets on Poetry series. Hummer has been the recipient of a Guggenheim Fellowship in poetry, a National Endowment for the Arts fellowship in poetry, the Hanes Prize for Poetry, the Richard Wright Award for Artistic Achievement, and two Pushcart Prizes. He has served as editor in chief of the *Kenyon Review, New England Review,* and *Georgia Review.*

TJ Jarrett is a software engineer and author of *Zion,* winner of the 2013 Crab Orchard Open Poetry Competition, and *Ain't No Grave.* Her poems have appeared in *Poetry, Beloit Poetry Review, Boston Review, Virginia Quarterly Review,* and elsewhere.

Rodney Jones, born in Alabama and educated at the University of Alabama and the University of North Carolina at Greensboro, has published widely in leading magazines, *The Oxford Book of Contemporary American Poetry,* and eight editions of *Best American Poetry.* His books include *Imaginary Logic* (2011); *Salvation Blues: 100 Poems, 1985–2005* (2006), which won the Kingsley Tufts Prize and was shortlisted for the Griffin International Poetry Prize; *Elegy for the Southern Drawl* (1999), a Pulitzer Prize finalist; *Things That Happen Once* (1996), a *Los Angeles Times* Book Award finalist; and *Transparent Gestures* (1989), winner of the National Book Critics Circle Award. Other honors include a Guggenheim Fellowship and the Jean Stein Award of the American Academy of Arts and Letters. A professor and distinguished scholar emeritus at Southern Illinois University Carbondale, he is a member of the Fellowship of Southern Writers and teaches in the MFA program at Warren Wilson College.

Judy Jordan's first book of poetry, *Carolina Ghost Woods,* won the National Book Critics Circle Award, the Academy of American Poets Walt Whitman Award, the Thomas Wolfe Literary Award, the Oscar Arnold Young Book Prize of the Poetry Council of North Carolina, and the Utah Book of the Year Award for Poetry. Her second volume, the book-length poem *60 Cent Coffee and a Quarter to Dance,* was published in 2005.

Her third book of poetry, *Hunger,* which centers on two years of semi-homelessness during which she lived in a half-collapsed greenhouse, is scheduled to be published. Jordan currently lives off the grid, surrounded by the Shawnee National Forest in a Thoreau-sized cordwood cabin she built herself, and is completing an eco-friendly, passive-solar-heated, hybrid earthbag and cob house. She is nearing completion of a fourth book of poetry and is working on a memoir and a work of nonfiction concerning global climate change. She is a professor of poetry at Southern Illinois University Carbondale.

TERRY L. KENNEDY is the author of the poetry collection *New River Breakdown* and the limited-edition chapbook *Until the Clouds Shatter the Light That Plates Our Lives,* selected by Thomas Lux for Jeanne Duvall Editions. His work has appeared in a variety of literary journals and magazines, including *Cave Wall, Southern Review,* and *Waccamaw,* and has been honored with a Randall Jarrell Fellowship as well as fellowships from the Virginia Center for the Creative Arts. He currently serves as the associate director of the Graduate Program in Creative Writing at the University of North Carolina at Greensboro and is editor of the online journal *storySouth.* You can find him online at www.terrylkennedy.com.

YUSEF KOMUNYAKAA was born in Bogalusa, Louisiana, in 1947. His numerous books of poems include *Pleasure Dome: New and Collected Poems, 1975–1999* (Wesleyan University Press, 2001); *Talking Dirty to the Gods* (2000); *Thieves of Paradise* (1998), which was a finalist for the National Book Critics Circle Award; *Neon Vernacular: New and Selected Poems 1977–1989* (1994), for which he received the Pulitzer Prize and the Kingsley Tufts Poetry Award; *Magic City* (1992); *Dien Cai Dau* (1988), which won the Dark Room Poetry Prize; *I Apologize for the Eyes in My Head* (1986), winner of the San Francisco Poetry Center Award; and *Copacetic* (1984).

JOHN LANE is the author of a dozen books of poetry and prose. His latest, *Abandoned Quarry: New and Selected Poems,* was published in 2011. The book includes much of Lane's published poetry over the past thirty years, plus a selection of new poems. In 2012 *Abandoned Quarry* won the SIBA (Southeastern Independent Booksellers Alliance) Poetry Book of the Year prize. His latest prose books are *My Paddle to the Sea,* published 2011, and *Begin with Rock, End with Water,* published in 2014. He teaches environmental studies at Wofford College.

Born in 1956 in Warren, Ohio, in what was then called the Steel Valley, NATON LESLIE put himself through college, earning a BA from Youngstown State University and an MA and PhD from Ohio University. Though his upbringing was set amid factory smokestacks, he had strong roots in the Appalachian Mountains of Pennsylvania, and these disparate backgrounds are the locales of much of what he wrote. Leslie was also a highly skilled craftsman and woodworker and an expert antique collector and restorer, all recurrent subjects in his creative work. He was a professor of creative writing at Miami University (Ohio) and, from 1990–2013, at Siena College. His publications include seven books of poetry, a nonfiction work about secondhand culture in the United States, *That Might Be Useful,* and a collection of short stories, *Marconi's Dream,* which won the George Garrett Fiction Prize. An eclectic and versatile author, Leslie was first and foremost a poet, with more than three hundred poems published nationwide and overseas. He was both an NEA and NYFA fellow. Leslie was a prolific essayist, and his work has been included in *Best American Essays* and recognized as notable since 1997. He also leaves behind a large body of work yet to be published.

Ed Madden grew up on a rice and soybean farm in northeast Arkansas, where he learned to carry a shovel and a grudge. He is the author of three books of poetry—*Signals, Prodigal: Variations,* and *Nest*—and his work has appeared in *Best New Poets 2007, The Book of Irish American Poetry,* and elsewhere. He is also coeditor of *Out Loud: The Best of Rainbow Radio,* a collection of radio essays from the first gay radio show in South Carolina. Sometimes he thinks he should have been a preacher.

Al Maginnes is the author of ten collections or chapbooks of poems, most recently *Music from Small Towns* (2014), winner of the annual Jacar Press contest, and *Inventing Constellations* (2012). His poems have appeared in *Poetry, Georgia Review, New England Review, Southern Review,* and many other journals. He lives with his family in Raleigh, North Carolina, where he teaches composition, literature, and creative writing at Wake Technical Community College.

Jeff Mann's books include four collections of poetry, *Bones Washed with Wine, On the Tongue, Ash: Poems from Norse Mythology,* and *A Romantic Mann;* two books of personal essays, *Edge: Travels of an Appalachian Leather Bear* and *Binding the God: Ursine Essays from the Mountain South;* the novellas *Devoured,* included in *Masters of Midnight: Erotic Tales of the Vampire,* and *Camp Allegheny,* included in *History's Passion: Stories of Sex before Stonewall;* two novels, *Fog: A Novel of Desire and Reprisal,* winner of the Pauline Réage Novel Award, and *Purgatory: A Novel of the Civil War,* winner of a Rainbow Award; a collection of poetry and memoir, *Loving Mountains, Loving Men;* and two volumes of short fiction, *Desire and Devour: Stories of Blood and Sweat* and *A History of Barbed Wire,* winner of a Lambda Literary Award. He teaches creative writing at Virginia Tech in Blacksburg.

Jeff Daniel Marion has published nine poetry collections, four poetry chapbooks, and a children's book. His poems have appeared in the *Southern Review, Southern Poetry Review, Shenandoah, Atlanta Review, Tar River Poetry,* and many others. In 1978 Marion received the first literary fellowship awarded by the Tennessee Arts Commission. *Ebbing and Flowing Springs: New and Selected Poems and Prose, 1976–2001* won the 2003 Independent Publisher Award in Poetry and was named Appalachian Book of the Year by the Appalachian Writers Association. His collection *Father* received the 2009 Quentin R. Howard Poetry Prize, and in 2011 he was awarded the James Still Award for Writing about the Appalachian South by the Fellowship of Southern Writers. Marion served as the Jack E. Reese Writer-in-Residence for the University of Tennessee Libraries, Knoxville, from 2009–2011. In spring 2013 his work and career were celebrated at Carson-Newman University and Walters State Community College.

Linda Parsons Marion is an editor at the University of Tennessee Press and the author of three poetry collections, the most recent of which is *Bound.* She served as poetry editor of *Now and Then* magazine for many years and has received literary fellowships from the Tennessee Arts Commission as well as the Associated Writing Programs' Intro Award and the 2012 George Scarbrough Award in Poetry, among others. Marion's work has appeared in journals such as the *Georgia Review, Iowa Review, Poet Lore, Asheville Poetry Review, Shenandoah, Louisiana Literature,* and *Birmingham Poetry Review;* and Ted Kooser's syndicated column "American Life in Poetry"; and in numerous anthologies, including *Listen Here: Women Writing in Appalachia* and *The Southern Poetry Anthology, Volume III: Contemporary Appalachia.*

Christopher Martin is the author of the poetry chapbook *A Conference of Birds* (New Native Press, 2012). Martin's poems and essays have appeared or are forthcoming in *Shambhala Sun, Ruminate Magazine, Thrush Poetry Journal, Drafthorse, Still: The Journal, Buddhist Poetry Review, Adventum, Poecology, Museum of Americana: A Literary Review, Loose Change Magazine, Revolution House, Pale Ale Press,* American Public Media's "On Being" blog, and elsewhere. His poems "Revelation on the Cherokee County Line" and "Antidote to Narcissus" were selected to appear in the *Southern Poetry Anthology, Volume V: Georgia,* published in 2012. His poem "Marcescence," published as a broadside in October 2012, was nominated for a Pushcart Prize. Martin is the founder and editor-in-chief of the online literary magazine *Flycatcher* and is a contributing editor to *New Southerner,* where he writes the monthly blog "*Kairos and Crisis*" on race, religion, and social justice in the South.

Chris Mattingly is the author of *A Light for Your Beacon* and *Scuffletown.* His poems have appeared most recently in *River Styx, Lumberyard, Still, Louisville Review, Sawmill,* and *Forklift, OHIO.* Equally important, Mattingly cultivates a big vegetable garden, plays the fretless banjo, and is the eighth-generation Mattingly to live in Kentucky. He holds an MFA in poetry from Spalding University and lives and teaches in southeast Georgia.

Michael McFee has published fourteen books, most recently a collection of poetry, *That Was Oasis* (2012); a chapbook of one-line poems, *The Smallest Talk* (2007); and a collection of prose, *The Napkin Manuscripts: Selected Essays and an Interview* (2006). He has received the James Still Award for Writing about the Appalachian South from the Fellowship of Southern Writers, the Thomas Wolfe Literary Award from the Western North Carolina Historical Association, and the R. Hunt Parker Memorial Award for lifetime literary achievement from the North Carolina Literary and Historical Association. A native of Asheville, North Carolina, he has taught in the Creative Writing Program at the University of North Carolina at Chapel Hill for several decades.

Ray McManus is the author of three books of poetry: *Driving through the country before you are born* (University of South Carolina Press, 2007), *Left Behind* (2008), and *Red Dirt Jesus* (2011). His poetry has appeared in many journals, including, most recently, *Natural Bridge, Barely South, Pea River Review,* the *Pinch, Hayden's Ferry,* and *moonShine Review.* Ray is the creative writing director for the Tri-District Arts Consortium in South Carolina, and he is an assistant professor of English in the Division of Arts and Letters at University of South Carolina Sumter, where he teaches creative writing, Irish literature, and southern literature.

Thorpe Moeckel is the author of *Odd Botany, Making a Map of the River,* and *Venison.* He teaches at Hollins University and lives in northern Botetourt County, Virginia, where he helps his wife, daughter, and many animals tend a small, mostly self-sufficient modern homestead.

Robert Morgan is the author of eleven books of poetry, including, most recently, *The Strange Attractor: New and Selected Poems* and *October Crossing.* He has also published eight volumes of fiction, including the novel *Gap Creek,* a *New York Times* bestseller and winner of the Southern Book Award, and *Brave Enemies: A Novel of the American Revolution.* In addition he has published *Boone: A Biography,* also a bestseller and winner of the Kentucky Book Award. At present he is at work on new poems and a study of the Westward Expansion from Thomas Jefferson to James K. Polk and the Mexican War. A member of the Fellowship of Southern Writers, he received the Fellowship's Hanes Prize for Poetry in 1991. In 2007 he was honored with the Academy Award in Literature from the American Academy of Arts and Letters. A native of western North Carolina, Morgan has taught since 1971 at Cornell University, where at present he serves as Kappa Alpha Professor of English.

Ricardo Nazario y Colón is a co-founder of the Affrilachian Poets. He was featured in the PBS documentary *Coal Black Voices* produced by the Media Working. He is the author of the collection *Of Jíbaros and Hillbillies* and the chapbook *The Recital.* His work has been anthologized in *Kentucky: Poets of Place* (2012), edited by Matthew Nickle, and *The Southern Poetry Anthology, Volume III: Contemporary Appalachia* (2011), edited by William Wright, Jesse Graves, and Paul Ruffin. An environmental justice advocate and diversity consultant from the South Bronx area of New York City, he has lived, worked, and played in Kentucky for the last twelve years. In 2011, the Governor of Kentucky Hon. Steven Beshear appointed him to serve on the state's Native American Heritage Commission. He has a BA in Spanish Literature and Latin American Studies from the University of Kentucky and a MST from Pace University (NY). He is a doctoral student at the University of Kentucky and currently serves as the Director of Student Activities, Inclusion and Leadership Development at Morehead State University in Eastern Kentucky.

Tara Powell is an associate professor of English at the University of South Carolina. She is the author of *Physical Science* (2010), a chapbook of poems from Finishing Line Press, and *The Intellectual in Twentieth-Century Southern Literature* (2012), a book of literary scholarship from Louisiana State University Press. A coedited essay collection, *Reading in the Kitchen: Essays on Foodways and Southern Literature,* is forthcoming.

Ron Rash is the Parris Distinguished Professor in Appalachian Cultural Studies at Western Carolina University. In 1994 he published his first book, a collection of short stories titled *The Night the New Jesus Fell to Earth.* Since then Rash has published three collections of poetry, three short story collections, and four novels. Rash's poems and stories have appeared in more than one hundred magazines and journals. His collection of short stories *Burning Bright* (2010) won the Frank O'Connor International Short Story Award.

Writer, naturalist and activist Janisse Ray is author of four books of literary nonfiction and a collection of nature poetry. She is on the faculty of Chatham University's low-residency MFA program and is a Woodrow Wilson Visiting Fellow. She holds an MFA from the University of Montana and in 2007 was awarded an honorary doctorate from Unity College in Maine.

Paul Ruffin holds the rank of Texas State University System Regents' Professor and Distinguished Professor of English at Sam Houston State University, where he directs the creative writing program, serves as director of *Texas Review Press,* and edits the *Texas Review.* His published books include two novels, three collections of short stories (with a fourth, *Living in a Christ-Haunted Land,* to be released in translation by a French publisher late this year), three books of essays (including, *Travels with George in Search of Ben Hur,* published by the University of South Carolina), and seven collections of poetry (the latest, *Paul Ruffin: New and Selected Poems,* published in 2010; one of his collections, *Circling,* won the 1997 Mississippi Institute of Arts and Letters Poetry Award). He is also the editor or coeditor of eleven other books, including studies on the work of John Steinbeck and Texas novelist William Goyen. Ruffin writes a weekly newspaper column, "Ruffin-It," for the *Huntsville Item.* Ruffin's work has appeared widely in such journals as *Alaska Quarterly Review, Georgia Review, Michigan Quarterly Review, New England Review, Paris Review, Poetry,* and *Southern Review,* and his fiction and poetry has appeared in a number of major university texts published by Little, Brown, Harcourt, and Norton. He was the poet laureate of Texas in 2009.

Steve Scafidi is the author of *Sparks from a Nine-Pound Hammer* (2001), *For Love of Common Words* (2006), *The Cabinetmaker's Window* (2014), and *To the Bramble and the Briar* (2014). He is a cabinetmaker and lives with his family in Summit Point, West Virginia.

James Seay teaches at the University of North Carolina at Chapel Hill. His poems and essays have appeared in *Antaeus, Esquire,* the *Southern Review,* among other venues. He cowrote the film *In the Blood* with director George Butler.

Poet, novelist, critic, and editor Dave Smith was born in Portsmouth, Virginia. The first member of his family to graduate from college, Smith received a BA from the University of Virginia, an MA from Southern Illinois University, and a PhD from Ohio University. He has published more than a dozen volumes of poetry, including *Little Boats, Unsalvaged: Poems 1992–2004,* and *The Wick of Memory: New and Selected*

Poems, 1970–2000, which was chosen as the Dictionary of Literary Biography's Book of the Year in Poetry. Influenced by Robert Penn Warren, James Dickey, and A. R. Ammons, Smith writes layered, expansively narrative free-verse poems that deal with history and regional identity. His prose includes the novel *Onliness* (1981), the story collection *Southern Delights* (1984), and the essay collection *Hunting Men: Reflections on a Life in American Poetry* (2006). Smith has been an editor of the *Southern Review,* the *New Virginia Review,* the University of Utah Poets Series, and the Southern Messenger Signature Poets series of Louisiana State University Press. He edited *The Essential Poe* (1991), *The William Morrow Anthology of Younger American Poets* (1985), and *The Pure Clear Word: Essays on the Poetry of James Wright* (1982). Smith has received fellowships from the National Endowment for the Arts, the John Simon Guggenheim Foundation, the Bread Loaf Writers' Conference, the Lyndhurst Foundation, and the Rockefeller Foundation. He has also won the Virginia Prize in Poetry, the *Prairie Schooner* Poetry Prize, an Award in Poetry from the American Academy and Institute of Arts and Letters, and a Pushcart Prize. He has twice been a finalist for the Pulitzer Prize.

R. T. Smith is the former editor of *Southern Humanities Review,* as well as former Alumni Writer-in-Residence at Auburn University. His books of poems include *Brightwood* and *Outlaw Style,* both recipients of the Library of Virginia Poetry Book of the Year Award, and his poetry has also been published in *Best American Poetry.* He has published four collections of stories, including *Sherburne* (2012), and his stories have appeared in *Best American Mystery Stories, The Pushcart Prize Anthology, New Stories from the South,* and *Best American Short Stories.* Smith's collection of poetry *The Red Wolf: A Dream of Flannery O'Connor* was published in 2013. He has edited *Shenandoah* since 1995 and in 2009 was named Washington and Lee's writer-in-residence. His latest book of poems is *In the Night Orchard: Selected Poems.*

A native of New Orleans, Sheryl St. Germain has taught creative writing at the University of Texas at Dallas, the University of Louisiana at Lafayette, Knox College, and Iowa State University. She currently directs the MFA program in creative writing at Chatham University, where she also teaches poetry and creative nonfiction. Her work has received several awards, including two National Endowment for the Arts fellowships, a National Endowment for the Humanities fellowship, the Dobie-Paisano Fellowship, the Ki Davis Award from the Aspen Writers Foundation, and most recently the William Faulkner Award for the personal essay. Her poetry books include *Going Home, The Mask of Medusa, Making Bread at Midnight, How Heavy the Breath of God,* and *The Journals of Scheherazade.* She has also published a book of translations of the Cajun poet Jean Arceneaux, *Je Suis Cadien.* A book of lyric essays about growing up in Louisiana, *Swamp Songs: The Making of an Unruly Woman,* was published in 2003. Her most recent book is *Let It Be a Dark Roux: New and Selected Poems,* published in 2007.

Leon Stokesbury has lived his entire life in the South, first in Texas and Arkansas and for the past twenty-five years as a teacher in the graduate creative writing program at Georgia State University in Atlanta. His first book, *Often in Different Landscapes,* was a cowinner of the first AWP Poetry Competition in 1975. He has also edited several anthologies, including *The Made Thing: An Anthology of Contemporary Southern Poetry* and *Articles of War: American Poetry about World War II.* His *Autumn Rhythm: New and Selected Poems* won the Poets' Prize in 1998.

Richard Tillinghast is the author of eleven books of poetry and four of creative nonfiction. His most recent poetry books are *Wayfaring Stranger* (2013), and three collections published in 2009: *Sewanee Poems, Selected Poems,* and *Dirty August,* translations of works by the Turkish poet Edip Cansever in collaboration with his daughter, Julia Clare Tillinghast. Tillinghast was born in Memphis, spent part of his childhood on a farm near Brownsville, Tennessee, graduated from Sewanee, and is the recipient of an honorary Doctor of Letters from there. He was a 2010–11 Guggenheim Fellow in poetry. His new travel book, *Istanbul, City of Forgetting and Remembering,* was recently published in England. He currently divides his time between Tennessee and Hawaii.

Deno Trakas is the Hoy Professor of American Literature and the chair of the English Department at Wofford College. In addition to his book *Because Memory Isn't Eternal: A Story of Greeks in Upstate South Carolina,* he has published fiction, poetry, and essays in magazines such as the *Denver Quarterly* and *Oxford American,* as well as in a half dozen anthologies. Holocene Press published two of his poetry chapbooks, *The Shuffle of Wings* and *human and puny.* He has won five South Carolina Fiction Project prizes and an individual artist grant from the South Carolina Arts Commission.

Natasha Trethewey is the author of four collections of poetry: *Domestic Work* (2000); *Bellocq's Ophelia* (2002); *Native Guard* (2006), for which she was awarded the 2007 Pulitzer Prize; and *Thrall* (2012). She is also the author of a book of creative nonfiction, *Beyond Katrina: A Meditation on the Mississippi Gulf Coast* (2010). *Domestic Work* won the inaugural 1999 Cave Canem poetry prize (selected by Rita Dove), a 2001 Mississippi Institute of Arts and Letters Book Prize, and the 2001 Lillian Smith Award for Poetry. *Bellocq's Ophelia* received the 2003 Mississippi Institute of Arts and Letters Book Prize, was a finalist for both the Academy of American Poets' James Laughlin and Lenore Marshall prizes, and was named a 2003 notable book by the American Library Association. She is the recipient of fellowships from the Guggenheim Foundation, the Rockefeller Foundation, the Bunting Fellowship Program of the Radcliffe Institute for Advanced Study at Harvard University, and the National Endowment for the Arts. During the 2005–6 academic year, she was Lehman Brady Joint Chair Professor of Documentary and American Studies at Duke University and the University of North Carolina at Chapel Hill, and in 2009 she was the James Weldon Johnson Fellow in African American Studies at the Beinecke Library at Yale University. Trethewey is also the recipient of the 2008 Mississippi Governor's Award for Excellence in the Arts and was named the 2008 Georgia Woman of the Year. In 2009 she was inducted into the Fellowship of Southern Writers and in 2011 into the Georgia Writers Hall of Fame. In 2012 she was named poet laureate of the state of Mississippi and the nineteenth poet laureate of the United States. She was also named a 2013 member of the American Academy of

Arts and Sciences, one of the nation's oldest and most prestigious honorary societies and a center for independent policy research.

Adam Vines is an assistant professor of English at the University of Alabama at Birmingham, where he is editor of the *Birmingham Poetry Review*. He has recently published poems or has poems forthcoming in *Poetry*, *Southwest Review*, *32 Poems*, and *Gulf Coast*, among others. His collection of poetry *The Coal Life* was published in 2012. The Alabama State Council on the Arts awarded him a 2013 individual artist fellowship.

Ellen Bryant Voigt grew up in Virginia, lives in Vermont, and teaches in the MFA Program for Writers at Warren Wilson College in Asheville, North Carolina. She has published seven volumes of poetry, including *Kyrie* (1995), a National Book Critics Circle Award finalist; *Shadow of Heaven* (2002), a National Book Award finalist; and *Messenger: New and Selected Poems 1976–2006* (2007), winner of the Poets' Prize and a finalist for both the National Book Award and the Pulitzer Prize. Her essays on craft have been published as *The Flexible Lyric* (1999) and *The Art of Syntax* (2009), and the poetry collection *Headwaters* was published in 2013. A member of the Fellowship of Southern Writers, she has received fellowships from the Guggenheim Foundation, the Lila Wallace–*Reader's Digest* Foundation, and the National Endowment for the Arts; the O. B. Hardison Jr. Prize for poetry and teaching from the Folger Shakespeare Library; and the Merrill Fellowship from the Academy of American Poets, for which she was subsequently elected a chancellor.

G. C. Waldrep was born in South Boston, Virginia, and grew up there and in the Carolinas. His most recent books are *Your Father on the Train of Ghosts* (2011), a lyric collaboration with John Gallaher; *The Arcadia Project: North American Postmodern Pastoral* (2012), coedited with Joshua Corey; and a chapbook, *Susquehanna* (2013). He teaches at Bucknell University, edits the journal *West Branch*, and serves as editor-at-large for the *Kenyon Review*.

Frank X Walker, from Danville, Kentucky, coined the word *Affrilachia*, signifying the importance of the African American presence in Appalachia: the "new word . . . spoke to the union of Appalachian identity and the region's African-American culture and history." In 2013 he was the poet laureate of Kentucky.

Robert West's poems have appeared in *Southern Poetry Review*, *Poetry*, *Christian Science Monitor*, *Pembroke Magazine*, *Light*, Ted Kooser's syndicated column and website *American Life in Poetry*, *The Best American Nonrequired Reading*, and other venues. His latest collection is the chapbook *Convalescent* (2011). He teaches in the Department of English at Mississippi State University and lives in Starkville with his wife and daughter.

James Whitehead was an American poet and novelist. He published four books of poetry and one critically acclaimed novel, *Joiner*.

Amy Wright is nonfiction editor of Zone 3 Press and the author of four poetry chapbooks. She received a Peter Taylor fellowship for the Kenyon Review Writers'

Workshop and an individual artists fellowship from the Tennessee Arts Commission and was recognized as an emerging writer at the Southern Women Writers' Conference. Her work has appeared in a number of journals, including *Bellingham Review, Brevity, CALYX, Denver Quarterly, Drunken Boat,* the *Kenyon Review, Passages North, The Southern Poetry Anthology,* vols. 3 and 6, and *Tupelo Quarterly.*

Charles Wright as born in Pickwick Dam, Tennessee, in 1935 and was educated at Davidson College and the University of Iowa. His books include *Sestets: Poems* (Farrar, Straus & Giroux, 2010); *Littlefoot: A Poem* (2008); *Scar Tissue* (2007), which was the international winner of the Griffin Poetry Prize; *Buffalo Yoga* (Farrar, Straus & Giroux, 2004); *Negative Blue* (2000); *Appalachia* (1998); *Black Zodiac* (1997), which won the Pulitzer Prize and the *Los Angeles Times* Book Prize; *Chickamauga* (1995), which won the 1996 Lenore Marshall Poetry Prize; *The World of the Ten Thousand Things: Poems 1980–1990; Zone Journals* (1988); *Country Music: Selected Early Poems* (1983), which won the National Book Award; and *Hard Freight* (1973), which was nominated for the National Book Award. He has also written two volumes of criticism and has translated the work of Dino Campana (*Orphic Songs*) and Eugenio Montale (*The Storms and Other Poems,* which was awarded the PEN Translation Prize). He was Souder Family Professor of English at the University of Virginia in Charlottesville. In 2014, Wright began his appointment as poet laureate of the United States.

William Wright is author of eight collections of poetry: four full-length books, including *Tree Heresies* (2015), *Night Field Anecdote* (2011), *Bledsoe* (2011), and *Dark Orchard* (2005). Wright's chapbooks are *April Creatures* (2015); *Sleep Paralysis,* winner of the South Carolina Poetry Initiative Prize, selected by Kwame Dawes (2012); *Xylem & Heartwood* (2013), and *The Ghost Narratives* (2008). Wright is series editor and volume coeditor of *The Southern Poetry Anthology,* a multivolume series celebrating contemporary writing of the American South, published by Texas Review Press. Additionally he serves as assistant editor for *Shenandoah,* translates German poetry, and is editing several volumes, including *The World Is Charged: Poetic Engagements with Gerard Manley Hopkins* (with Daniel Westover). Wright won the 2012 Porter Fleming Prize in Poetry.

Jake Adam York authored four books of poems: *Murder Ballads* (2005), *A Murmuration of Starlings* (2008), *Persons Unknown* (2010), and *Abide,* which was published posthumously in 2014. Originally from Alabama, he was educated at Auburn and Cornell Universities. He received fellowships to serve as a poet in residence at the University of Mississippi (2009), as the Thomas Visiting Professor in Creative Writing at Kenyon College (2011), and, from the Mellon Foundation, to serve as a visiting faculty fellow at the James Weldon Johnson Institute for Advanced Study at Emory University (2011–12). He was an associate professor of English at the University of Colorado Denver and edited the journal *Copper Nickel.*

SUGGESTIONS FOR FURTHER READING

Anthologies of Contemporary Southern Poetry

Abbott, Dorothy, ed. *Mississippi Writers: An Anthology.* Jackson: University Press of Mississippi, 1991.

Allen, Gilbert, and William Rogers, eds. *45/96: The Ninety-Six Sampler of South Carolina Poetry.* Greenville, S.C.: Ninety-Six Press, 1994.

———. *Millennial Sampler of South Carolina Poetry.* 2005.

Beggs, Marck L., ed. *Eightieth Anniversary Anthology: Poets' Roundtable of Arkansas.* Maynard, Ark.: Mockingbird Lane, 2013.

Biespiel, David, ed. *Poems of the American South.* New York: Knopf, 2014.

Chappell, Fred, ed. *A New Pléiade: Selected Poems, Seven American Poets.* Baton Rouge: Louisiana State University Press, 1998.

Dobie, Ann Brewster, ed. *Uncommonplace: An Anthology of Contemporary Louisiana Poets.* Baton Rouge: Louisiana State University Press, 1998.

Ellison, George, ed. *High Vistas: An Anthology of Nature Writing from Western North Carolina and the Great Smoky Mountains, Volume II, 1900–2009.* Charleston, S.C.: History Press, 2011.

Garin, Marita, ed. *Southern Appalachian Poetry: An Anthology of Works by 37 Poets.* Jefferson, N.C.: McFarland, 2008.

Garrett, George, ed. *The Yellow Shoe Poets: Selected Poems 1964–1999.* Baton Rouge: Louisiana State University Press, 1999.

Horne, Jennifer, ed. *Working the Dirt: An Anthology.* Montgomery, Ala.: New South, 2003.

Owen, Guy, and Mary C. Williams, eds. *Contemporary Southern Poetry: An Anthology.* Baton Rouge: Louisiana State University Press, 1980.

Rigsbee, David, and Steven Ford Brown, eds. *Invited Guest: An Anthology of Twentieth-Century Southern Poetry.* Charlottesville: University Press of Virginia, 2001.

Serpas, Martha, ed. *Improbable Words: An Anthology of Texas and Louisiana Poets.* Houston: Mutabilis, 2011.

Stokesbury, Leon, ed. *The Made Thing: An Anthology of Contemporary Southern Poetry.* 2nd ed. Fayetteville: University of Arkansas Press, 2000.

Stone, Nancy, and Robert Waters Grey. *White Trash: An Anthology of Contemporary Southern Poets.* 2nd ed. Los Angeles: New South, 1976.

Watson, Randall, ed. *The Weight of Addition: An Anthology of Texas Poetry.* Houston: Mutabilis, 2007.

Wright, William, and Stephen Gardner, eds. *The Southern Poetry Anthology, Volume I: South Carolina.* Huntsville: Texas Review Press, 2007.

———. *The Southern Poetry Anthology, Volume II: Mississippi.* Huntsville: Texas Review Press, 2010.

Wright, William, Jesse Graves, and Paul Ruffin, eds. *The Southern Poetry Anthology, Volume III: Contemporary Appalachia.* Huntsville: Texas Review Press, 2011.

———. *The Southern Poetry Anthology, Volume VII: North Carolina.* Huntsville: Texas Review Press, 2014.

———. *The Southern Poetry Anthology Volume VI: Tennessee.* Huntsville: Texas Review Press, 2013.

Wright, William, and Paul Ruffin, eds. *The Southern Poetry Anthology, Volume IV: Louisiana.* Huntsville: Texas Review Press, 2012.

———. *The Southern Poetry Anthology, Volume V: Georgia.* Huntsville, Texas Review Press, 2012.

Critical Sources on Contemporary Southern Poetry

Bendixen, Alfred, and Stephen Burt, eds. *The Cambridge History of American Poetry.* New York: Cambridge University Press, 2014.

Cartwright, Keith. *Sacral Grooves, Limbo Gateways: Travels in Deep Southern Time, Circum-Caribbean Space, Afro-creole Authority.* Athens: University of Georgia Press, 2013.

Chappell, Fred. "'Not as a Leaf': Southern Poetry and the Innovation of Tradition." *Georgia Review* 51, no. 3 (1997): 477–89.

Daniels, Kate. "Porch-Sitting and Southern Poetry." In *The Future of Southern Letters,* edited by Jefferson Humphries and John Lowe, 61–71. New York: Oxford University Press, 1996.

Dungy, Camille T. "Introduction: The Nature of African American Poetry." In *Black Nature: Four Centuries of African American Nature Poetry,* edited by Camille T. Dungy, xix–xxxv. Athens: University of Georgia Press, 2009.

Handley, George B. *New World Poetics: Nature and the Adamic Imagination of Whitman, Neruda, and Walcott.* Athens: University of Georgia Press, 2007.

Harmon, William. "Is Southern Poetry Southerner than Southern Fiction?" *Mississippi Quarterly* 46, no. 2 (1993): 273–78.

Kirby, David. "Is There a Southern Poetry?" *Southern Review* 30, no. 4 (1994): 869–80.

Lang, John. *Six Poets from the Mountain South.* Baton Rouge: Louisiana State University Press, 2010.

Mattison, Mike, and Ernest Suarez. "'You Say You Want a Revolution': The Blues, Poetry, and Rock." *Five Points: A Journal of Literature and Art* 15, no. 3 (2013): 145–67.

Olney, James, and Dave Smith, eds. "Contemporary Southern Poetry." Special issue. *Southern Review* 30, no. 4 (1994).

Prunty, Wyatt. "At Home and Abroad: Southern Poets with Passports and Memory." *Southern Review* 30, no. 4 (1994): 745–50.

Ramazani, Jahan. *The Hybrid Muse: Postcolonial Poetry in English.* Chicago: University of Chicago Press, 2001.

Schneider, Steven P., ed. *The Contemporary Narrative Poem: Critical Crosscurrents.* Iowa City: University of Iowa Press, 2012.

Smith, Dave. *Hunting Men: Reflections on a Life in American Poetry.* Baton Rouge: Louisiana State University Press, 2006.

———. *Local Assays: On Contemporary American Poetry.* Urbana: University of Illinois Press, 1985.

Suarez, Ernest. "Robert Penn Warren and the Younger Southern Poets." In *The Legacy of Robert Penn Warren,* edited by David Madden, 60–70. Baton Rouge: Louisiana State University Press, 2000.

———. "Southern Verse in Poetry and Song." In *The Cambridge Companion to the Literature of the American South,* edited by Sharon Monteith, 72–87. New York: Cambridge University Press, 2013.

———. "Towards a New Southern Poetry: Southern Poetry in Contemporary American Literary History." *Southern Review* 33, no. 1 (1997): 181–96.

Suarez, Ernest, with T. W. Stanford III and Amy Verner. *Southbound: Interviews with Southern Poets.* Columbia: University of Missouri Press, 1999.

Turner, Daniel Cross. *Southern Crossings: Poetry, Memory, and the Transcultural South.* Knoxville: University of Tennessee Press, 2012.

West, Robert, ed. "Southern Poetry." Special issue. *Mississippi Quarterly* 58, no. 2 (2005).

Weathers" reprinted with permission of Robert Snyderman, literary executor of the Besmilr Brigham Estate. Kathryn Stripling Byer: "Dagger," "Bait," and "Delivery" are printed with permission of the author. Fred Chappell: "The Artful Dodger out of the Bag" is printed with permission of the author. Kelly Cherry: "Wild Dogwood" and "The Heat Down South (Richmond, 1955)" are from *Hazard and Prospect: New and Selected Poems.* © 2007 by Kelly Cherry. Reprinted with the permission of Louisiana State University Press. "Gulfport" printed with permission of the author. Michael Chitwood: "A Childhood," "The One Day," and "Skinning" are printed with permission of the author. Jim Clark: "Black Dog Shadrick Mayhew," "Waking Up Drunk," and "Once More, the Night" are printed with permission of the author. Allison Adelle Hedge Coke: "The Change" is from *Dog Road Woman.* © 1997 by Allison Adelle Hedge Coke. Reprinted with the permission of Coffee House Press. "Packin' Four Corner Nabs" is from *Off-Seasons City Pipe.* © 2005 by Allison Adelle Hedge Coke. Reprinted with the permission of Coffee House Press. Daniel Corrie: "Sleeping and Waking" is printed with permission of the author. Kate Daniels: "Autobiography of a White Girl Raised in the South" and "The Figure Eight" from *A Walk in Victoria's Secret.* © 2010 by Kate Daniels. Reprinted with the permission of Louisiana State University Press. "Louisiana, Late Summer" printed with permission of the author. Kwame Dawes: "Thief" and "Reburial" are printed with permission of the author. James Dickey: "Cherrylog Road" and "The Sheep Child" are from *The Whole Motion: Collection Poems.* © 1998 by James Dickey. Reprinted by permission of Wesleyan University Press. "Canebrake" reprinted from *Striking In: The Early Notebooks of James Dickey,* edited by Gordon Van Ness. © 1996 by the Curators of the University of Missouri. R. H. W. Dillard: "A Friday Night Kind of Sonnet" and "Event; A Gathering; Vastation" are printed with permission of the author. Claudia Emerson: "Ephemeris," "Practice Blood," and "Third" are printed with permission of the author. Tarfia Faizullah: "Nocturne in Need of a Bitch" and "The Streetlamp above Me Darkens:" are printed with permission of the author. Forrest Gander: Sections from *Life of Johnson Upside Your Head* are reprinted with permission of the author; these sections were first printed in *Lynchburg* (University of Pittsburgh Press). © 1993 by Forrest Gander. "Lovegreen" is from *Core Samples from the World.* © 2007 by Forrest Gander. Reprinted by permission of New Directions Publishing Corp. George Garrett: "Whistling in the Dark," "Buzzard," and "Luck's Shining Child" are from *Days of Our Lives Lie in Fragment: New and Old Poems, 1957–1997.* © 1998 by George Garrett. Reprinted with the permission of Louisiana State University Press. Jesse Graves: "River Gods," "Firing Order," and "Elegy for a Hay Rake" from are *Tennessee Landscape with Blight Pine.* © 2011 by Jesse Graves. Reprinted with permission from Texas Review Press; Jeff Hardin: "On the Eve of a New Millennium" is printed with permission of the author. Ashley Mace Havird: "At Stonewall" and "Lunar Eclipse" are printed with permission of the author. David Havird: "In Seventh Grade" and "Downriver with Uncle Paul" are printed with permission of the author. Terrance Hayes: "Ode to Big Trend" and "Palmetto State" are printed with permission of the author. Hastings Hensel: "Jump-Start," "The Rope in the Motor," and "Filet" are printed with permission of the author. Ron Houchin: "Meanwhile," "Outhouse," and "The Broken Eye" are printed with permission of the author. Rebecca Gayle Howell: "No One Was Born Here," "We're on a Need to Know Basis," and "The Quick and the Dead" are printed with permission of the author. David Huddle: "Even Then I Knew," "Evidence Contributing to a Late Illumination," and "Trotlines" are printed with permission of the author. Andrew Hudgins: "The Names of the Lost" and "My Daughter" are from *American Rendering: New and Selected Poems.* © 2010 by Andrew Hudgins. Reprinted by permission from Houghton Mifflin Harcourt Publishing Company. All rights reserved. "In" and "Out" are printed with permission of the author. T. R. Hummer: "Slow Train through Georgia," "The Antichrist in Arkansas," and "Greek" are published with permission of the author. TJ Jarrett: "Of Late, I Have Been Thinking about Despair," "Late That Summer," and "Meridian, MS, 1978: Miss Polly Attends the Altar at Mt. Zion" are printed with permission of the author. Rodney Jones: "The Power of the Quote" is printed with permission of the author. Judy Jordan: Sections from *Pete's Lake* are printed with permission of the author. Terry L. Kennedy: "Concerning the Hunt" and "Concerning the Puppies" are printed with permission of the author. Yusef Komunyakaa: Section from *Requiem,* "The White Handkerchief," and "Augury at Sunset" are printed with permission of the author. John Lane: "The Day Andy Griffith Died," "Tommy Dorsett and His Band," and "Wreckage" are printed with permission of the author. Naton Leslie: "Completion" and "Country" are printed with permission of Susan Leslie, literary executor of the Estate of Naton D. Leslie Jr; Ed Madden: "Inferno" from *Nest.* © 2014 by Ed Madden. Reprinted with permission of Salmon Poetry, Ltd. via Siobhán Hutson, editor. Al Maginnes: "Pornography," "Firefly Gospel," and "Music from Small Towns" are printed with permission of the author. Jeff Mann: "A Brief Christian Visit; or, The Butch Bottom Sends Old Ladies Packing" and "The Shepherdstown Sweetshop" are printed with permission of the author. Jeff Daniel Marion: "Hand-Me-Down Days," "Orpha," and "Winter Watch" are printed with permission of the author. Linda Parsons Marion: "Chicken Pickin'," "My Stepmother Takes Me to the Fair," and "Repossessed" are printed with permission of the author. Christopher Martin: "Parable of the Carolina Chickadee" and "Visiting Wildman's Civil War and Herb Shop" are printed with permission of the author. Chris Mattingly: "No 'Count" and "Summertime" are printed with permission of the author. Michael McFee: "Yaller," "Breaks," and "Cottonmouth" are printed with permission of the author. Ray McManus: "Dog Box," "Disturbing Remains," and "Staying in the Truck" are printed with permission of the author. Thorpe Moeckel: "Spitoono Lily" and "Cold Range, Hot Range" are printed with permission of the author. "Living by Water" is from *Odd Botany.* © 2002 by Thorpe Moeckel. Reprinted with the permission of Silverfish Review Press. Robert Morgan: "Manure Pile," "The Gift of Tongues," and "Man and Machine" are printed with permission of the author. Ricardo Nazario y Colón: "Mi Nuevo Hogar: Kentucky" is printed with permission of the author. Tara Powell: "Watching *Deliverance* with My Students" is from *Physical Science.* © 2010 by Tara Powell. Reprinted with permission of Finishing Line Press. Ron Rash: "The Skeleton in the Dogwood," "Winter Lightning," and "Animal Hides" are printed with permission of the author. Janisse Ray: "Land of Milk and Honey" is printed with permission of the author. Paul Ruffin: "Frozen Over," "Circling," "Gigging Frogs," and

"Sawdust Pile" are printed with permission of the author. Steve Scafidi: "To Whoever Set My Truck on Fire" is from *Sparks from a Nine-Pound Hammer.* © 2001 by Steve Scafidi. Reprinted with the permission of Louisiana State University Press. "The West Virginia Copper-Wing" from *The Cabinetmaker's Window.* © 2014 by Steve Scafidi. Reprinted with the permission of Louisiana State University Press. "The Hillbilly Break-Dance and the Talking Crow" is printed with permission of the author. James Seay: "It All Comes Together outside the Restroom in Hogansville" and "Kelly Dug a Hole" are from *Open Field, Understory: New and Selected Poems.* © 1997 by James Seay. Reprinted with the permission of Louisiana State University Press. Dave Smith: "How to Get to Green Springs," "In the Yard, Late Summer," and "The Tire Hangs in the Yard" are from *The Wick of Memory: New and Selected Poems, 1970–2000.* © 2000 by Dave Smith. Reprinted with the permission of Louisiana State University Press. R. T. Smith: "A Local Doc, over Rocky Lunchtime Bourbon, Speaks of Barter and Hopeful Home Remedies" is from *In the Night Orchard: New and Selected Poems.* © 2014 by R. T. Smith. Reprinted with the permission of Texas Review Press. "Horton's Store" is from *Brightwood.* © 2004 by R. T. Smith. Reprinted with the permission of Louisiana State University Press. "Dar He" is from *Outlaw Style.* © 2007 by University of Arkansas Press. Reproduced with the permission of the University of Arkansas Press, www.uapress.com. Sheryl St. Germain: "Addiction," "Always Wear Clean Underwear, You Never Know When You Might Get in a Car Accident" (from "Things My Mother Always Told Me"), and "Wild Ones" are from *Let It Be a Dark Roux: New and Selected Poems.* © 2007 by Sheryl St. Germain. Reprinted with the permission of the Permissions Company, Inc., on behalf of Autumn House Press, www.autumnhouse.org. Leon Stokesbury: "To Laura Phelan: 1886–1906" and "Midway" are printed with permission of the author. Richard Tillinghast: "Lost Cove & the Rose of San Antone" and "Allen's Station: They" are printed with permission of the author. Deno Trakas: "End of August, 2005" and "Walking to Work on a Snowy Morning" are printed with permission of the author. Natasha Trethewey: "Disclosure" is from *Bellocq's Ophelia.* © 2002 by Natasha Trethewey. Printed with the permission of the Permissions Company, Inc., on behalf of Graywolf Press, Minneapolis, Minnesota, www.graywolfpress.org. Excerpt from "Native Guard" is from *Native Guard: Poems by Natasha Trethewey.* © 2006 by Natasha Trethewey. Reprinted by permission of Houghton Mifflin Harcourt Publishing Company. All rights reserved. "Dr. Samuel Adolphus Cartwright on Dissecting the White Negro, 1851" is from *Thrall: Poems by Natasha Trethewey.* © 2012 by Natasha Trethewey. Reprinted by permission of Houghton Mifflin Harcourt Publishing Company. All rights reserved. "Onlookers Gathered at the Traveling Chair's Arrival" is printed with permission of the author. Adam Vines: "Prologue and Return," "Mine Rats," and "The Old Salt's Brag" are from *The Coal Life.* © 2012 by the University of Arkansas Press. Reproduced with the permission of the University of Arkansas Press, www.uapress.com. Ellen Bryant Voigt: "Bright Leaf" and "The Trust," © 1987 by Ellen Bryant Voigt, are from *Messenger: New and Selected Poems, 1976–2006.* © 2007 by Ellen Bryant Voigt. Printed by permission of W. W. Norton & Company, Inc. "Cow" and "Owl" are from *Headwaters: Poems.* © 2013 by Ellen Bryant Voigt. Printed by permission of W. W. Norton & Company, Inc. G. C. Waldrep: "Elberta" and "Vertigo" are reprinted from *Goldbeater's Skin.* © 2003 by G. C. Waldrep. Reprinted by permission of the Center for Literary Publishing and the author. "Sustainable Agriculture" is printed with permission of the author. Frank X Walker: "Spell to Give the Woman a Head," "How to Swallow an Elephant," "Cure to Eliminate the N-Word" are printed with permission of the author. Robert West: "Mountaintop Removal" and "Cornfield" are printed with permission of the author. James Whitehead: "A Local Man Remembers Betty Fuller" and "The Alabama Man Remembers All He Can about the Battered Children and the Woman with Almost Perfect Skin in Mobile Seven Years Ago" are from *Local Men and Domains: Poems.* © 1987 by James Whitehead. Printed with permission of the University of Illinois Press. Amy Wright: "In That Place" is printed with permission of the author. Charles Wright: "Driving through Tennessee" and "Lost Bodies" from *The World of the Ten Thousand Things: Poems 1980–1990.* © 1990 by Charles Wright. Reprinted by permission of Farrar, Straus and Giroux, LLC; William Wright: "Trumpet Creeper" and "Rabid Cat" are from *Night Field Anecdote.* © 2011 by William Wright. Reprinted with permission of Louisiana Literature Press. "Triptych for the Days before Her Passage" is printed with permission of the author. Jake Adam York: "Collect" and "Self Portrait in a Plate-Glass Window" are from *Person's Unknown.* © 2010 by Jake Adam York. Reprinted with permission of Southern Illinois University Press. "Letter Written on a Hundred Dollar Bill" and "Inscription for Air" are from *Abide.* © 2014 by the Estate of Jake Adam York. Reprinted with permission of Southern Illinois University Press.

INDEX OF AUTHORS AND TITLES

"Acknowledgments" (Turner and Wright), xiii-xiv
Adcock, Betty, xi, 6, 11–14, 265
"Addiction" (St. Germain), 215–16
"After an All-Nighter Camping with a Young Friend at Cape Romain Wildlife Refuge, South Carolina" (Allen), 21–22
"Alabama Man Remembers All He Can about the Battered Children and the Woman with Almost Perfect Skin in Mobile Seven Years Ago, The" (Whitehead), 245–46
Albergotti, Dan, 6, 15–18, 265
Allen, Paul, 19–22, 265
"Allen's Station: They" (Tillinghast), 223–25
"Altar Call" (Allen), 19–20
"Always Wear Clean Underwear, You Never Know When You Might Get in a Car Accident" (St. Germain), 217
Ammons, A. R., xii, 6, 7
"Animal Hides" (Rash), 190
"Antichrist in Arkansas, The" (Hummer), 120–21
"Artful Dodger Out of the Bag, The" (Chappell), 48–50
"At Stonewall" (A. Havird), 97
"Augury at Sunset" (Komunyakaa), 140
"Autobiography of a White Girl Raised in the South" (Daniels), 68–69
Aviram, Amittai F., 4
"Bait" (Byer), 45–46
Barker, Brian, xi, 6, 23–26, 266
Barks, Coleman, 27–31, 266
Barrax, Gerald, xii
Bedell, Jack B., 32–34, 266
Bernstein, Charles, 4
Birdsong, Destiny O., 35–36, 266
"Black Dog Shadrick Mayhew" (Clark), 57–58
Bottoms, David, xii, xiii, 6, 37–41, 266
Bowers, Cathy Smith, xii
"Breaks" (McFee), 172–73
"Brief Christian Visit; or, The Butch Bottom Sends Old Ladies Packing, A" (Mann), 156
Brigham, Besmilr, xii, 6, 42–43, 266–67
"Bright Leaf" (Voigt), 234–35
"Broken Eye, The" (Houchin), 109
"Burnt Offerings" (Adcock), 11
"Buzzard" (Garrett), 90–91
Byer, Kathryn Stripling, xii, 3, 6, 44–47, 267

"Canebrake" (Dickey), 78–79
Carpenter, Brian, xi, 1
Chappell, Fred, 6, 48–50, 267
Cherry, Kelly, 6, 51–53, 267–68
"Cherrylog Road" (Dickey), 74–76
"Chicken Pickin'" (L. Marion), 161
Chitwood, Michael, 54–56, 268
"Childhood, A" (Chitwood), 54
"Circling" (Ruffin), 193–94
Clark, Jim, 57–60, 268

Coke, Allison Adelle Hedge, 8, 61–66, 268
"Cold Range, Hot Range" (Moeckel), 179–80
"Collect" (York), 259–60
"Completion" (Leslie), 148
"Concerning the Hunt" (Kennedy), 134
"Concerning the Puppies" (Kennedy), 134–35
"Cornfield" (West), 244
Corrie, Daniel, 67, 268
"Cottonmouth" (McFee), 173
"Country" (Leslie), 149
"Cow" (Voigt), 236
"Cure to Eliminate the N-Word" (Walker), 242–43

"Dagger" (Byer), 44–45
Daniels, Kate, 68–70, 269
"Dar He" (R. Smith), 212–14
Dawes, Kwame, xii, 8, 71–73, 269
"Day Andy Griffith Died, The" (Lane), 141–43
"Delivery" (Byer), 46–47
Dickey, James, xii, 2, 6, 74–79, 269
Dillard, R. H. W., 80–81, 269
"Disclosure" (Trethewey), 228
"Disturbing Remains" (McManus), 176
"Dog Box" (McManus), 174–76
"Dog Gospel" (Barker), 25–26
"Downriver with Uncle Paul" (D. Havird), 100–2
"Dr. Samuel Adolphus Cartwright on Dissecting the White Negro, 1851" (Trethewey), 229
"Driving through Tennessee" (C. Wright), 249

"Elberta" (Waldrep), 238–39
"Elegy for a Hay Rake" (Graves), 95
Eliot, T. S., 3
Emerson, Claudia, 82–84, 269
"End of August, 2005" (Trakas), 226
"Ephemeris" (Emerson), 82–83
"Even Then I Knew" (Huddle), 112
"Event; A Gathering; Vastation" (Dillard), 80–81
"Evidence Contributing to a Late Illumination" (Huddle), 113

Faizullah, Tarfia, 8, 85–87, 270
"Figure Eight, The" (Daniels), 69–70
"Filet" (Hensel), 107
"Firefly Gospel" (Maginnes), 153–54
"Firing Order" (Graves), 94–95
Franklin, Tom, xi, 1
Freud, Sigmund, 4
"Friday Night Kind of Sonnet, A" (Dillard), 80
Frost, Robert, 3
"Frozen Over" (Ruffin), 193

Gander, Forrest, xii, 7, 88–89, 270
Garrett, George, 90–92, 270
"Gift of Tongues, The" (Morgan), 182–83
"Gigging Frogs" (Ruffin), 195
"Grace" (Barks), 28
Graves, Jesse, 3, 93–95, 270
"Greek" (Hummer), 121–22
Grit Lit: A Rough South Reader, xi, 1
"Gulfport" (Cherry), 52–53

"Hand-Me-Down Days" (J. Marion), 158
Hardin, Jeff, 96, 270–71
Haupt, Jonathan, xiii
Havird, Ashley Mace, 97–98, 271
Havird, David, 99–102, 271
Hayes, Terrance, 103–4, 271
"Heat Down South (Richmond, 1955), The" (Cherry), 51–52
Hensel, Hastings, 105–7, 271
"Hillbilly Break-Dance and the Talking Crow, The" (Scafidi), 199–200
"Horton's Store" (R. Smith), 210–11
Houchin, Ron, 108–9, 271

"How to Get to Green Springs" (D. Smith), 204
"How to Swallow an Elephant" (Walker), 241–42
Howell, Rebecca Gayle, 110–11, 271–72
Huddle, David, 112–15, 272
Hudgins, Andrew, 6, 116–18, 272
Hummer, T. R., 7, 119–22, 272
"Hurricane, The" (Brigham), 42

"If Their Voices Were Visible Entities" (Adcock), 13–14
"In" (Hudgins), 117
"In a U-Haul North of Damascus" (Bottoms), 39–41
"In Seventh Grade" (D. Havird), 99–100
"In That Place" (A. Wright), 247–48
"In the City of Fallen Rebels" (Barker), 23–24
"In the Yard, Late Summer" (D. Smith), 204–5
"Inferno" (Madden), 150–51
"Inscription for Air" (York), 263–64
"Introduction: Rough Rhythms" (Turner), 1–9
"It All Comes Together outside the Restroom in Hogansville" (Seay), 201–2

Jagger, Mick, 4
Jarrett, TJ, 8, 123–25, 272
Jones, Rodney, xii, 6, 126–29, 272
Jordan, Judy, 6, 130–33, 272–73
"Jump-Start" (Hensel), 105

"Kelly Dug a Hole" (Seay), 202–3
Kennedy, Terry L., 134–35, 273
Komunyakaa, Yusef, xii, 6, 7, 8, 136–40, 273
Kristeva, Julia, 4

Lacan, Jacques, 4
"Land of Milk and Honey" (Ray), 191–92
Lane, John, xi, xiii, 6, 141–47, 273
"Lard Gourd" (Barks), 27–28
"Late That Summer" (Jarrett), 124
Leslie, Naton, 8, 148–49, 273–74
"Lesson of the Elements: Fire" (Albergotti), 16–17
"Lesson of the Elements: Earth" (Albergotti), 17–18
"Letter Written on a Hundred Dollar Bill" (York), 262–63
Life of Johnson Upside Your Head (Gander), 88–89
"Living by Water" (Moeckel), 180–81
"Local Doc, over Rocky Lunchtime Bourbon, Speaks of Barter and Hopeful Home Remedies, A" (R. Smith), 209–10
"Local Man Remembers Betty Fuller, A" (Whitehead), 245
"Lost Bodies" (C. Wright), 249–52
"Lost Cove & the Rose of San Antone" (Tillinghast), 222–23
"Louisiana, Late Summer" (Daniels), 69
"Loup Garou" (Bedell), 33–34
"Lovegreen" (Gander), 89
"Luck's Shining Child" (Garrett), 91–92
"Luke and the Duct Tape" (Barks), 29–31
"Lunar Eclipse" (A. Havird), 98

Madden, Ed, 150–51, 274
Maginnes, Al, 152–55, 274
"Man and Machine" (Morgan), 183–84
Mann, Jeff, 156–57, 274
"Manure Pile" (Morgan), 182
Marion, Jeff Daniel, xii, 158–60, 274
Marion, Linda Parsons, 161–63, 275
Martin, Christopher, 164–66, 275
Mattingly, Chris, 167–70, 275
McFee, Michael, 171–73, 275
McManus, Ray, 174–77, 275–76
"Meanwhile" (Houchin), 108
"Meridian, MS, 1978: Miss Polly Attends the Altar at Mt. Zion" (Jarrett), 124–25

"Mi Nuevo Hogar: Kentucky" (Nazario y Colón), 185–86
"Midway" (Stokesbury), 220–21
Miller, Jim Wayne, xii
"Mine Rats" (Vines), 232–33
Moeckel, Thorpe, 178–81, 276
Morgan, Robert, xii, 6, 182–84, 276
"Mountaintop Removal" (West), 244
"Music from Small Towns" (Maginnes), 154–55
"My Daughter" (Hudgins), 116–17
"My Stepmother Takes Me to the Fair" (L. Marion), 161–62

"Names of the Lost, The" (Hudgins), 116
"Native Guard" (Trethewey), 228
Nazario y Colón, Richardo, 8, 185–88, 276
Nietzsche, Friedrich, 4
"No 'Count" (Mattingly), 167–68
"No One Was Born Here" (Howell), 110
"Nocturne in Need of a Bitch" (Faizullah), 85–86
"Notes for a Poem in Which God Does Not Appear" (Albergotti), 15–16

"Ode to Big Trend" (Hayes), 103
"Of Late, I Have Been Thinking about Despair" (Jarrett), 123
"Off-Season" (Hedge Coke), 61–62
"Old Salt's Brag, The" (Vines), 233
"On the Eve of a New Millennium" (Hardin), 96
"Once More, the Night" (Clark), 59–60
"One Day, The" (Chitwood), 54–55
"Onlookers Gathered at the Traveling Chair's Arrival" (Trethewey), 229–30
"Orpha" (J. Marion), 158–59
"Out" (Hudgins), 118
"Outhouse" (Houchin), 108
"Owl" (Voigt), 236–37

"Packin' Four Corner Nabs" (Hedge Coke), 62–66
"Palmetto State" (Hayes), 103–4
"Parable of the Carolina Chickadee" (Martin), 164
Pete's Lake (Jordan), 130–33
Poe, Edgar Allan, 3–4
"Pornography" (Maginnes), 152–53
Powell, Tara, 187–88, 276
"Power of the Quote, The" (Jones), 126–29
"Practice Blood" (Emerson), 83–84
"Preface: Brutal Grace" (W. Wright), xi-xii
"Prologue and Return" (Vines), 231

"Quick and the Dead, The" (Howell), 111

"Rabid Cat" (W. Wright), 256
Rash, Ron, xii, xiii, 6, 189–90, 277
Ray, Janisse, xii, 191–92, 277
"Reburial" (Dawes), 72–73
"Repossessed" (L. Marion), 162–63
Requiem (Komunyakaa), 136–38
Richards, Keith, 4–5, 6
"Rising Star, 1985" (Adcock), 11–12
"River Gods" (Graves), 93
"Rope in the Motor, The" (Hensel), 106
Ruffin, Paul, 193–96, 277

"Saturday Night Crab Boils" (Bedell), 33
"Sawdust Pile" (Ruffin), 196
Scafidi, Steve, 197–200, 277
Seay, James, 201–3, 277
"Self-Portrait in a Plate-Glass Window" (York), 260–61
"Sheep Child, The" (Dickey), 77–78
"Shepherdstown Sweetshop, The" (Mann), 157
"Shooting Rats at the Bibb County Dump" (Bottoms), 37
Singleton, George, xiii
Smith, Dave, xii, 6, 204–8, 277–78
Smith, R. T., xii, 209–14, 278

"Skeleton in the Dogwood, The" (Rash), 189
"Skinning" (Chitwood), 55–56
"Sleeping and Waking" (Corrie), 67
"Slow Train through Georgia" (Hummer), 119
"Spell to Give the Woman a Head" (Walker), 241
"Spittoono Lily" (Moeckel), 178
St. Germain, Sheryl, 215–18, 278
"Staying in the Truck" (McManus), 176–77
Stokesbury, Leon, 219–21, 278–79
"Streetlamp above Me Darkens, The" (Faizullah), 86–87
"Sugar" (Birdsong), 35–36
"Summertime" (Mattingly), 168–70
"Sustainable Agriculture" (Waldrep), 240

"Thief" (Dawes), 71–72
"Third" (Emerson), 84
Tillinghast, Richard, 222–25, 279
"Tire Hangs in the Yard, The" (D. Smith), 205–8
"To Laura Phelan: 1886–1906" (Stokesbury), 219
"To Whoever Set My Truck on Fire" (Scafidi), 197–98
"Tony Dorsett and His Band" (Lane), 143–44
Trakas, Deno, 226–27, 279
"Travail" (Bedell), 32
"Trees of the South, The" (Barker), 24–25
Trethewey, Natasha, xii, 6, 7, 8, 228–30, 279–80
"Triptych for the Days before Her Passage" (W. Wright), 256–58
"Trotlines" (Huddle), 114–15
"Trumpet Creeper" (W. Wright), 253–55
"Trust, The" (Voigt), 235–36
Turner, Daniel Cross, xi, xiii, xiv, 1–9

"Under the Boathouse" (Bottoms), 38–39
"Under the Vulture-Tree" (Bottoms), 37–38

"Vertigo" (Waldrep), 239–40
Vines, Adam, 231–33, 280
"Visiting Wildman's Civil War Surplus and Herb Shop" (Martin), 164–66
Voigt, Ellen Bryant, xii, 234–37, 280

"Waking Up Drunk" (Clark), 58–59
Waldrep, G. C., xi, xiii, 238–40, 280
Walker, Frank X, 8, 241–43, 280
"Walking to Work on a Snowy Morning" (Trakas), 227
Warren, Robert Penn, xii, 6
"Watching *Deliverance* with My Students" (Powell), 187–88
"We're on a Need to Know Basis" (Howell), 110
West, Robert, 244, 280
"West Virginia Copper-Wing, The" (Scafidi), 201–2
"Whistling in the Dark" (Garrett), 90
"White Handkerchief, The" (Komunyakaa), 138–40
Whitehead, James, 245–46, 280
"Wild Dogwood" (Cherry), 51
"Wild Ones" (St. Germain), 217–18
"Winston Weathers" (Brigham), 43
"Winter Lightning" (Rash), 189–90
"Winter Watch" (J. Marion), 159–60
"Wreckage" (Lane), 144–47
Wright, Amy, 247–48, 280–81
Wright, Charles, xii, 2–3, 6, 7, 8, 249–52, 281
Wright, William, xi-xii, xiii-xiv, 1, 253–58, 281

"Yaller" (McFee), 171–72
Yeats, W. B., 3
York, Jake Adam, xii, 6, 259–64, 281